Economic Espionage and Industrial Spying

In view of the recent revolution in information technology, this book investigates the current state of industrial espionage, showing the far-reaching effects of advances in computing and wireless communications. Synthesizing views from leading national and international authorities, Professor Hedieh Nasheri explains the historical and conceptual underpinnings of economic espionage, trade secret theft, and industrial spying. She shows how these activities have impacted society, and she tracks the legislative and statutory efforts to control them.

Advance Praise for *Economic Espionage and Industrial Spying*:

"We criminologists and academic criminal lawyers have been slow to turn our attention to non-traditional crimes and criminals, thereby missing extraordinarily important developments. Hedieh Nasheri has given us a wake up call. Her work on theft of intellectual property should be incorporated into our courses and research agendas."
– James B. Jacobs, New York University

"Hedieh Nasheri skillfully shows us the dimensions of economic espionage in this era of ever increasing interconnectedness and globalization. She provides a fascinating account of the criminalization of economic espionage, and offers a compelling analysis of the impact and possible evolution of important criminal statutes. Her book also raises complex issues about the use of criminal sanctions in an electronic environment, making it required reading for anyone studying or fighting cyber crime today."
– Alan J. Lizotte, The University at Albany

"This is a fascinating and timely account of the ways in which new technologies are being employed to steal information in twenty-first century America. It provides a carefully-researched analysis of the appropriateness and effectiveness of criminalization of economic espionage, particularly under the *Economic Espionage Act* 1996, and considers alternative approaches that may yield greater benefits in terms of prevention and deterrence. An essential reference work for cyber-criminologists and corporate regulators in the information age."
– Russell G. Smith, Australian Institute of Criminology

Hedieh Nasheri is Associate Professor of Justice Studies at Kent State University.

Cambridge Studies in Criminology

Editors

Alfred Blumstein, H. John Heinz School of Public Policy and Management, Carnegie
   Mellon University
David Farrington, Institute of Criminology, Cambridge University

Other books in the series:

Economic Espionage and Industrial Spying

Hedieh Nasheri
Kent State University

PUBLISHED BY THE PRESS SYNDICATE OF THE UNIVERSITY OF CAMBRIDGE
The Pitt Building, Trumpington Street, Cambridge, United Kingdom

CAMBRIDGE UNIVERSITY PRESS
The Edinburgh Building, Cambridge CB2 2RU, UK
40 West 20th Street, New York, NY 10011-4211, USA
477 Williamstown Road, Port Melbourne, VIC 3207, Australia
Ruiz de Alarcón 13, 28014 Madrid, Spain
Dock House, The Waterfront, Cape Town 8001, South Africa

http://www.cambridge.org

First published 2005

Printed in the United States of America

Typeface ITC New Baskerville 10/12 pt.   *System* LaTeX 2_ε [TB]

A catalog record for this book is available from the British Library.

Library of Congress Cataloging in Publication Data
Nasheri, Hedieh.
    Economic espionage and industrial spying / Hedieh Nasheri.
        p.   cm. – (Cambridge studies in criminology)
    Includes bibliographical references and index.
    ISBN 0-521-83582-8 – ISBN 0-521-54371-1 (pb.)
        1. Business intelligence.   2. Trade secrets.   3. Computer crimes.
    4. Intellectual property.   5. Commercial crimes.   I. Title.   II. Series.
    HD38.7.N37   2004
    364.16'8 – dc22   2004045889

ISBN 0 521 83582 8 hardback
ISBN 0 521 54371 1 paperback

To my parents

Contents

Preface

The idea for this book developed in October 1996 on the eve of the passage of the Economic Espionage Act (EEA) in discussions with a colleague who specialized in intellectual property law and had been practicing for some 15 years, litigating patents, trade secrets, and infringement cases domestically and internationally in this area. We engaged in an ongoing debate with respect to factors that had contributed to the passage of this new legislation. Our discussions were fruitful because we each had unique perspectives, mine from an academic social science background and his from a practitioner's legalistic point of view dealing with these issues, not on an abstract level but rather day in and out handling disputes among corporate entities.

I began analyzing and interpreting the legislative actions at both state and federal levels regarding past and postcriminalization efforts. Accordingly, the objective was to examine the available records on legislative evolution and legislative history that gave rise to the enactment of this statute and Congress' initiatives. I systematically began reviewing and tracing all prosecutions brought to date under the EEA legislation. Furthermore, I began examining the impact of this law in the United States and related legal regimes in Central and Eastern Europe as well. My project in Central Europe was made possible through a research grant from the State Department of the United States, which provided me with an opportunity to analyze this topic from a comparative perspective in order to gain a better understanding of what some European countries were doing with respect to these issues and their potential impact on western nations. This analysis, however, is still evolving and is not within the scope of the materials presented in this book.

For a number of years, I have been in close contact and collaboration with government officials in the Department of Justice, Federal Bureau of Investigation, who play key roles in prosecution and investigation of these criminal activities under the EEA, as well as members of the private sector. Furthermore, members of the law enforcement and prosecutorial community were queried regarding their activities related to these types of crimes. This provided an enriching opportunity for understanding the enforcement initiatives that have been taking place in the United States in the past and the present.

The criminalization of trade secret theft raises several important implications for future research and theorizing about the formation of laws at national and international levels. However, any opinions, findings and conclusions, or recommendations expressed in this book are those of the author and do not necessarily reflect the views of any government officials or granting entities.

My research results for the past 10 years have addressed the trends in criminal activities in connection with the rapid growth of computing and communications technologies and the increasingly global nature of commerce and business, both of which have caused an increase in technologically sophisticated criminal activity as well as international economic espionage. My work has concentrated on issues related to economic and industrial espionage. My research has revolved around the following question: Should the taking of information be criminalized as it has been in the United States by the EEA? The U.S. Congress enacted the EEA in 1996, which meant to establish a comprehensive approach to economic espionage, facilitating investigations and prosecution. This enactment raises complex issues about the use of criminal sanctions and civil penalties in the rapidly changing world of technology. Federal criminal prosecution is a powerful weapon, and one that should not be taken lightly. Criminal penalties imposed for the misappropriation of trade secrets under the EEA are far more severe than any other criminal liability for violations of other intellectual property rights. Persons engaged in misappropriation in the United States will no longer have their liability limited to civil remedies and damages imposed for such misconduct.

Economic espionage can be characterized as a new form of white-collar crime that includes technology-related crimes and/or cybercrimes. It has been argued that this will be a defining issue of the twenty-first century for policy makers – as defining as the Cold War was for the twentieth century. My work concentrates on issues related to technology changes. For example, the Internet itself provides opportunities for various kinds of theft, ranging from online banks to intellectual property. However, it also offers new means of committing old crimes, such as fraud, and offers new vulnerabilities relating to communications and data that provide attractive targets for extortion, a crime that has always been a staple of criminal organizations. The synergy between organized crime and the Internet is not only very natural, but it is also likely to flourish and develop even more in the future. The Internet provides both channels and targets for crime and enables them to be exploited for considerable gain with a very low level of risk. For organized crime figures and white-collar criminals, it is difficult to ask for more.

This topic has generated debate among policy makers, the courts, lawmakers, and the intelligence community worldwide. Criminologists, however, acknowledge that economic espionage is an important topic in the context of cybercrimes and transnational crimes, but very few have even addressed crimes that arise out of electronic communications such as economic espionage. Peter Grabosky points out that the basic principles of criminology apply to computer-related crime no less than they do to bank robbery or to shoplifting. As James Finckenauer pointed out, the whole panoply of so-called cybercrimes are almost by definition transnational crimes because cyberspace is not constrained within borders. Accordingly, Finckenauer noted that ignoring the transnationalization of crime would be akin to adopting a "head in the sand" strategy. Criminologist David Wall asserted that criminologists have been slow to explore these emerging fears and new criminal behaviors, and to engage in debate about them in order to develop useful bodies of knowledge that could enlighten the public and provide the basis for informed policy. In the criminologists' defense, however, Wall argued that there is wisdom in exercising caution and in waiting for reliable trends of behavior to emerge. He further pointed out that the time has arrived to address these issues. Most recently, Peter Drahos and John Braithwaite argued against expansion of intellectual property rights as a form of "information feudalism" that entrenches economic inequalities. They chronicle examples that, in their view, show an improper balance being struck between individual property rights in knowledge and the interests of society. It is inevitable that social scientists, including criminologists, economists, political scientists, and the like, will need to analyze and address these topics.

My book is designed to provide an analytic overview and assessment of the changing nature of crime in the burgeoning information society, where significant technological advances have revolutionized the nature of criminal activity across national borders, and increasing interconnections and interdependence have created new risks. Bringing together views from leading national and international authorities, it explains the historical and theoretical background surrounding issues of economic espionage, trade secret theft and industrial spying, and its impact on society. It looks at legislative history, the progression of electronic and corporate criminal behavior by introducing the concept of information theft and computer crimes, exploring its definition, its identification, and its development within criminology.

Currently, no countries have enacted legislation similar to the EEA of the United States. The most basic question that Congress and the EEA face is to what extent the legislation will extend in "extraterritorial" application. The book examines issues such as whether expansive extraterritorial legislation will likely irritate many countries, including those that are not involved in the theft of sensitive materials. One of the main objectives of the book is to lay out the legislative initiatives that the United States has taken to combat criminal activities that fall under the EEA. I hope that discussions on these and related issues will provide insight for legislatures and policy makers in other countries to examine similar issues that they encounter and to provide them with some basis for assessment of their existing laws or lack thereof.

The research for this book was made possible, in part, by a grant from the International Center at the National Institute of Justice on intellectual property as part of its research agenda on transnational crime, and through a Research Fellowship at the Institute of Advanced Legal Studies (IALS) at the University of London. The institute's reputation and emphasis on economic crime and commercial criminal law were an ideal match for my research agenda and interest. I want to acknowledge, too, the help of a number of people and institutions. I want to thank the anonymous reviewers for their helpful comments on the preliminary draft of this project. Special thanks go to the staff at the IALS Library at the University of London for providing assistance with research materials and I thank Kent State University for allowing me the time for my research in the U.K. I am indebted to my colleagues Jay Albanese, James Finckenauer, Peter Grabosky, Henry Pontell, and David Wall for their expertise, insight, and support as this manuscript was progressing. Finally, I am grateful to David Farrington whose guidance and encouragement was invaluable in shaping my thinking.

Acronyms and Abbreviations

ARPA	Advanced Research Projects Agency
ASIS	American Society of Industrial Security
CCIPS	Computer Crime and Intellectual Property Section
CERT/CC	Computer Emergency and Response Team Coordination Center
CFAA	Computer Fraud and Abuse Act
CHIP	Computer Hacking and Intellectual Property
CIA	Central Intelligence Agency
COE	Council of Europe
CSI	Computer Security Institute
CSIS	Canadian Security Intelligence Service
DCI	Director of Central Intelligence
DHS	Department of Homeland Security
DIS	Defense Investigative Service
DoD	Department of Defense
DOE	Department of Energy
DSS	Defense Security Service
EC	European Commission
ECPA	Electronic Communications Privacy Act
FOIA	Freedom of Information Act
GATT	General Agreement on Tariffs and Trade
IFCC	Internet Fraud Complaint Center
ITSPA	Interstate Transportation of Stolen Property Act
MID	Military Intelligence Department
NACIC	National Counterintelligence Center
NAFTA	North American Free Trade Agreement
NCCS	National Computer Crime Squad
NIPC	National Infrastructure Protection Center

NSA	National Security Agency
NSPA	National Stolen Property Act
OECD	Organization for Economic Cooperation and Development
OIA	Office of International Affairs
SCIP	Society of Competitive Intelligence Professionals
SEC	Securities and Exchange Commission
TRIPS	Trade-Related Aspects of Intellectual Property Rights
UTSA	Uniform Trade Secrets Act
WIPO	World Intellectual Property Organization
WTO	World Trade Organization

CHAPTER ONE

Dimensions of Economic Espionage and the Criminalization of Trade Secret Theft

WE LIVE in a world in which the economic health of nations and the competitiveness of businesses are determined largely by the ability to develop, commercialize, and capture the economic benefits from scientific and technological innovations. As the Internet and technological advances continue to reshape the way we do business in government and industry, and as competition and economic pressures create quicker and more efficient ways to do business, the reality of increased economic crimes has a serious impact. The connectivity of the Internet has made the concept of borders and jurisdictions an incredible challenge in combating this problem. Organized groups of criminals can easily commit economic crimes and avoid sanctions across what were once clearly defined jurisdictions, necessitating increased cooperation among the global criminal justice agencies. A greater understanding of how technology, competition, regulation, legislation, and globalization interact is needed to successfully manage the competition between economic progress and criminal opportunity.

The reach of criminal sanctions has expanded in the realm of technology. The revolution in information technologies has changed society fundamentally and will continue to do so in the foreseeable future. The development of information technology has given rise to unprecedented economic and social changes, which also have a dark side. The new technologies challenge existing legal concepts. Information and communications flow more easily around the world. Borders are no longer boundaries to this flow. Criminals are increasingly located in places other than where their actions produce their effects.

Today's information age requires businesses to compete on a worldwide basis, sharing sensitive information with appropriate parties while protecting that information against competitors, vandals, suppliers, customers, and foreign governments. Lawmakers are increasingly resorting to criminal codes to establish economic and social policies regarding the use and dissemination of technology. Many fear that technological advances are making corporate spying and theft of "intellectual capital" both easier and cheaper. In the global economy, there is less distinction between the need to protect the interests of the state and the need to protect commercial interests. A nation's economic status makes up a large part of its national security. This economic status is dependent on a nation's ability to compete effectively in the world market.

Intellectual property crimes are serious crimes in their own right, not because they inflict physical injury or death upon a person, but rather because they steal a creative work from its owner. Intellectual property theft is rampant, but largely silent, so corporations and law enforcement alike have trouble grasping its enormous impact on profitability – not to mention on national economies. Although civil remedies may provide compensation to wronged intellectual property rights holders, criminal sanctions are often warranted to ensure sufficient punishment and deterrence of wrongful activity. Indeed, because violations of intellectual property rights often involve no loss of tangible assets and, for infringement crimes, do not even require any direct contact with the rights holder, the rights holder often does not know it is a victim until a defendant's activities are specifically identified and investigated.

In the United States, Congress has continually expanded and strengthened criminal laws for violations of intellectual property rights specifically to ensure that those violations are not merely a cost of doing business for defendants. However, domestic laws are generally confined to a specific territory. Thus, solutions to the problems posed must be addressed by international law and international cooperation, necessitating the adoption of adequate international legal procedures. Law enforcement officials in the United States, apparently viewing the U.S. economy as the most likely target, have begun to focus on this new form of crime and the U.S. Congress has handed them a new enforcement tool in the Economic Espionage Act (EEA). This law, although relatively new, has far-ranging international implications. It is a trap for unwary foreign competitors who compete aggressively with U.S.-based companies. It also may serve as a model that will be followed by other nations with similar legislative or law enforcement initiatives. In those countries where the government plays a role in encouraging industrial activity, the conflict between economic nationalism and international competition will be an ongoing problem. It remains to be seen whether U.S. initiatives in this area are the start of an international trend or whether the United States will stand alone.

The most obvious legislative deficiency with which law enforcement has to deal is the absence of comprehensive legislation relating to offenses committed in an electronic environment. Some countries have none at all, some have adopted measures that have been integrated awkwardly into existing legislation, but relatively few have adequately updated their penal codes. Even after legislation is introduced at the national level, many problems will remain unless governments at the same time address the transnational nature of high-tech crime, which may originate in one country and have consequences in a second, while the evidence may be spread through many more. At present, there are no guidelines concerning which country's laws should prevail in pursuing an offense, how court decisions can be enforced if defendants reside abroad, and which protocols govern cross-border investigations.

Criminal Consequences of Trade Secret Theft

The American people have had contradictory views of economic crimes for some time, seeing these crimes as either a minor issue or a major crisis. Since the mid-1980s, there have been times when they have been in the limelight because of a financial crisis (e.g., the savings and loan scandal and the insider trading problems in the 1980s). Usually, they have taken a backseat to a strong national focus on more conventional crimes, specifically violent crimes.

For example, even a cursory evaluation of internal corporate security operations and protection procedures demonstrates that U.S. corporations view the issue of security as one of protecting people and tangible, physical assets rather than intellectual property. Given such a traditional approach to security, this particular attitude is not readily adaptable to providing protection against economic espionage. Many companies do not even recognize the significant loss that is suffered when trade secrets are pilfered by foreign intelligence services; they may simply view it as a process that is going to occur regardless of what they do.

Economic espionage and trade secret theft are considered white-collar offenses. The phrase *white-collar crime* was coined in 1939 during a speech given by Edwin Sutherland to the American Sociological Society. Sutherland defined the term as "crime committed by a person of respectability and high social status in the course of his occupation." Although there has been some debate as to what qualifies as a white-collar crime, the term today generally encompasses a variety of nonviolent crimes usually committed in commercial situations for financial gain. Many white-collar crimes are especially difficult to prosecute because the perpetrators are sophisticated criminals who have attempted to conceal their activities through a series of complex transactions. According to the Federal Bureau of Investigation (FBI), white-collar crime is estimated to cost the United States more than $300 billion annually. However, the protection of trade secrets is considered to be increasingly important to the competitiveness of the world's industrial sector.

At the same time, the world has been undergoing a computer revolution. Since at least the beginning of the 1990s, the power of information technology has grown exponentially, resulting in increasingly powerful means for the theft and transfer of protected information. This technological evolution in open societies facilitates the emergence of certain kinds of criminal and subversive activities, such as economic espionage. Thus, security (both economic and physical) in light of the recent evolution in technology and changes in geopolitical tensions is the broader topic surrounding this book.

The central focus of this book revolves around the following questions: Should the taking of information be criminalized as it has been, for example, in the United States by the EEA? Does the prospect of the threat of prosecution serve as a true deterrent for corporate espionage under the EEA? How can economic espionage be made less appealing? Which would be more effective, prosecution or heavier fines? For example, should violator companies be sanctioned internationally, whereby they cannot reap any benefits from the stolen information? Are criminal laws in this area indispensable to competitiveness? Is it unnecessary? Or is it perhaps even counterproductive? The book's focus on economic espionage reflects an underlying belief in the importance of industrial policy as a topic in the broader context of national and international security concerns.

Furthermore, the lack of agreed-upon definitions regarding economic and high-tech crimes has resulted in a paucity of data and information on the size and scope of the problem. There are no national mechanisms, such as the *Uniform Crime Reports*, for the reporting of economic crimes by law enforcement. Academics have not been able to agree on definitions and have, for the most part, continued to focus on white-collar crime. However, although most social scientists acknowledge that economic espionage is a major problem, especially in the digital age, the topic remains underrepresented in the social science literature, including criminological and sociological literature.

This book brings together a wide variety of materials that deal with the frequently neglected criminological dimension of economic espionage. The book's purpose is twofold: first, to present an assessment of the state of economic espionage activities within a criminological context and, second, based on that assessment, to address areas where additional research, legislative action, training, cooperation between law enforcement and the private sector, and international cooperation are required.

The data presented in this book are a result of years of interaction with practitioners, industry representatives, and government officials prosecuting and investigating these types of crimes. The data presented provide the basis for a discussion to address the topic of economic espionage, both as a crime and as a national security issue. It points out the challenges that lie ahead in today's contemporary global economy for the law enforcement community, policy makers, and legislators. There is a need for a critical discussion about the definition of this problem, the source of the problem, and the purpose behind the enactment of the EEA legislation. The material presented here is intended to encourage a dialogue about what is meant by criminalization of intellectual property crimes, such as information theft and trade secret theft, whether information should be considered "property," and the role of law enforcement in policing economic espionage activities. Beyond these concerns, the book draws attention to a variety of issues raised by economic espionage and technological development. Many of these problems are derived from an environment in which there is little face-to-face interaction and identification of the perpetrator is difficult to establish. It is not only the environment that poses problems for law enforcement but also the technology itself. The discussions address the need for the education and training of law enforcement personnel who deal with these problems. Such educational initiatives should be extended to effect change in the attitudes of the judiciary and the wider public concerning prevention of information theft and technology crimes.

Economic espionage is not merely an intelligence issue; it involves fundamental questions about a nation's economic interests, which in turn are part of its national security. For example, the arrest of the senior FBI official Robert Hanssen in February 2001 reminded America of the dangers of foreign spying against U.S. national security interests.[1] As the legislative history to the EEA stated: "typically, espionage has focused on military secrets. But as the Cold War came to an end, this classic form of espionage evolved. Nations around the world recognize that economic superiority is increasingly as important as military superiority."

Theoretical Perspectives

One philosophical rational for regarding knowledge as property is the labor reward theory, a theory that finds foundation in the work of John Locke.[2] Locke, in his famous *Two Treatises of Government*, stated: "Whatsoever then he removes out of the State that Nature hath provided, and left it in, he hath mixed his Labor with, and joined to it something that is his own, and thereby makes it his Property."[3] This reasoning applies to the creation of new scientific knowledge.

Two prominent and competing theories, retribution and utilitarianism, might justify the punishment of information thieves as criminals. Both retributive and utilitarian arguments are useful in understanding the conflict that seems to have arisen between two sets of social values: those who seek to protect private rights by means of the criminal justice system and those that argue that society benefits more with the basic principles of freedom from interference, freedom of information, freedom of expression, and the like. The question then becomes whether either traditional retributive or utilitarian theory provides a justification for the imposition of criminal punishment.

Proponents of retribution argue that, regardless of the effects of punishment, society is always justified in imposing criminal sanctions on those who violate the moral order. All retributive arguments in favor of punishment assume that we can define the moral order we seek to protect. In light of utilitarian theories of punishment, the question becomes what kind of behavior do we want to deter and what kind of behavior do we want to encourage to arrive at utilitarian gain?

In a civil suit, the issue before the court is usually how much harm the plaintiff has suffered at the hands of the defendant and what remedies, if any, are appropriate to compensate the victim for his or her loss. The goal of civil litigation is compensation. By contrast, a criminal case requires the court to determine whether and to what extent the defendant has injured society. The result of criminal conviction is a sentence designed to punish. Criminal law seeks to punish because society recognizes that we cannot adequately respond to certain courses of action merely by rendering compensation to the victim.

Legal theories about the justification for punishment can be grouped into two main categories: retributionism and utilitarianism. Retribution is an ancient concept. Opponents of the theory have argued that it is an outmoded, even barbaric, idea, inappropriate in an enlightened society.[4] The classic, modern statement of the concept of retributive justice is found in Kant's *The Philosophy of Law*:

> Juridical punishment can never be administered merely as a means of promoting another good, either with regard to the Criminal himself or to Civil Society, but must in all cases be imposed only because the individual on whom it is inflicted has committed a Crime.... The Penal Law is a Categorical Imperative; and woe to him who creeps through the serpent-windings of Utilitarianism to discover some advantage that may discharge him from the Justice of punishment, or even from the due measure of it, according to the Pharisaic maxim: "It is better that one man should die than that the whole people should perish." For if Justice and Righteousness perish, human life would no longer have any value in the world.[5]

Most utilitarian arguments on the value of punishment can be categorized as a theory of deterrence, restraint, or reformation. According to Jeremy Bentham, punishment serves the purpose of deterring socially undesirable behavior due to a "spirit of calculation" we all possess:

> Pain and pleasure are the great springs of human action. When a man perceives or supposes pain to be the consequence of an act, he is acted upon in such a manner as tends ... to withdraw him ... from the commission of that

act. If the apparent magnitude, or rather, value of that pain be greater than the apparent magnitude or value of the pleasure or good he expects to be the consequence of the act, he will be absolutely prevented from performing it.[6]

Jeremy Bentham formulated the principle of utility as part of such a theory in *Introduction to the Principles of Morals and Legislation* in 1789. An action conforms to the principle of utility if and only if its performance will be more productive of pleasure or happiness, or more preventive of pain or unhappiness, than any alternative. Instead of "pleasure" and "happiness" the word "welfare" is also apt: The value of the consequences of an action is determined solely by the welfare of individuals.

A characteristic feature of Bentham's theory is the idea that the rightness of an action *entirely* depends on the value of its consequences. This is why the theory is also described as consequentialist. Bentham's theory differs from certain other varieties of utilitarianism (or consequentialism) by its distinctive assumption that the standard of value is pleasure and the absence of pain, by being an act-utilitarian, and by its maximizing assumption that an action is not right unless it tends toward the optimal outcome.

These theories provide useful tools for examining the topics of this book. They are reexamined in connection with some of the conclusions in the final chapter, where policy choices are analyzed. These theories provide justification for the move toward criminalization of certain intellectual property theft.

Spies Target Our Know-How

Trade secret theft, or economic espionage as it is often called, commonly occurs in one of two ways: (1) a disgruntled employee misappropriates the company's trade secrets for his or her own financial benefit or to harm the company or (2) a competitor of the company or a foreign nation misappropriates the trade secret to advance its own financial interests.[7] The manner in which these thefts occur ranges from the complex (computer hacking, wire interception, spy devices) to the mundane (memorization, theft of documents, photocopying).

There are many varieties of spies. Some of the more common international snoops include competitors, vendors, investigators, business intelligence consultants, the press, labor negotiators, and government agencies.[8] Espionage employees are often talented people with highly analytical skills who excel at quickly collecting and synthesizing significant quantities of information.[9] Some countries hire individuals, rather than large organizations or intelligence agencies, to do their spying for them.[10] Other countries hire teams of individuals to enter foreign companies and steal ideas. The tools of the espionage community include scanning trade-show floors,[11] combing through web sites,[12] reviewing filings with regulatory agencies,[13] eavesdropping in airline terminals and on airline flights,[14] taking photographs of factories and business offices,[15] using data-mining software to search the Internet at high speeds for information,[16] using "shadow teams,"[17] stealing laptop computers,[18] tuning in to computer monitors from a nearby location using surveillance equipment,[19] attending competitors' court trials,[20] and even "dumpster diving."[21] However, in all instances, the owner – who often has invested hours of hard work and millions of dollars in developing the trade secret – is deprived of the commercial advantage he or she would have obtained by keeping the trade secret unavailable to his or her competitors and the public.

Economic Espionage Becoming Big Business

A number of factors have contributed to the increase in trade secret theft in recent years, such as the end of the Cold War, increased access to and use of computer technology, greater profitability, and the lack of company resources to investigate and pursue such theft.[22] The increasing importance of economic factors in defining a nation's security has resulted in the widespread theft of proprietary information in the form of trade secrets. The level of trade secret theft appears to have skyrocketed in recent years, and it includes more capers than the celebrated Amazon.com–Wal-Mart employee poaching case,[23] the improper use of the Sabre computer system by an American Airlines employee,[24] and the Oracle–Microsoft "dumpster diving" case.[25] Realistically, no business is immune from economic espionage. Targets include two main forms: industry and proprietary business information.[26] Government and corporate financial and trade data are also stolen on a regular basis.

The United States leads the world in developing new products and new technologies.[27] Per capita, the United States produces the majority of the world's intellectual property capital, including patented inventions, copyrighted material, and proprietary information.[28] Within the United States, economic espionage occurs with the greatest frequency in regions with high concentrations of technology and research and development activities. The FBI has reported that at least twenty-three foreign governments actively target the intellectual property of U.S. corporations.[29] Another FBI study also found that of 173 countries, 100 were spending resources to acquire U.S. technology.[30] Of those 100 countries, 57 were engaging in covert operations against U.S. corporations.[31] According to the FBI study, the following countries allegedly are extensively engaged in espionage activities against American companies: France, Israel, Russia, China, Iran, Cuba, the Netherlands, Belgium, Germany, Japan, Canada, India, and several Scandinavian countries.[32] Examples of the most targeted regions for spying include Silicon

Valley, Detroit, North Carolina, Dallas, Boston, Washington, DC,[33] and the Pennsylvania–New Jersey area,[34] where many pharmaceutical and biotechnology companies are headquartered.[35] Silicon Valley, according to some experts, is the most targeted area. It offers an ideal setting for economic espionage because of its concentration of electronics, aerospace, and biotechnology industries; its national ties to the Far East; and its mobile, multinational workforce. In Silicon Valley alone, more than twenty FBI agents are assigned full time to investigations of trade secret theft. In particular, high-tech businesses, pharmaceutical companies, manufacturing firms, and service industries are the most frequent targets of corporate spies.[36] The most frequently targeted industries appear to include aerospace, biotechnology, computer software and hardware, transportation and engine technology, defense technology, telecommunications, energy research, advanced materials and coatings, stealth technologies, lasers, manufacturing processes, and semiconductors.[37] Victims are not just the naïve and unsophisticated – they include such corporate giants as General Motors, Intel, Lockheed Martin, and Hughes Aircraft.[38] Further, it is not just "high-technology" information that is a target. Proprietary and confidential business information such as customer lists and information, product development data, pricing data, sales figures, marketing plans, personnel data, bid information, manufacturing costs analyses, and strategic planning information are also sought out by intelligence agents.[39] Japan, Taiwan, South Korea, China, the former Soviet Union, and the Russian Republic have devoted the most resources to stealing Silicon Valley technology.[40] Nearly every major U.S. company now has a competitive intelligence office that is designed to discover the trade secrets of competitors.[41] Some firms, such as Motorola, have intelligence units located around the world.[42]

Computers Spark Surge in Trade Secret Theft

No single reason can be given for the increase in trade secret theft. However, one reason for the dramatic increase is undoubtedly the world's ever-expanding use of the computer. Increasing public use and access to computers has allowed people who harbor criminal intentions to copy sensitive information or to enter confidential areas to which they previously had no access. For example, a disgruntled employee who wants to take the company's most attractive new plan or product to his or her next employer no longer needs to spend hours clandestinely duplicating documents. He or she can now download the plans, schematics, or documents to a 3.5-in. computer disk in a matter of seconds.[43] Every time a new computer is linked to a network, or a company network is linked to the Internet, the points of entry through which a hacker may gain access to a company's confidential system are increased. Each new addition increases the chance that someone will not follow the proper security instructions or will allow access to an unauthorized user.[44]

Not only has confidential and proprietary business information become easier to steal, but stealing it is also potentially very lucrative.[45] For example, a group of Russian computer hackers stole $10 million from Citibank by infiltrating its computer network.[46] One businessman has stated: "if I want to steal money, a computer is a much better tool than a handgun . . . it would take me a long time to get $10 million with a handgun."[47]

Proprietary Information

Generally, such information concerns business and economic resources, activities, research and development, policies, and critical technologies. Although it may be unclassified, the loss of this information could impede the ability of a nation to compete in the world marketplace and could have an adverse effect on its economy, eventually weakening its national security. Commonly referred to as "trade secrets," this information typically is protected under both state and federal laws in the United States. A misappropriation of trade secrets, or industrial espionage, occurs when a trade secret is obtained by a breach of a confidential relationship or through improper means, when such information is used, and when such use causes the trade secret owner to sustain damages.

Global Competition and Intellectual Property Rights

Economic espionage especially threatens intellectual property rights (IPRs), which have become the most valuable asset of global business.[48] IPRs can be owned or stolen for profit and are a vital issue in today's competitive market economy. IPRs have become an area of international interest and controversy as the rate and cost of technological progress have increased and as national borders have become ever more transparent. Intellectual property refers to the legal rights that correspond to intellectual activity in the industrial, scientific, and artistic fields.[49] These legal rights, most commonly in the form of patents, trademarks, and copyright, protect the moral and economic rights of the creators, in addition to the creativity and dissemination of their work.[50] Industrial property,[51] which is part of intellectual property, extends protection to inventions and industrial designs.

The costs of product development in the innovation and expression industries are high. For example, filmmaking, music producing, and research-oriented pharmaceuticals manufacturing are risky businesses that survive with three successes out of ten tries. In contrast, the costs of product imitation (or outright theft) are relatively low. The theft in question is not, of course, of the actual pills themselves (i.e., the tangible asset), but of the creative idea that produced them, in other words, the invention, which is something intangible.

The following incidents further demonstrate this point. In 1995, an employee of high-technology giant Intel attempted to steal blueprints for the Pentium processor developed through years of research and development at great cost.[52] Mr. Ow, 31, a resident of Sunnyvale, California, and a citizen of Malaysia, was originally indicted by a federal grand jury on March 29, 2000. A superseding indictment was filed on March 14, 2001, which charged him with three counts of theft of trade secrets in violation of Title 18, U.S. Code, Sections 1832(a)(2) and (a)(3); one count of computer fraud in violation of Title 18, U.S. Code, Section 1030(a)(4); and one count alleging the criminal forfeiture pursuant to Title 18, U.S. Code, Section 1834(a)(2). He pled guilty on September 14, 2001, to a superseding information charging him with the copying of a trade secret in violation of Title 18, U.S. Code, Section 1832(a)(2), and he admitted to the criminal forfeiture.

According to the information and plea agreement, Mr. Ow copied computer files relating to the design and testing of the Merced microprocessor (now known as the Itanium microprocessor). At the time, Mr. Ow knew that the materials contained trade secrets belonging to Intel Corporation. He copied the trade secret information with intent to convert it to his own economic benefit by using it at his then-new employer, Sun Microsystems. He also knew at the time that his act would injure Intel Corporation, in that he – as a former employee of Intel – possessed Intel's extremely valuable trade secret information without its knowledge. He also agreed that the information he copied was in fact a trade secret and that it was related to a product that was produced for and later placed in interstate and foreign commerce. The Itanium microprocessor was under joint development by Intel and Hewlett-Packard Co. since 1994 and was released in 2001. Mr. Ow also agreed to the criminal forfeiture of his interest in the computer system that was located at his residence and that he used to commit and facilitate the commission of the copying. Prior to imposing the 2-year prison sentence, Judge Fogel stated that the key point in a case such as this is the gravity of what happens when people steal intellectual property of such enormous value.

Although this employee was arrested prior to transmitting the data to an Intel competitor, he could have provided the information necessary to create an identical competing product and put a billion-dollar company out of business.[53] In recent years, Microsoft's network was invaded by industrial hackers using a computer virus that allowed them to steal pending Microsoft products; the hackers were traced to an electronic mail (e-mail) address in Russia.[54] These attacks against two sophisticated technology giants demonstrate that all businesses are vulnerable to economic espionage.

What Is Industrial Espionage ?

The key difference between economic espionage and industrial espionage is that the former involves a government's efforts to collect information.[55] Spying remains irresistible to leaders and fascinating to the public. It is occasionally of spectacular value, particularly in wartime. Opposing sides in World War I searched for secret weapons, knowing that such weapons would be available in a foreign country's industrial sector. Spies gained information on how to create weapons such as poison gas.[56] Spying saved countries time and financial resources that they would have spent developing poison gas on their own. The spies stole the secret from the Germans, and shortly afterward many countries used poison gas against each other during warfare.[57]

The practice commonly known today as "industrial espionage," including state-sponsored espionage, has been carried out for centuries. Proof of this can be found in the 1474 laws of the Republic of Venice. The leaders of Venice understood that new technologies were being developed throughout the civilized world that were not yet available in Venice. If enterprising Venetians could be encouraged to travel the world and bring these inventions back home, Venice would prosper. To promote such espionage, Venice enacted a form of monopoly law that would reward the enterprising adventurers. Under the law, if a man brought a new machine or process to Venice from another land, only that man could use the machine or process within the boundaries of Venice for a number of years; all others were excluded. In this manner, that man prospered and Venice gained new technology.

Patents and copyrights were devised by the Venetians to stimulate innovation and expression in a city-state that was losing its trade hegemony in the eastern Mediterranean and the capacity to compete with Florence and other city-states. The institutions gradually spread northward, developing certain distinctive characteristics in France, Germany, and England. The authoritarian French government came to view patents and copyrights as royal favors to be bestowed at whim. Eighteenth-century French revolutionaries established instead that they were "natural rights" of the creative process of innovation and expression and were not to be subject to government intervention other than ratification. Early seventeenth-century English reformers reacted to the perversion of the patent and copyright into royal monopolies by codifying into law that these were rights bestowed by government to stimulate innovation and expression. Thus, the institutions in England kept to the original Venetian intent.

The framers of the U.S. Constitution rejected the French assumptions in favor of the British, and laws regarding patents and copyrights were promulgated by the new Congress during George Washington's first presidential term through the leadership of Thomas Jefferson on patents and Noah Webster on copyrights. The aim of U.S. intellectual property policy has always been to promote public welfare; private property rights have been the means toward that end.[58]

Traditionally speaking, espionage was the way in which spies acquired an enemy's military secrets. Some famous incidents of espionage in a military context included England's use of spies to acquire military information in defeating the Spanish Armada in 1588; other examples were the Allies' use of spies during World War II in defeating the Axis powers and the former Soviet Union's use of spies in stealing atomic bomb secrets from the United States and Great Britain.[59]

Today, an example of industrial espionage would be a South Korean company eavesdropping on Intel's communications. If, however, the South Korean government supplied the listening equipment or owned the company, then the Korean company's activities would be considered economic espionage. Despite some overlap, economic, industrial, and traditional espionage, in theory, are mutually exclusive terms, although their usage in the literature is inconsistent.[60]

According to the U.S. Department of Justice, industrial espionage is defined "as activity conducted by a foreign ... government or by a foreign company with the direct assistance of a foreign government against a private United States company for the sole purpose of acquiring commercial secrets." This definition does not extend to the activity of private entities without foreign government involvement, nor does it pertain to lawful efforts to obtain commercially useful information, such as information available on the Internet. As demonstrated in later chapters, although some open-collection efforts may be a precursor to clandestine collection, they do not constitute industrial espionage. Some countries have a long history of ties between government and industry; however, it is often difficult to ascertain whether espionage has been committed under foreign government sponsorship.[61]

Contrary to many media reports, commercial enterprises and individuals account for the bulk of international industrial espionage activity. For example, in the defense industry, 58% of industrial espionage is practiced by corporations and individuals, whereas only 22% is attributed to foreign government-sponsored efforts, according to the FBI's 2001 Annual Report to Congress on Foreign Economic Collection and Industrial Espionage. The significance surrounding the classes of parties involved in economic espionage is twofold. First, friendly and allied nations commit espionage against one another. In the world of economic espionage, there are no true friendly relations, largely due to the fact that countries that engage in the activity are vying for a rung on the global market ladder.[62] As former French intelligence chief Pierre Marion pointed out, "it is an elementary blunder to think we're allies. When it comes to business, it's war."[63] Second, developing nations are heavily involved in the trade, due to recent political developments, especially the decline of communism. Formerly communist states strive to quickly catch up with the West, and economic espionage often provides an avenue to do just that. Without communism, intelligence agents from Eastern bloc countries are unemployed and available in the open market. The involvement of Eastern bloc agents is threatening because their intelligence activities are not restricted by traditional notions of international business ethics.[64] Therefore, such agents may go to any lengths to acquire the information they seek.

Many foreign nations dedicate significant resources to gathering intelligence about other governments or elements thereof, and to gathering counterintelligence information to protect against other nations' intelligence activities. The problem of foreign economic espionage has grown significantly since the end of the Cold War. A 1994 Report to Congress on Foreign Acquisition of and Espionage Activities Against United States Critical Technology Companies reported that the intelligence organization of one ally ran an espionage operation that paid a U.S. government employee to obtain U.S. classified military intelligence documents. Citizens of that ally were found to be stealing sensitive U.S. technology used in manufacturing artillery gun tubes within the United States. Other agents of that ally stole design plans for a classified reconnaissance system from a U.S. company and gave them to a defense contractor in their home country. A company based in the territory of the ally was suspected of surreptitiously monitoring a Defense Department telecommunications system to obtain classified information for the intelligence organization of its government. Citizens of that country were investigated for passing advanced aerospace design technology to unauthorized scientists and researchers.

According to the 1994 report, another country that did not maintain its own intelligence service relied on private companies to do that kind of work. Those firms operate abroad and collect data for their own purposes, but also gather classified documents and corporate proprietary information for use by their government. For example, electronics firms from that nation directed their data-gathering efforts at U.S. firms in order to increase the market share of companies in that country in the semiconductor industry.

In 1993, Peter Schweizer aroused considerable interest with his book, *Friendly Spies: How America's Allies Are Using Economic Espionage to Steal Our Secrets*. Appearing in the wake of a number of sensational cases, Schweizer's book began to make the American public and industry aware of a growing problem. Schweizer offered a broader perspective on the subject of economic espionage, from Pierre Marion, a longtime senior official of the French Intelligence Service:

> I think you have to separate very clearly what are the fields which are covered by an alliance and the fields which are not covered by an alliance. It's clear that

when you are allies, you have certain sectors. I'm speaking of the armaments. I'm thinking of diplomatic matters where normally you should not try to gather intelligence. But in all of the other fields, being allied does not prevent the states from being competitors. Even during the Cold War, the economic competition between the states is moving from the political-military level to the economic and technological level. In economics we are competitors, not allies. I think even during the Cold War getting intelligence on economic, technological, and industrial matters from a country with which you are allied is not incompatible with the fact that you are allies.[65]

Peter Schweizer exposed the fact that U.S. allies are targeting U.S. industry and stealing trade secrets to benefit their countries. He implicated France, Israel, Germany, South Korea, and Japan and asserted that these "friendly" nations have been involved in economic and technological espionage against the United States for the past 45 years.

Schweizer's revelations were recognized by the U.S. government in August 1996, when the Central Intelligence Agency (CIA) accused American allies, including France and Israel, of engaging in economic espionage. The accusation was the result of a list compiled by the National Counterintelligence Center (NACIC) that included only those countries they believe are extensively engaged in economic espionage.[56] The CIA made the accusation in written answers to questions by members of the Senate Intelligence panel. The Senate report is a rare public endorsement of the CIA charges and was the first time the U.S. government had ever publicly confirmed Israel's involvement.[67] This revelation about Israel touched a sensitive area, given the historic close ties between the United States and Israel and the periodic allegations that Israel targets U.S. military and commercial secrets.[68] The report also included testimony by a General Accounting Office national security specialist, David E. Cooper, before the committee. He reported that "according to the Federal Bureau of Investigation and intelligence agencies, some close United States allies actively seek to obtain classified and technical information from the United States through unauthorized means." The agencies determined that foreign intelligence activities directed at U.S. critical technologies pose a significant threat to national security.[69]

Although the report only uses terms such as "Country A" and "Country B," the descriptions of the countries and the incidents overwhelmingly suggest that Country A is Israel and Country B is France.[70] According to the report, Israel "conducts the most aggressive espionage operation against the United States of any United States ally." The report declares that classified military information and sensitive military technologies are high-priority targets for Israel's intelligence agencies. The report also documented how France began an aggressive and massive espionage effort against the United States. The lessening of East–West tensions in the late 1980s and early 1990s enabled French intelligence services to allocate greater resources to collect sensitive U.S. economic information and technology. France's "government organization that conducts these activities does not target United States national defense information such as war plans, but rather seeks United States technology."

The information concerning France's espionage activities was nothing new to the U.S. intelligence community. According to CIA and FBI officials, French agents have gone as far as bugging seats on Air France to listen to conversations of American businessmen as well as ransacking their hotel rooms.[71] In 1993, the CIA warned American defense contractors against attending the Paris Air Show because French operatives were lying in wait to steal their trade secrets.[72]

The NACIC's Annual Report submitted to Congress in March 2001 confirmed a number of new trends in the way economic espionage is practiced in the United States by foreign companies, individuals, businessmen, and indeed government agencies. The NACIC survey was based on reports from the leading American intelligence agencies and a handful of specialized units, such as the U.S. Air Force's Office of Special Investigations, the State Department's Bureau of Diplomatic Security, or the Naval Criminal Investigative Service. The survey established that most bids to dig out commercial or financial information were instigated by private persons or companies. Indeed, some 58% of economic intelligence collected in the United States was the work of firms and/or individuals acting on their own initiative, whereas 22% was instigated by government agencies and 20% by state-owned or state-run establishments (research centers, universities, and the like). With regard to the method of collection, NACIC underlined the increasing use of software that specializes in processing open sources. The report cited "highly assertive open source collection" conducted under programs that can analyze output from hundreds of discussion groups or screen price lists, catalogues, annual reports, patent data, and marketing materials.[73] In pinpointing the problem, the NACIC implied that U.S. intelligence agencies had found ways of monitoring the software in question, which is in wide use among business intelligence professionals. However, the report also went into some detail about illegal collection of data through the open theft of trade secrets, acquisition of export-controlled technologies, and the recruitment of U.S. nationals as spies.

Economic Espionage

Economic espionage has been defined as one nation collecting economic data about another nation.[74] Simply put, economic espionage is the "outright theft of private information."[75] It is a widespread form of attack that is conducted by employees against their own employers, by competing private companies, and by governments seeking to protect or expand their national economies.[76] Economic data may include such information as national gross domestic product and inflation rate figures, which may be obtained from published sources, or more privileged information such as budgetary allocations for defense and national research and development expenditures, which are usually acquired through illicit means. Technological espionage involves one nation collecting data about another's technological development programs, usually those of critical industries such as electronics, aerospace, defense, or biotechnology.

A different and somewhat more definitive description comes from the Canadian Security Intelligence Service (CSIS). According to CSIS, economic espionage is "illegal, clandestine, coercive or deceptive activity engaged in or facilitated by a foreign government designed to gain unauthorized access to economic intelligence, such as proprietary information or technology, for economic advantage."[77] Still another, far more complex definition is contained in the United States' EEA,[78] one of the few forms of legislation enacted to help suppress economic espionage. Economic espionage entails the unlawful compilation and use of data with economic consequences, although technological developments can, on occasion, obscure the distinction between economic and military targets.[79]

An important concept related to economic espionage is economic intelligence. According to CSIS, economic intelligence is "policy or commercially relevant economic information, including technological data, financial, proprietary commercial and government information, the acquisition of which by foreign interests could, either directly or indirectly, assist the relative productivity or competitive position of the economy of the collecting organization's country." Those who conduct economic espionage specifically target this class of information.

In Japan, the ministry for international trade and industry identifies foreign high-tech companies that are likely to produce significant products in the near future. The ministry supplies crucial information to Japanese companies, leading them toward purchasing the foreign companies through front organizations, false flag operations, or overt means.[80] In another case, a firm in the United States lost a contract bid for international electronics. Shortly thereafter, it learned that a European intelligence agency somehow intercepted its pricing information. The European agency turned this critical data over to another company, which eventually won the contract bid. In still another incident, the CSIS discovered that a handful of "flight attendants" on Air France were actually agents of the French intelligence service, strategically positioned to spy on companies' executives and gather their trade secrets. These present-day examples, together with the aforementioned historical evidence, illustrate a crucial point that economic espionage has been and continues to be on the rise.[81]

Trolling for Secrets Past and Present

Although the end of the Cold War seemingly brought a surge of economic espionage activity, stealing the ideas of a business competitor is not a new game in the world market. Indeed, economic espionage is a practice that has existed for thousands of years. An early instance of economic espionage occurred more than 1,500 years ago and involved the secret of silk. A Chinese princess traveled abroad, wearing a flowered hat. She hid the silkworms in the flowers and gave them to a man in India. Thus, through economic espionage, the secret of silk escaped from China.[82]

In the eighteenth century, China again lost a secret because of economic espionage. After China had spent centuries making high-quality porcelain through a process known only to its alchemists, the French Jesuit, Father d'Entrecolles, visited the royal porcelain factory in China, where he learned the secrets of porcelain production and described the process in writings he sent to France.[83]

In his book, *War by Other Means: Economic Espionage in America*, John Fialka introduces the readers to the subject by reciting the story of Francis Cabot Lowell of Massachusetts, who traveled to Great Britain in 1811 and returned with the secrets of the Cartwright loom. This act of economic espionage revolutionized the New England textile industry and greatly enriched Lowell. From these early roots, technology theft has evolved with the changes in technology. Fialka further points out:

> Spies are normally associated with wartime and the theft of military technology. In the vast popular literature, there is hardly a mention of the peacetime industrial spy. One reason may be because spy stories tend to blossom when wars end. War is relatively clear-cut; there is a winner and an eventual loser, a beginning and an end. The end is normally the signal for the memoir writers to begin, but the economic struggle that attracted Lowell's stealthy genius is not clear-cut. Winners win quietly, and losers are often unconscious of loss, or too embarrassed to admit it. And it is a war that does not end. The stage for the studiously low-key dramas of economic espionage is set, as one perceptive French writer puts it, in a kind of perpetual limbo, where there is "neither war nor peace."[84]

The early twentieth century and the reality of worldwide conflict led to significant incidents of economic espionage, proving that economic and military intelligence were equally important. Perhaps no other company has been targeted by foreign intelligence agents as many times as International Business Machines (IBM). A leader in both computer hardware and software, IBM produces many products of strategic interest to other governments. According to IBM's internal documents, foreign agents illegally sought to acquire business secrets twenty-five times over a 10-year period.[85] A retired French spymaster has even admitted to spying on IBM.[86]

The most famous attempt to steal trade secrets from IBM mirrored that of an old Soviet operation. In 1980, an IBM employee stole some of the Adirondack Workbooks, a series of valuable books containing computer specifications and strategic planning, and sold them to Hitachi, a Japanese computer maker.[87] Not content with a partial set of the workbooks, Hitachi sought the remaining workbooks and other confidential material from other sources. Over the next 2 years, the FBI, in conjunction with IBM, set up an elaborate sting operation. In the end, Hitachi's efforts were thwarted, the conspirators were arrested, the Japanese government's involvement was revealed, and Hitachi paid IBM a considerable out-of-court settlement. Still, the conspirators did not receive any jail time, and Hitachi greatly benefited from the workbooks.

Cold War's End and Spies Shift to Corporate Espionage

As Cold War structures – from NATO to the KGB and the CIA – seek to redefine themselves and to assume new roles and new functions, economic espionage is an attractive option. During the Cold War, both intelligence[88] and counterintelligence[89] focused on military and political targets.[90] For example, a typical case of espionage might involve an American scientist selling military technology to the Soviet Union or an Eastern European nation.[91] Increasing state involvement in modern economies also has blurred the traditional lines between the private and public sectors. Many businesses are state owned, state financed. Many businessmen double as politicians, and numerous politicians serve on corporate boards.[92] With the end of the Cold War, nations have refocused domestic and foreign policies and programs to increase economic standards for their citizens.[93] Economic superiority has become as important as military superiority, and the espionage industry has been retooling with this in mind.[94] In a recent decision by the U.S. Court of Appeals[95] for the Third Circuit, the court echoed this notion, stating that "the end of the Cold War sent government spies scurrying to the private sector to perform illicit work for businesses and corporations and by 1996, studies revealed that nearly $24 billion of corporate intellectual property was being stolen each year."[96]

Shift in Espionage Trends

With the fall of communism, the U.S. intelligence community was forced to redefine its mission and role in order to meet the new realities of the post–Cold War climate. Different forms of espionage evolved. Now, espionage activities have largely shifted to concentrate on technology, manufacturing processes, and other trade secrets that sometimes have dual use, but often only civilian applications.[97]

Foreign intelligence services have increasingly devoted their resources to stealing U.S. technology.[98] Shortly after CIA officer Aldrich "Rick" Ames began selling secrets to the Soviet KGB in 1985, a scientist named Ronald Hoffman also began peddling classified information. Ames, the last known mole of the Cold War, received $4.6 million for names of CIA informants before he was apprehended in early 1994. Hoffman, a project manager for a company called Science Applications, Inc., made $750,000 selling complex software programs developed under secret contract for the Strategic Defense Initiative. Hoffmann, who was caught in 1992, sold his wares to Japanese multinationals – Nissan Motor Company, Mitsubishi Electric, Mitsubishi Heavy Industries, and Ishikawajima-Harima Heavy Industries wanted the information for civilian aerospace programs.

Ames received the more dramatic and sensational coverage, as he should have, given that his betrayal led to the loss of life. However, the Hoffman case represents the future of intelligence. Although one spied for America's chief military rival, the other sold information to a major economic competitor.[99]

Economic Intelligence – A New Battlefront

Economic and technological strength are the keys to power and influence.[100] Trade talks have replaced arms control as the most critical form of diplomacy.[101] Government agencies now have a growing role in surreptitious data collection. Perhaps most surprising about this trend is that the perpetrators are often longtime U.S. allies.[102] These countries steal U.S. economic and technological information, despite their friendly diplomatic and cultural relations with the United States. Taking advantage of their access to U.S. information, many U.S. allies have obtained valuable confidential information with more success than the United States' traditional enemies. Ironically, the U.S. intelligence community often trained and supplied the very services now spying on the United States.

Even during the Cold War, countries that were formally allied with the United States spied on U.S. corporations.[103] Some U.S. allies adopted a "two-track" approach under which they worked with the United States against the Soviet Union while stealing trade secrets from U.S. corporations.[104] In fact, the practice of economic spying by allied intelligence services was an open secret among many FBI and CIA professionals during the Cold War. The U.S. government did not consider espionage from friendly countries to be a serious national security concern.[105] The U.S. intelligence community kept these activities secret to ensure that allied intelligence services continued to spy on the Soviet Union. Victimized U.S. companies rarely revealed the theft of their confidential information. Thus, few people outside of the counter-intelligence community were aware that many U.S. allies stole information from U.S. corporations.

As economic competition replaces military confrontation in many global affairs, spying for high-tech secrets will continue to grow.[106] How the United States elects to deal with this troubling issue will not only determine the direction of the American intelligence community, but also set the tone for commercial relations in the global marketplace.[107]

With such significant national effects of economic espionage, intelligence agencies have had to confront the issue vigorously. This has led to another kind of arms race in which some national intelligence agencies spend billions of dollars each year in their economic espionage efforts, and counterintelligence agencies spend billions of dollars trying to thwart those efforts.[108]

Episodes of Intelligence Failures

Since the fall of the Soviet Union, the U.S. intelligence community has experienced some embarrassing failures. These include the expulsion of CIA operatives from France and Germany, the failure to warn of Indian nuclear tests, the bombing of the Chinese embassy in Belgrade due to faulty data provided by the CIA, and computer failures that disrupted intelligence processing operations.[109]

In February 1995, the French government went public with its request that five CIA operatives, allegedly caught stealing economic and political secrets in Paris, leave the country.[110] The French Foreign Ministry summoned the U.S. Ambassador Pamela Harriman to the Quai d'Orsay to demand the recall of several CIA officers who allegedly had been involved in clandestine operations targeted against French government officials. The officials had access to information on telecommunications issues, including France's negotiating strategy and its international telecommunications structure. Two officials approached by the CIA reported their overtures to the Direction de la Surveillance du Territoire, the French security service.[111] U.S. officials responded angrily to France's public reaction to the spying. One U.S. official was quoted as saying that "this is not the way allies treat each other." The French officials claimed that the U.S. citizens were trying to bribe government officials to obtain French technology and trade secrets.[112]

Another CIA agent allegedly paid Henry Plagnol, an aide to then-French Premier Edouard Balladur, 500 francs each time he provided information on French positions on matters being negotiated in ongoing General Agreement on Tariffs and Trade (GATT) talks.[113] Two other CIA agents asked communications ministry officials for information about GATT and intelligence on telecommunications and audiovisual policy.

Although the five agents were eventually allowed to remain in France,[114] French Premier Edouard Balladur asked for the United States to respect France's "national interest" and suspended the CIA's long-standing liaison with French intelligence.[115] This suspension was particularly harmful as the

relationship between the United States and France is crucial for joint operations, such as tracking terrorists. To make matters worse, one top American
official stated that the information obtained was worthless.

The next failure occurred in the summer of 1995, during critical Japan–
United States automobile trade talks. U.S. trade representative Mickey
Kantor and his team of negotiators came to the table armed with information that the CIA and the National Security Agency (NSA) had gathered. During the talks in Geneva, the CIA's Tokyo station and the NSA were
eavesdropping on the Japanese delegation, including Japan's Prime Minister
Ryutaro Hashimoto.[116] The high-level trade negotiations were over possible
tariffs on Japanese luxury cars and for better access to Japan's markets for
American cars and car parts. Each morning, Kantor was briefed with descriptions of conversations between Japanese bureaucrats and auto executives from Toyota and Nissan. The surveillance was legal under U.S. law but
sparked controversy and criticism from Congress.

Another incident involved the American intelligence agents "hacking"
into the European Parliament and European Commission as part of an
international espionage campaign aimed at stealing economic and political
secrets.[117] Security experts at the European Union's (EU's) Luxembourg
offices said they found evidence that American agents had penetrated the
e-mail that links 5,000 EU elected officials and bureaucrats and used the
information they obtained during the GATT trade talks.[118] The breach was
detected after officials began to suspect that American negotiators had been
given advance warning of confidential EU positions. Lord Plum, leader of
the British Tory Members of the European Parliament, was shocked and
voiced his disgust to the American ambassador to the EU.[119]

In 1997, the German government also ordered a CIA officer to leave
the country. Although an initial account suggested the officer had been
trying to recruit senior German officials to provide information on high-
tech projects, a later report suggested that the officer was seeking to gather
information on a third country – probably Iran – and was expelled because
the operation had not been cleared with the German government.

In May 1998, the Indian government conducted multiple nuclear tests,
fulfilling the pledge made by the recently elected Bharatiya Janata Party
during the Indian election campaign. The tests, which were quickly followed
by Pakistani nuclear tests, came as a surprise to both the U.S. intelligence
community and policy makers. George Lauder, the director of the CIA's
Non-Proliferation Center, was first informed of the test on May 11, when he
was handed a wire service report by an aide. At first, Lauder believed it to
be a joke.[120]

On May 7, 1999, during Operation "Allied Force," the Chinese embassy
in Belgrade was bombed under the mistaken belief that it was the Yugoslav
Federal Directorate for Supply and Procurement (FDSP). The FDSP had

been nominated as a target by the CIA. Lacking the precise geographic coordinates needed for a bombing mission, a CIA contract officer used land navigation techniques and a street address to try to determine the precise location of the directorate – techniques that the Director of Central Intelligence (DCI) George Tenet later characterized as ones that "should not be used for aerial targeting because they provide only an approximate location." That error, plus the fact that multiple intelligence community and Defense Department databases indicated the old, pre-1996, location for the Chinese embassy, resulted in the embassy, rather than the FDSP headquarters, becoming the target. Three were killed in the attack, and the U.S. embassy in Beijing became the site of angry demonstrations. The already difficult relations between Beijing and Washington were strained further – with the People's Republic of China claiming that the attack on the embassy had been deliberate.[121]

In January 2000, computer problems struck U.S. imagery and signals intelligence (SIGINT) systems. A "Y2K" fix, intended to allow the uninterrupted and complete processing of advanced KH-11 satellite imagery data received at the Ft. Belvoir, Virginia, ground station, failed. As a result, imagery interpreters were forced to operate at less than full capability.

Late in January 2000, during heavy snowstorms, the computers at the NSA also failed. The failure did not restrict the NSA's massive collection operations, but it did make it impossible to retrieve the data collected. Two days later the storm abated, and NSA employees who had not been on duty the night of the failure returned to work and were told by the agency's new director, Lieutenant General Michael Hayden, of the failure and the need to keep it secret. "American lives were at stake," General Hayden cautioned them. It was only on the morning of Friday, January 27, that the NSA began to get some capability back. On Saturday, the story first appeared in newspapers, but by Friday night full capability had been restored. Fortunately, the United States escaped any damage due to the temporary collapse of a key component of its SIGINT system.[122]

To some extent these incidents are symptoms of deeper problems, such as the mismatch between intelligence collection and processing and analysis, and the emphasis on support to military operations. They are also indicative of the dramatic changes that have occurred since the mid-1990s – in the international political and economic system, in the availability of information, and in the nature of international communications.

Big Brother Named Echelon

Reports by France and Italy of industrial espionage by the United States sparked an inquiry in the European Parliament as to the actions of the CIA and its use of information from the Echelon system.[123] The Echelon system dates back to the Cold War and is generally believed to be able to intercept almost every modern form of communication. According to intelligence specialists, Echelon is a massive network of eavesdropping stations capable of monitoring billions of private phone conversations, e-mail, and fax transmissions around the world. It is a powerful tool, obviously, in the intelligence war against terrorism and other threats.[124] Echelon is an automated global interception and relay system reportedly operated by intelligence agencies in five nations: the United States, the United Kingdom, Canada, Australia, and New Zealand. It has been suggested that Echelon may intercept as many as 3 billion communications every day, including phone calls, e-mail messages, Internet downloads, and satellite transmissions. There has been a global response to the Echelon system, resulting in counter technological systems and code designed to attract the attention of the Echelon system. Many countries have also expressed concern regarding the parameters that participants in the Echelon system will follow in deciding whether to disclose information gathered by the system to third parties. The United States denies that it ever passes intercepted information to U.S. companies. Yet, Europeans note that officials in Washington have acknowledged that U.S. intelligence data about possible bribery figured in Saudi Arabia's decision to cancel a big airliner contract with Airbus Industries, the European consortium. The order eventually went to Airbus's U.S. competitor, Boeing Company.

The European Parliament, reflecting growing mistrust on the issue, voted in July 2000 to investigate whether the United States is spying on European businesses. A committee was appointed to scrutinize the Echelon spy system.[125]

Keeping Secrets

Trade secrets have been common to shaman priests in preliterate societies, and the concept has been intellectually rooted in Western thought in respect for individual liberty, confidentiality of relationships, common morality, and fair competition.[126] Trade secret law grows more out of the concepts of contract and trust than of property because information maintained as a trade secret may be legally safeguarded against misappropriation, but not against independent discovery or accidental leakage.[127]

Legal protection for trade secrets derives from two theories that are only partly complementary. The first is utilitarian in nature and is sometimes associated with the view that information is a form of property. Under this view, protecting against the theft of proprietary information encourages research investments. The second theory emphasizes deterrence of destructive acts and is therefore like a tort theory. Under this theory, the aim of trade secret law is to punish and prevent behavior that is offensive to reasonable standards of commercial behavior.

Although trade secret law is new by common law standards, it comes with respectable credentials.[128] Holders of trade secrets have sought the protection of common laws since the eighteenth century,[29] and a Massachusetts court recognized limited rights in secret information in 1837.[130]

The theory behind trade secrets maintains one core hypothesis: Innovators would not be inclined to spend labor, money, and equipment to create if the law did not give them some assurance that they could profit from their labors.[131] Based on this theory, the foundation of trade secret law is supported by three core public policies. First, trade secret law maintains commercial morality – an enforced standard of business ethics – so businesses can enter into good faith transactions, form stable business relationships, and share confidential information to gain assistance in product development.[132] Second, trade secret law encourages research by ensuring that innovators are the first on the market with their creations. Finally, trade secret law punishes industrial espionage by protecting the right of privacy of the trade secret owner.[133]

At common law, employers had a property right in their trade secrets, and the disclosure of such confidential information in violation of an employment relationship was a tort. Section 757 of the Restatement of Torts, entitled Misappropriation of Trade Secrets, continues to be cited as the guide to the law of trade secret misappropriation. According to the Restatement, misappropriation occurs once a secret is acquired either by improper means or with notice of its mistaken disclosure.[134]

The theft of corporate trade secrets[135] has largely been protected through the remedies provided in civil litigation.[136] However, for numerous reasons, these remedies fail to provide the equivalent deterrent of criminal laws.[137] First, the purpose of criminal sanctions is punitive and seeks to deter socially undesirable activity.[138] Criminal sanctions seek to provide a penalty with the goal of preventing the behavior from occurring in the future, while punishing the past behavior. In contrast, civil law sanctions serve the purpose of compensation and returning the party to a preexisting status quo. Second, criminal and civil sanctions produce different remedies. Criminal sanctions place an inherent stigma on the individual, with punishment being the conventional device for the expression of resentment and indignation.[139] Civil sanctions remedy the problem in an entirely different manner, most notably through monetary disbursements.[140] Criminal law serves as a proactive approach to deterring the problem before it occurs, whereas civil law only serves to compensate the victim for activity that has harmed the individual. For these reasons, civil litigation serves important interests in this area other than deterrence.[141] However, compared with other intellectual property laws, civil trade secret laws have the potential to provide more effective and comprehensive legal protection.[142] This dichotomous relationship has the potential to adequately protect corporations and businesses from theft and misappropriation of trade secrets through separate but related remedies. Civil trade secret laws provide an effective defensive approach, whereas criminal trade secret laws provide a powerful proactive deterrent to combat the growing simplicity and ease of theft. However, although state civil trade secret laws and remedies in this area provide an effective defensive response, current state criminal trade secret laws fail to provide an effective deterrent to the theft and misappropriation of trade secrets.

Although civil remedies that may provide compensation to wronged intellectual property rights holders are available, criminal sanctions are often warranted to ensure sufficient punishment and deterrence of wrongful activity. Indeed, because violations of intellectual property rights often involve no loss of tangible assets and, for infringement crimes, do not even require any direct contact with the rights holder, the rights holder often does not know it is a victim until a defendant's activities are specifically identified and investigated. Criminal penalties imposed for the misappropriation of trade secrets are far more severe than any other criminal liability for violations of other intellectual property rights. Persons engaged in misappropriation in the United States no longer will have their liability limited to civil remedies and damages imposed for such misconduct. Federal criminal prosecution is a powerful weapon, one that should not be taken lightly.[143]

A New Code of Commercial Conduct

Discouraged by the failure of civil remedies to prevent trade secret theft, the inability of prosecutors to effectively use other criminal statutes, and frequent efforts by foreign governments to obtain trade secrets from American companies, the U.S. Congress made the theft of trade secrets a federal crime by enacting the EEA in October 1996.[144]

The EEA criminalizes[145] activity by anyone who:

intending or knowing that the offense will benefit any foreign government, foreign instrumentality, or foreign agent, knowingly – (1) steals, or without authorization appropriates, takes, carries away, or conceals, or by fraud, artifice, or deception obtains a trade secret; (2) without authorization copies, duplicates, sketches, draws, photographs, downloads, uploads, alters, destroys, photocopies, replicates, transmits, delivers, sends, mails, communicates, or conveys a trade secret; (3) receives, buys, or possesses a trade secret, knowing the same to have been stolen or appropriated, obtained, or converted without authorization; (4) attempts to commit any offense described in any of paragraphs (1) through (3); or (5) conspires with one or more other persons to commit any offense described in any of paragraphs (1) through (3), and one or more of such persons do any act to effect the object of the conspiracy. (See Appendix A.)

A powerful example of the need for an economic espionage law is the experience of Dr. Raymond Damadian, who holds the first U.S. patent for a commercial magnetic resonance imaging (MRI) device. In testimony before the House Committee on the Judiciary Subcommittee on Crime on May 9, 1996, Dr. Damadian described how his Fonar Corporation frequently had been under attack from foreign competitors. Damadian told the committee how the absence of a law to repel the invasion of economic espionage cost Fonar a valuable advantage:

[A] gypsy service company servicing medical equipment hired Fonar service engineers, thereby acquiring a full set of our top secret engineering drawing and multiple copies of our copyrighted software. We obtained a temporary restraining order from a federal judge ordering this group not to use Fonar's schematics or software in the service of scanners. They ignored the judge's order. Through a modem connection we secured hard proof of them loading our diagnostic software on our scanner in violation of the judge's order. He cited them for contempt of court. When we complained there were no sanctions beyond the citation, the judge said, "What do you expect me to do, put them in jail?" The irony is if it had been someone's automobile instead of millions of dollars of technology, incarceration would have been automatic.[146]

One of Fonar's competitors, Toshiba Corporation, also lured a company engineer away so that he could provide technical data on Fonar products. The engineer's contract specified that he could not work for a competitor for a 2-year period after leaving Fonar.[147] Damadian soon learned that Toshiba was paying all the engineer's legal bills to fight Fonar's action to enforce the contract.

Damadian also testified that Fonar kept its magnet installation procedures behind locked doors in an effort to protect its most precious technology. An executive of Siemens, a German company, told Damadian that these precautions were easily overcome. The executive told him that the company had taken a technician out to dinner, filled him with alcoholic beverages, and thereby secured an invitation to enter the room and inspect the scanner, which they did, for as long as they wanted.[148]

Today, MRI is a multibillion-dollar industry. Even though the MRI is an American invention, only two of the eight companies selling in the American market today are American. Fonar is now, by far, the smallest of the nine companies that dominate the industry.[149] Most of the profits and thousands upon thousands of high-paying technical jobs created by this invention have gone to companies in Japan and Germany. Fonar's experience is a good example of the shortcomings of civil remedies in preventing the harm of economic espionage.

The EEA provides for criminal prosecution of an individual who "appropriates, takes, carries away, or conceals, or by fraud, artifice, or deception obtains a trade secret." Using a computer to download a trade secret without authorization or, alternatively, destroying a trade secret so as to make it no longer available to the bona fide owner, violates the statute. Appropriation alone – absent commercial use or even disclosure – may trigger criminal liability. In enacting the EEA, Congress created a trade secret law that differs from the common law by broadening both the kind of information covered and the type of conduct prohibited. The EEA thus expands and strengthens the rights of those who hold the trade secrets.

Congress has continually expanded and strengthened criminal laws for violations of IPRs specifically to ensure that those violations are not merely a cost of doing business for defendants. In addition, Congress is concerned with providing adequate protections for both foreign and domestic owners of intellectual property. Indeed, the U.S. government has committed, in a number of international agreements, to protecting IPR holders, including foreign rights holders, from infringement in the United States.[150]

Some misuse of intellectual property has not been criminalized. For example, infringement of a patent is not a criminal violation. Likewise, the laws protecting personally identifiable information do not generally provide for criminal penalties except in the most narrow of circumstances.[151]

Although the EEA addresses and criminalizes domestic economic espionage, such as one domestic firm misappropriating the trade secrets of another or a disgruntled employee stealing his or her employer's trade secrets, the single most important reason it was passed was to address the problem of foreign economic espionage.[152] Foreign economic espionage, where a foreign government or company targets the trade secrets of an American firm, was and continues to be viewed as more insidious, complex, and difficult to discover and track. Furthermore, prior to the passage of the EEA, the prevailing wisdom was that existing state and federal laws, not to mention the extraterritoriality and enforcement issues, made it virtually impossible to effectively prosecute foreign economic espionage.[153]

A problem with the current U.S. philosophy regarding economic espionage is that our European and Asian competitors have little separation between business and government. The EEA has nevertheless filled a significant gap in the protection of trade secrets and has been an important and positive step forward in the battle against trade secret theft. It will be interesting to see if over time the U.S. government loosens the leash on the act and becomes more aggressive in its enforcement efforts, such as by bringing actions under section 1831 (the foreign activity section). Should that occur, it will be yet another reason for American companies to familiarize themselves with the EEA.

The last decade of the twentieth century was marked in most countries of the world with a rising wave of terrorist acts, globalization, and transnational unification of criminal groups. In addition, the last decade was characterized by widespread economic and high-tech crimes, such as unauthorized access to computer networks, industrial and economic espionage, and information theft. These events have increased the importance of establishing a world stage to unify the efforts in combating threats, such as the dissemination of high-tech weaponry, international terrorism, transnational organized crime, and threats to the orderly development of countries and regions of the world.[154]

Transition to an Information Society – Increasing Interconnections and Interdependence

MODERN SOCIETY is increasingly dependent on networked computer systems. The development of information technology in cyberspace has changed our societies, commerce, and lifestyle. These information networks have led to numerous advances in the quality of life by improving the provision of vital services such as power, medicine, and public safety.[1]

The information age is enabled by computing and communications technologies, known as information technologies, whose rapid evolution is almost taken for granted today. Computing and communications systems appear in virtually every sector of the economy and, increasingly, in homes and other locations. These systems focus economic and social activity on information gathering; analyzing, storing, presenting, and disseminating information in text; and numerical, audio, image, and video formats as a product itself or a complement to physical or tangible products. Science and technology have further revolutionized geopolitical strategy, internationalized markets, created new possibilities for environmental or nuclear destruction, undermined totalitarian governments, and changed the conduct of warfare and the basis of economic and political power.

For some time, it has been clear that advances in science and technology are outdistancing the capacity of existing international organizations to deal with them. A glance at the daily newspaper is enough to convince even the most casual observer that there are international dimensions to almost every aspect of science and technology. These dimensions go well beyond the customary international teamwork that characterizes today's massive research and development projects. There are scientific or technical issues woven into the political, economic, and social concerns of international relations. The complexity of the issues at stake not only defies simplification or reduction, but it also challenges distinctions long held to be true between domestic and foreign, between national and international, and finally among the political, the social, and the economic.

Science and technology transform international relations by presenting problems requiring new strategies for decision making, new choices, and new assessments of risk. Not long after the fall of the Berlin Wall and communism, a Carnegie Commission Report called for the need "to adapt to a world in which the border between domestic and foreign affairs is crossed everywhere and most particularly by science and technology."[2]

From the end of World War II until the end of the Cold War, international issues in science and technology largely concerned arms and energy. The panoply of issues in science and technology that impact international affairs today is much broader. Traditional issues in arms control and energy production are still important, but they have been joined by new concepts of intelligence and security, by new technologies in international communications and information networks, and by expanding financial markets and international trade. Modern networked societies are challenged by increasingly complex, diffuse, and global threats. The world's economic globalization has intensified competition in every industrial sector, and with that has come a corresponding rise in industrial espionage.

The Rapid Growth of Computer Technology

As the world's most advanced countries enter into what has been termed the *information age*,[3] this new epoch is defined by the use of computers, particularly computers grouped into the network form[4] and used to facilitate human interactions. The 1980s saw the rapid development of computer technology, and with it the digitization of most forms of information. In the 1990s, this computerization trend led to the expansion of the Internet, which makes the distribution and transportation of information possible with the click of a button. The ability to digitize information and transport it worldwide with the click of a computer key creates a fertile ground for the movement of information protected by intellectual property laws.

For example, Intel, the computer chip maker, has revolutionized the computer industry through the invention of a single product, the Intanium microprocessor.[5] Intel developed this product through years of research, development, and modification.[6] However, through the unscrupulous acts of one person, the company's competitors could have obtained the information necessary to produce an identical product for a fraction of the cost, effort, and time, threatening to put Intel out of business.[7] Lye Ow, an employee at Intel, decided to steal the blueprints for a new processor. In 1998, Ow attempted to download the files about the design and testing of Intel's Merced microprocessor, now know as the Intanium processor, to a remote

site, his home computer. Although the computer files could be viewed remotely by authorized people, Intel's internal computer system would not
allow these critical files to be downloaded. However, this safeguard failed to
deter Ow. Rather than giving up, Ow displayed the files on the computer and
proceeded to videotape each screen. With the information stored on tape,
Ow possessed the information necessary to exactly duplicate the company's
flagship product after only spending minimal amounts of money, time, and
effort.[8] Although Ow was arrested prior to transmitting this information to a
third party, this narratives illustrates the rapidly growing threat of economic,
corporate, and industrial espionage on the welfare of corporations around
the world.[9]

New Crimes of the Information Age

The growth of the information age and the globalization of Internet communication and commerce have significantly impacted the manner in which
economic crimes are committed, the frequency with which those crimes
are committed, and the difficulty in apprehending the perpetrators. It
might start with a photo of a hot-looking convertible from Miami, promised
through an Internet auction and never delivered, or an e-mail from a
Nigerian businessman, offering a fat paycheck in return for a person's bank
account number.[10]

Technology has contributed to that increase in four major respects –
anonymity, security (or insecurity), privacy (or the lack of it), and globalization. In addition, technology has provided the medium or opportunity for
the commission of traditional crimes. Criminals in an electronic world can
ignore international boundaries because they can send information and execute commands via worldwide networks. Requiring no physical presence
and facilitated by the presence of the Internet, electronic crimes are readily
suited for international commission.

Although computer hacking is one good example of an international
crime in cyberspace, there are many other crimes that are facilitated by computer networks, such as forgery and counterfeiting, transmission of threats,
fraud, copyright infringement, theft of trade secrets, transmission of child
pornography, interception of communications, and transmission of harass-
ing communications. The computer hacking cases have repeatedly raised
issues that will be of concern in all international electronic crime cases. In
addition to their inability to prevent such attacks, both law enforcement and
the private sector lack effective enforcement tools and remedies to bring the
perpetrators to justice.

The widespread use of technology and the Internet, as well as the confluence of anonymity, security, privacy, and globalization, have exposed the
public and private sectors to a new array of cyberattacks. Privacy protections

enable thieves to take advantage of anonymity, thus hampering the efforts of law enforcement and private sector fraud investigators to track the thieves. Anonymity enables the criminal to submit fraudulent online applications for bank loans, credit card accounts, insurance coverage, brokerage accounts, and health care coverage. Anonymity also enables employees to pilfer corporate assets. For example, bank employees can embezzle money through electronic fund transfers and employees of credit card issuers can capture account numbers and sell them to outsiders, electronically transferring the account numbers to the co-conspirators. A survey conducted by the Gartner Group of 160 retail companies selling products over the Internet revealed that the amount of credit card fraud was twelve times higher online than in the physical retail world.[11] There is no reason to believe that this figure is unique to the credit card industry. Another study found that the number of search warrants issued by the U.S. federal government for online data had increased 800% over the past few years.[12] Further, anonymity provides enhanced opportunities for two types of perpetrators – the organized crime mobster and the teenage hacker. Last, the Internet enables communication and commerce to occur beyond or without borders presenting significant problems in the prevention, investigation, and enforcement of those crimes. Organized groups of criminals can easily commit economic crimes and avoid sanctions across what were once clearly defined jurisdictions, necessitating increased cooperation among the global criminal justice agencies. Other threats include the loss of credibility with world partners, the transference of proceeds of economic crime to conventional crimes, such as drug trafficking and gun running, and threats to the national security by increased victimization from assaults based in foreign jurisdictions.[13]

Internet Is Making It Easy

Crime knows few limits when greed is at stake and technology is a weapon.[14] The rise of new media, especially the Internet, has brought with it a host of new legal and ethical issues. Although these issues are variations on traditional legal themes, they require fundamentally new approaches.[15] The popularity of the Internet as a form of communication has placed a spotlight on the need to protect original ideas from improper use. Ironically, computer technology has also made it much easier for information to be stolen. In the case of computer crime or cybercrime, the need for legislation to prevent unauthorized access to data or information is more important than ever. Only a few years ago, stealing customer information was a cumbersome task. A prime example is Jose Lopez, the former General Motors executive in the United States who was indicted by a federal grand jury in Detroit for wire fraud for allegedly stealing boxes of confidential and proprietary information in 1993 from General Motors and transferring them to his new job at Volkswagen. Today, there is no need to steal the boxes; the information contained in those boxes is now stored on computers. Such information can be instantly sent anywhere in the world via the Internet. In fact, with the more recent trend of employees being permitted to work at home on their own personal computers, there may not even be a need to use the Internet to accomplish such a theft.

The connectivity of the Internet has made the concept of borders and jurisdictions an incredible challenge in most situations and meaningless in others. Laws, policies, and procedures that were once the purview of sovereign states are now becoming the focus of the world community. In the United States, both civil and criminal laws are now adapting to this reality.

Cybercrimes Are More Real

Most economic crimes have a cyberversion today. With computer networks now spanning the globe, law and law enforcement agencies must address the international dimensions of crimes in cyberspace. These cybercrimes offer more opportunities to the criminals, with larger payoffs and fewer risks. Web sites can be spoofed and hijacked. Payment systems can be compromised and electronic fund transfers to steal funds or launder money occur at lightning speeds. Serious electronic crimes and victimization of the public have caused consumer confidence to waiver. These issues have also lead to growing privacy concerns and demands.[16] For example, preventing and prosecuting cybercrime requires government agents to ascertain the identity of criminals in cyberspace. This is typically accomplished by tracing the Internet protocol (IP) address of each node along the path of the user's electronic trail and has been called the "fingerprint of the twenty-first century," only it is much harder to find and not as permanent as its more traditional predecessor. Surveillance technology makes such identification possible by searching networks for specific types of data, and by providing "backdoors" into suspect's systems and widescale monitoring of communications.

Hackers are employed to deface or disable web sites, attack networks, or disrupt programs by adding code;[17] this also allows competing companies to identify security weaknesses that are then used to gain access to more sensitive data.[18] Despite these attacks, information losses are not consistently reported to U.S. federal or state law enforcement agencies. This is primarily due to (1) the perception that intellectual property theft is a low priority compared with more violent crimes, (2) the fear of adverse publicity or a required disclosure of trade secrets to the defendant, and (3) the desire to pursue civil remedies.[19] Many of these fears are well-founded because information loss incidents are difficult to investigate. Without complete cooperation of the injured party, trained staff of both the business and the law enforcement agency, and a timely response, investigations are severely hindered.

Law Enforcement's Response in the United States

Changes to the criminal laws were made in response to technological changes that have created serious problems for protecting industrial property rights. Some countries do not value protecting IPRs as much as the United States does. Thus, it is possible that large-scale violations of U.S. copyright could take place in a foreign country without any prosecutable crime arising under that country's laws. The changes to criminal laws were also made in response to strong lobbying by the affected industries. In the United States, it was frequently the owners of trademarks and copyrighted works that brought the inadequacies of existing industrial property laws to the attention of Congress. In testimony before Congress and in press releases, industry groups warn of huge losses and dire consequences from counterfeit goods. Recognizing the importance of enforcement of industrial property crimes, the Department of Justice (DOJ) formed the Computer Crime and Intellectual Property Section (CCIPS) in 1995. The CCIPS is part of the DOJ's Criminal Division. Its responsibilities include dealing with a variety of computer-related crimes as well as "the coordination of the federal criminal enforcement of intellectual property rights."[20]

U.S. law enforcement already has substantial experience with one kind of international electronic criminal – hackers.[21] Perhaps the most well-known example of international computer crime was described by Clifford Stoll in his book *The Cuckoo's Egg*.[22] In 1986, Stoll had just started working on a computer system at the Lawrence Berkeley Laboratory near San Francisco when he noticed a $.75 discrepancy between the charges printed by two accounting programs responsible for charging people for machine use. What he first believed was a bug turned out to be the beginning of a chase that led him from California to West Germany via the FBI, the CIA, and the NSA, which led to the arrest of a group of German hackers who had been scouring American military systems for material to sell to the KGB.

Markus Hess, the hacker Stoll was tracking, exploited a variety of simple loopholes in computer security systems to break into machines belonging to both the military and civilian defense contractors through the Internet, a network created by the U.S. government that links thousands of academic, industrial, and (unclassified) military computers

Once Stoll realized he was dealing with a tenacious intruder, rather than a casual amateur out for a joyride, he contacted his local FBI office. The attitude he encountered was to plague him throughout his chase: Nothing had been stolen, no one had been kidnapped, and there was less than $1 million at stake, so the FBI could not help, although they wanted to be kept informed. The CIA could not help either, although they also wanted to be kept informed. The NSA's National Computer Security Center (whose responsibility was how to design secure computers, not investigating holes in existing ones) and the Air Force Office of Special Investigation gave the same answers – no one organization, it seemed, was responsible for computer security. However, many individuals within those organizations understood and feared the erosion of the trust upon which computer networks are built that hacking was causing. Federal law enforcement authorities initially showed no interest in the case in the absence of a clear monetary loss. Thus, Stoll launched his own investigation, which eventually led to the conviction of three hackers in Germany. The investigation revealed that the hackers used access to the Lawrence Berkeley computers to obtain access to many other U.S. computers. The hackers had obtained sensitive information – such as munitions information, information on weapons systems, and technical data – and then sold it to the KGB. This case demonstrated the importance of confidentiality of information on computer systems and the difficulty of determining a loss figure for a computer intrusion case at the beginning of an investigation.

Technological Challenges and New Vulnerabilities

For years, national security experts have warned of the dangers posed by foreign and domestic terrorists or government-sponsored hackers that may attempt to exploit vulnerabilities in the relatively insecure, bug-ridden software that dominates the companies that safeguard the national infrastructure. A General Accounting Office report warns that cyberterrorists could "severely damage" national security and the nation's power and telecommunications networks. Now, companies recognize that their computer networks may very well become the objects of attacks by terrorist groups or others as the nation responds to the attacks against it.[23] However, even more mundane attacks, through self-propagating viruses, extortion threats, e-mail bombs, and malicious programs, may cause substantial damage and create ongoing daily risks for businesses in our interconnected society.[24]

Economic security affects our national security. Economic intelligence reporting helps us expose activities that may support terrorism, narcotics trafficking, proliferation, and gray arms dealing.[25] Technical innovation provides new ways to resolve international problems, but also creates new foreign policy headaches. For example, satellite surveillance can help verify compliance with arms control treaties, but the commercial market in high-resolution imagery and global positioning data also can provide rogue nations or terrorist groups with critical intelligence. Advanced database management techniques can be used to track and deter terrorist groups such as al-Q'aeda, even as these techniques have triggered a dispute between the United States and the European Commission (EC) regarding data privacy.

Technical innovation has fundamentally challenged the way foreign policy is conducted. Recombinant DNA techniques hold out the promise of resolving the world's food crisis, but they also caused a major trade blowup between the United States and the EC regarding transgenic food exports. In the wrong hands, these same genetic engineering techniques can turn the already dangerous smallpox variola into an unstoppable "killer germ." More positively, the communications revolution of the Internet has enabled non-state actors to erode governments' monopoly over interstate arms control measures, as advanced monitoring techniques allowed university seismologists to debunk the alleged Novaya Zemlya nuclear test and nongovernmental organizations to rally support for the Land Mine Convention.

As worldwide usage of the Internet has increased so too have the vast resources available to anyone online. Search engines and similar technologies have made arcane and seemingly isolated information quickly and easily retrievable to anyone with access to the Internet. Although society is entering an era abounding with new capabilities, many societal practices today remain similar to those of the earlier decades; they have not always evolved to reflect the introduction of personal computers, portable computing, and increasingly ubiquitous communications networks. Thus, even though people continue to relinquish control over substantial amounts of personal information through credit card transactions, proliferating uses of social security numbers, and participation in frequent buyer programs with airlines and stores, these organizations implement trivial or no protection for proprietary data and critical systems, trusting legal policies to protect portable storage media or relying on simple passwords to protect information.

As the availability and use of computer-based systems grows, so too does their interconnection. The result is a shared infrastructure of information, computing, and communications resources that facilitate collaboration at a distance, geographic dispersal of operations, and sharing of data. With the benefits of a shared infrastructure also comes costs. Changes in the technology base have created more vulnerability, as well as the potential to contain them. For example, greater access for bona fide users implies easier access for unauthorized users. The design, mode of use, and nature of a shared infrastructure create vulnerabilities for all users. Among the information available to Internet users are details on critical infrastructures, emergency response plans, and other data of potential use to persons with criminal intent. For national institutions such as banks, new risks arise as the result of greater public exposure through such interconnections. For example, a criminal who penetrates one bank interconnected to the world's banking system can steal much larger amounts of money than are stored at the one bank. Reducing vulnerability to breaches of security will depend on the ability to identify and authenticate people, systems, and processes and to assure with high confidence that information is not improperly manipulated, corrupted, or destroyed.

Information Warfare

Dependence on information networks also places those countries reliant on them in a position of vulnerability.[26] If vital information networks stopped functioning, an information age society would be paralyzed and could quickly collapse into chaos. Attacks on information networks, or information warfare (IW), could inflict damage rivaled only by other weapons of mass destruction. A concerted IW attack could devastate a modern society by crippling the information networks crucial to providing power, transportation, national defense, and medical services. The destructive capability of IW presents a significant threat to the international community and creates a need for consideration of a mechanism to respond to IW attacks.[27]

IW is especially troublesome for the international community because relative to chemical, biological, or nuclear weapons, the technology required to attack information networks is simple to acquire. Information networks can also be sabotaged via the manufacture of purposely defective equipment and, given the wide manufacturing base for computers, there exists significant opportunity for such sabotage to occur.[28] The United States and several European countries have recognized the potential threat posed by IW and are developing their own IW capabilities in answer to the threat.[29] As Alvin Toffler pointed out in his book *Powershift: Knowledge, Wealth and Violence at the Edge of the 21st Century:*

> The 21st century will be marked by information wars and increased economic and financial espionage. All sorts of knowledge will become strategic intelligence in the struggle for power and dominance. The race for information of all kinds will be motivated not only by a desire to lead, but will be required to avoid obsolescence. It is information that will be the moving force in the 21st century.[30]

Information wars will drag businesses into the fray, causing massive loss not only of business, but also of sensitive information and the businesses' critical information infrastructure. To name a few, among them are

• The continued increase and globalization of the Internet, and the connections to the businesses' and government agencies' intranets for e-commerce

- The increasing threats of Netspionage
- The increasing threats of technocriminals
- The concern and potential threats of IW.

Hacktivism

Hacking is well-known – it means getting unauthorized access to a computer. Sometimes the hacker will use spyware or key-logging software to capture password information in order to gain entry to a system. When a hacker gets access, he or she may do something destructive and/or leave a "calling card." It may be difficult to tell that the system has been breached. The following incidences illustrate the extent of destructive harm that can be accomplished by launching an attack.

Danish Hackers Attack Weather Computers

In 1993, the National Weather Service in Maryland detected hacker activity in its systems. Because air traffic and shipping operations rely on National Weather Service data, this attack threatened to cause substantial damage. The intrusion was traced back to computers at the Massachusetts Institute of Technology (MIT) and then back to Denmark. U.S. and Danish investigators identified thirty-two U.S. systems as well as systems in other countries, including Denmark, that hackers had penetrated. Danish authorities made seven arrests, including two juveniles. Six convictions resulted in Denmark, for attacks on both Danish and U.S. computer systems.[31]

Vladimir Levin's Bank Fraud from Russia

Between June and October 1994, a theft ring headed by a computer hacker in St. Petersburg, Russia, broke into a Citibank electronic money transfer system and attempted to steal more than US $10 million by making approximately forty wire transfers to accounts in Finland, Russia, Germany, the Netherlands, the United States, Israel, and Switzerland. All these transfers, except US $400,000, were recovered by Citibank.[32] The leader, Vladimir Levin, was arrested in London, England, and successfully extradited to the United States 2 years later. In February 1998, Levin was sentenced to 3 years' imprisonment and was ordered to pay US $240,000 in restitution to Citibank. Several accomplices were also convicted.

Julio Cesar Ardita's Intrusion from Argentina

From August 1995 until February 1996, the U.S. Naval Criminal Investigative Service and the FBI investigated a hacker who successfully obtained unauthorized access to multiple military, university, and other private computer systems, many of which contained sensitive research.[33] The hacker acquired unlimited access to those systems, including the ability to read the sensitive materials stored in them.

U.S. authorities tracked the hacker to Argentina and notified a local telecommunications carrier. The telecommunications company contacted local law enforcement, which began its own investigation. An Argentine investigating judge authorized the search of the hacker's apartment and the seizure of his computer equipment as the first step in an investigation of his potential criminal violations of Argentine law. The hacker was first identified to law enforcement by his user name "griton" (Spanish for "screamer") and eventually identified as Julio Cesar Ardita.

Ardita was investigated by the Argentineans for his intrusions into Argentine telecommunications systems, but Argentine law did not extend to cover his crimes against computers in the United States. For those crimes, only the United States could prosecute him. In the absence of an extradition treaty with Argentina for these offenses, Ardita eventually agreed, in May 1998, to come to the United States and plead guilty to felony charges of unlawfully intercepting communications and of damaging files on U.S. Department of Defense (DOD) and National Aeronautics & Space Administration (NASA) computers. He was fined US $5,000 and sentenced to 3 years of probation.

Florida 911 Attack from Sweden

In February 1996, the FBI investigated suspicious phone calls placed to the Northern Florida Emergency 911 system. The hacker had been able to obtain direct telephone numbers that corresponded to the lines used to receive 911 calls for eleven counties. He used them to tie up emergency lines and harass operators. A trace initiated by one affected phone company identified a potential suspect in Sweden. Swedish authorities, cooperating with the Washington, DC, Field Office of the FBI, executed a search warrant on the residence of the subject, who turned out to be a minor. The hacker was convicted of a misdemeanor in Sweden and given a suspended sentence.[34]

Miami Internet Service Provider Takeover from Germany

In July 1996, a hacker gained complete control over an Internet service provider in Miami, Florida, and captured credit card information of the service's subscribers.[35] He threatened to destroy the system and distribute the credit card numbers unless the victim provider paid US $30,000. Following investigation by the U.S. Secret Service, German authorities arrested the hacker, Andy Hendrata, when he tried to pick up the money at a post office box. A 27-year-old Indonesian computer science student, Hendrata was prosecuted and convicted in Germany. He was given a 1-year suspended sentence and a US $1,500 fine.

Ehud "The Analyzer" Tenebaum's Pentagon Penetration from Israel

On March 18, 1998, the Israeli National Police arrested Ehud "The Analyzer" Tenenbaum, an Israeli citizen, for illegally accessing computers belonging to the Israeli and U.S. governments, as well as hundreds of other commercial and educational systems in the United States and elsewhere.[36] The arrest of Tenenbaum led to several weeks of investigation into a series of computer intrusions into U.S. military systems that occurred in February 1998. As part of this investigation, the U.S. DOJ formally requested legal assistance from the Israeli Ministry of Justice, and U.S. law enforcement agents traveled to Israel to present Israeli law enforcement officials with evidence. As part of this evidence, U.S. investigators also presented the Israelis with evidence of Tenenbaum crimes against Israeli computer systems.

On February 9, 1999, Tenenbaum was indicted by an Israeli court, along with four accomplices. They were charged with illegal entry into computers in the United States and Israel, including U.S. and Israeli academic institutions and the Israeli Parliament.[37]

The Electronic Disturbance Theater

Since the mid-1990s, several politically minded groups have used a variety of hacking tools that they program themselves or download from the Internet to shut down or disrupt their opposition online. One such group, the Electronic Disturbance Theater (EDT), is best known for its support of the Zapatista insurgency in Mexico. The EDT produced an "electronic civil disobedience" device called Flood Net, URL-based software used to flood and block an opponent's web site. As a Java applet reload function, this software acts in much the same way as manually striking the reload key of the targeted web site – the more people that log on to the web site at a particular time and do this, the more likely the web site is going to crash or be "blockaded."[38] In the tradition of civil disobedience protests, they encourage mass participation and use their real names. The software they use to attack web sites disrupts Internet traffic, but does not destroy data. Targets have been Mexican President Ernesto Zedillo and the United States Department of Defence. Stefan Wray, one of its founders, asserts that such tactics are "a form of electronic civil disobedience ... transferring the social-movement tactics of trespass and blockade to the Internet."[39] In 1998, EDT members organized a number of "virtual sit-ins" against the web sites of financial and government institutions, including the Pentagon, which they believe were sympathetic to the Mexican crackdown against the rebels.

A Need for International Cooperation

Although the development of cyberspace offers much promise for international interaction and growth, it also facilitates the commission of international crime. By identifying the critical international issues relating to crimes in cyberspace and addressing them, countries can try to maintain for their citizens the same security in the information society that they have traditionally enjoyed.

The global interconnection of vulnerable computer systems may require a uniform transnational legal framework for addressing multinational computer-related crimes. A large step toward such a transactional framework took place in 1998, when Britain, Canada, France, Germany, Italy, Japan, Russia, and the United States agreed to coordinate efforts to investigate and prosecute Internet crimes.[40,41] In addition to increased multinational governmental cooperation, international organizations and private corporations are also working to combat international computer crimes.[42] International organizations have contributed to the drive to harmonize national legislation.

Conflicting Laws and Investigatory Challenges

Substantive criminal law may actually conflict between various countries. What is criminal activity in one country may be specifically protected in another. Although such differences arise without the involvement of computers, the often-recognized tendency of computer networks to make the world seem "smaller" can exacerbate these differences and bring them into conflict.[43]

Until more recently, computer crime has not received the emphasis that other international crimes have engendered. Even now, not all affected nations recognize the threat that computer crime poses to public safety or the need for international cooperation to respond effectively to the problem. Consequently, many countries have weak laws, or no laws, against computer hacking, and they may decline to assist other countries on the basis of lack of dual criminality.[44] Although the Internet knows no borders, criminal law and law enforcement agencies are constrained by the limits of their authority. Those limits are usually reached at national borders. Even if relevant substantive laws have been enacted in all the jurisdictions where a person perpetrates electronic crime, the precise scope and application of those laws can be as complex as the underlying technology. Because the substantive laws are sure to vary, the "dual criminality" requirement discussed previously is not necessarily satisfied by dual enactment of relevant criminal provisions. Those laws must incorporate the precise crime particularly at issue. For example, even if two countries have criminal copyright infringement laws, copyright infringement without a commercial motive may be a crime in one country, but not in another.

Jurisdictional Constraints

Although limitations related to national sovereignty are often described as "jurisdictional," these jurisdictional limitations arise in many different forms. A criminal can perpetrate an electronic crime against a victim without ever entering the country. Applying the domestic law of a country where the victim is located against a non-national perpetrator who has never even visited the country and may not even have known where his or her victim was located raises questions about the extraterritorial reach of national laws. International law can permit extraterritorial reach of criminal law under an "effects test" – where the non-national has engaged in extraterritorial conduct with the intention or the likelihood that it will have effects in the country whose law is to be applied or, possibly, where a crime is committed against a nation's citizens.[45] Whether extraterritorial reach of a nation's substantive law is permitted depends on the particular law at issue, the particular nation's jurisprudence, and most important the particular facts of the case.[46,47] Substantive laws may apply to domestic activity only, and even if they are given extraterritorial effect, cooperation from a foreign country is more likely with regard to activity that violates its own domestic law. Although some countries, such as Denmark, Israel, and Sweden, may prosecute criminals for attacks on foreign victims, other countries may be limited by their legal authority to do so, as Argentina was in the Ardita case.[48] Procedural laws, such as those provisions that permit tracing of telephone calls or other communications, have clear jurisdiction over domestic processes only. At the operational level, law enforcement agents only have jurisdiction to investigate domestic crime.

A single electronic crime case can often raise a comprehensive set of international issues. When international legal assistance, such as extradition, is sought, it is not necessarily sufficient that a victim country's laws criminalize the conduct at issue, even if they are capable of extraterritorial application. Rather, it is frequently necessary that the substantive law of the other country where investigative support is sought criminalizes the conduct in its own laws. Such parallelism is called "dual criminality" (or "double criminality"). Unless the dual criminality condition is present, a nation may be unwilling to extradite an individual to the victim country, or may be unwilling to execute searches or take other investigative steps.

The complexity and rapid development of technology can give rise to complex or evolving laws that govern electronic crimes. Electronic crime statutes from various countries are, of course, subject to their own evolution.[49] Consequently, it is predictable that such laws will differ in scope.

For electronic violations that occur in countries where no similar laws have been enacted, the crime may not be prosecutable. Consequently, with the United States at the forefront of the information age, it makes sense that Congress adapts federal law to technological development far earlier than the legislatures of some foreign countries.

Thus, problems created by the ease of commission of international electronic crimes are exacerbated by a variety of jurisdictional constraints on law enforcement in protecting the public against such crime. This confluence facilitates and indeed invites commission of international crime because of the reduced risk of penalty. Commentators and criminals have recognized the ability to exploit safe havens. These concerns demand a coherent response from the public agencies that are charged with protecting public safety by enforcement of the criminal laws.

A detailed framework of procedural laws can be valuable to investigations, create powers and limits, and provide clear guidance for collection of evidence by law enforcement agents. In addition, they can ensure for the public both an appropriate level of protection against unwarranted government intrusion and an expectation of regularity in government action. For example, the United States has a relatively detailed statutory scheme governing law enforcement's access to stored wire and electronic communications.[50] This statute provides direct guidance in investigations relating to any crimes where such data are stored by third parties. Many other countries do not have such a detailed framework.

Other differences in national procedural laws also can impede investigation of a computer crime case. These differences arise due to differences in national policy or history and idiosyncrasies related to the history of the laws governing procedure, among other reasons. For example, whereas certain evidence or certifications may be necessary in one country to obtain an order to trace a telephone call, entirely different showings may be required in another country.[51] Obtaining the necessary information to procure a foreign court order to trace a transmission may be very difficult if domestic authorities do not know what information will be needed in a foreign court.

As more companies take advantage of computer networks to operate internationally, those companies increasingly become subject to the laws of multiple nations. As more investigations of crime committed over those networks are conducted – and as the laws regulating privacy of electronic data evolve – more conflicts are sure to arise.

Even procedures to obtain information domestically may have international implications. For example, a search of computer data on a domestic branch of a foreign corporation may be authorized pursuant to a search warrant. Upon executing the search, however, the law enforcement officers may discover that the data are actually stored on a file server in the home country of the corporate headquarters (or some other country). The foreign search might also take place without the officers' recognizing that the data are stored abroad. Either way, investigations of international electronic crime can give rise to unusual questions of national sovereignty without a law enforcement agent ever leaving his or her home country's soil. It may be legitimate and important for law enforcement to be allowed to conduct a remote search of computers in a foreign country. At present, however, there is no way to know how often such searches take place, and the laws governing them are uneven and conflicting.[52]

An investigation that uncovers substantial crime in a victim country and successfully identifies a perpetrator in a foreign country may nevertheless be subject to certain limits. For example, a home country may be unwilling or unable to extradite its national for many crimes, particularly because there is substantial variation regarding enforcement and punishment of electronic crimes.[53] Even if a country is willing to extradite a criminal, it can extradite him or her to only one country at a time. This is problematic because a criminal in cyberspace could have committed crimes in many countries without leaving home.

Law enforcement officers are hampered in investigating such attacks due to nonexistent laws, lack of jurisdiction, difficulty in getting cooperation from law enforcement officers of other countries because of politics, and different laws. As noted previously, what may be illegal in Indonesia may not be illegal in the Netherlands. Therefore, extradition would not be possible, as the citizen of the Netherlands violated no law of their home country. The investigation processes of technocrimes are complicated enough. When they are internationally accomplished, it is almost impossible to bring these criminals to justice.

Operational Challenges

In addition to the formal concerns related to substantive laws and procedural laws, international computer crime investigations are hampered by a variety of operational issues. Among these concerns are expertise and coordination, communication, and timeliness. Communication is essential to cooperative electronic crime investigations. Law enforcement agents can be stymied by language barriers and time differences that do not necessarily deter criminals in cyberspace. The common language of the Internet is English (and, to a lesser extent, Unix), and networked computers are often in operation 24 hours a day, 7 days a week. With the Internet, instantaneous access can be achieved with ease, regardless of the target computer's locale. Thus, a criminal from an English-speaking country could easily commit a crime on a victim in a Spanish-speaking, Chinese-speaking, or Hebrew-speaking country (or vice versa) located on the other side of the world. For law enforcement agents to respond to such an attack effectively would require communication among people of two or more different languages at odd hours. Many countries are not yet well-equipped to meet this challenge.

In traditional physical world crimes, law enforcement is not often asked to respond with such speed. One commentator has observed that computer crime requires law enforcement to be coordinated at a speed and to a degree never before maintained "or even envisioned."[54] Law enforcement specialists are not necessarily available 24 hours a day. Moreover, legal requirements, such as those for the issuance of a search warrant, and law enforcement policies are not designed to initiate an immediate law enforcement investigation. Investigations of international cases, which can sometimes move at the speed of the slowest country, are particularly prone to delay.

Investigators in computer crime cases rely heavily on third-party communications providers to provide information regarding both computer connections and content. This information is often provided only in response to court orders issued pursuant to established criminal procedures. Such court orders can give law enforcement the ability to search stored data, to access e-mail, to trace the source and destination of communications, and to intercept communications in real time. Procedures to obtain information, and procedural safeguards to restrict access to information, are not available in computer cases in some countries, and such processes may vary from country to country. However, procedures to obtain information domestically may result in transborder searches with international implications.

Each of these circumstances aggravates the others. The time spent finding and informing the technically literate law enforcement personnel in a foreign country who are authorized to address the crime under investigation makes it more difficult for law enforcement to combat crime quickly. The technical nature of the subject heightens the potential for problems arising because of language barriers. Those language barriers can further slow law enforcement response to computer crime. Differences in language, culture, and national interests create situations ripe for misunderstandings to arise. For all these reasons, operational issues are among the most intractable that arise in the course of an international computer crime case.

Resources and Technical Training

Law enforcement's response to the rapid evolution of the Internet technocriminals has been slow. In large part, this is because of the prevalence of other, according to some, more serious crimes. So, the public's priority has been to use the limited, budgeted resources for fighting gangs, drugs, and violent crimes. It is beyond dispute that economic and electronic crime investigations require specialized training and experience on the part of law enforcement agents and prosecutors. Investigators must understand how these types of crimes effect specific industries. Without an understanding of how specific industries function, it is difficult to investigate or prosecute economic and electronic crimes. Substantial computer equipment and resources are needed. In the United States and in numerous other developed countries, the need for such training and resources has been recognized for some time.[55] Elsewhere, comparatively fewer law enforcement agents and prosecutors are trained to address such crimes.[56] In certain cases, it may be crucial to find the law enforcement personnel in another country who have been trained or who have experience in computer cases. Without well-developed coordination, this task can be difficult.

Threat of a New World Disorder

The world has also shifted dramatically toward a more computer networked environment. Thus, financial transactions, electrical power, communications systems, health services, air traffic control, record-keeping functions, and many other aspects of modern day life are largely controlled by or interact with computer systems and computer networks. Therefore, the potential impact of failing to protect the intellectual property and information infrastructure upon which this world-leading economy is increasingly dependent poses potentially serious risks.

Internet criminals will become more sophisticated as the computers become more sophisticated. Threats to valuable business and public assets are increasing while the public demands more time spent pursuing violent crimes, allowing less time to be spent pursuing technocriminals.

Netspionage, high-technology crimes, and frauds are considered victimless and thus receive a low priority. This priority order will continue for the foreseeable future. Preventing, detecting, investigating, and prosecuting economic crimes must become a priority, in an effort to lessen their impact on the economy and the public's confidence. However, both law enforcement and the private sector, as it stands now, is in danger of slipping further behind the highly sophisticated criminals. A greater understanding of how technology, competition, regulation, legislation, and globalization interact is needed to successfully manage the balance between economic progress and criminal opportunity.

The enactment of international laws is far behind the technology, making it extremely difficult to identify, apprehend, and prosecute Internet criminals across national boundaries. There have been some successes, for example, in the international fight against child pornography. However, the more sophisticated, financially based, Internet crimes will grow in number due to the lack of security professionals to prevent them and the lack of capabilities of the law enforcement professionals to investigate and apprehend the technocriminals.

The international focus for the next two decades must be directed toward Internet crime and cybercrime. That focus cannot be limited to procedural remedies. Many countries lack substantive laws specifically designed to combat computer and Internet crimes. For example, the alleged perpetrators of the "Love Bug" virus in the Philippines could not be charged with a crime because that country had no computer crime laws. The international community must establish a more aggressive and comprehensive approach to cybercrime, including treaties that provide for uniform laws on cybercrime and cyberterrorism. That approach should be inspired and led by the United States.

Adapting to an Information Society

New technologies promise many advances for human development. Gene therapy could tackle diseases such as cystic fibrosis and cancer. Genetically altered crops could reduce the need to use polluting herbicides and pesticides. The information and communications industry could provide entry points for developing countries into producing for the knowledge-intensive economy.

The Internet will continue its rapid growth and expansion around the world. It will play a major role in changing nations, societies, business, and technology, as well as changing the responsibilities of corporate managers, security, and law enforcement professionals. Nations around the world must create a framework for understanding the relationship among technology, law, and policy in this networked world. Although the development of cyberspace offers much promise for international interaction and growth, it also facilitates the commission of international crime. By identifying the critical international issues relating to crimes in cyberspace and addressing them, countries can try to maintain the same security for their citizens in the information society that they have traditionally enjoyed.[57] Nations must work together to identify their weaknesses, propose viable solutions, and rise to meet the challenges that face the increasingly connected society.[58]

CHAPTER THREE

International Dimensions of Business and Commerce

BUSINESS FIRMS increasingly operate in a global environment, obtaining goods and services from companies worldwide, participating in a global virtual corporation, and working as part of international strategic alliances. One key dimension of increasing globalization has been the dismantling of barriers to trade and investment. From the 1950s to 1993, for example, world trade grew at an average compound rate of 10% annually. Investment also has grown rapidly in recent decades, stimulated by the removal of restrictions and by international rules that provide assurances to investors against discriminatory or arbitrary treatment.

A second international dimension is the enormous growth in recent years of multinational enterprises. Such firms operate across national boundaries, frequently in multiple countries. Therefore, in today's global marketplace, it may be difficult to decide, for example, what constitutes an American company. Is Chrysler an American company or a foreign company? Is a U.S.-based multinational company that derives more than one-half its revenues and profits from operations outside U.S. borders an American company? Just because a company is incorporated in Delaware does not make it an "American" company. Such a company may be principally doing business outside U.S. borders and for the benefit of foreign nations. All these changes complicate the problems of economic espionage.

Effects of the New Technology and Threats to Business Interests

Global markets are increasingly affected by issues of trade secret protection.[1] Safeguarding intellectual property has become an increasingly visible responsibility in more recent years,[2] largely because the Internet allows the transfer of information at high speeds.[3] Increasing numbers of countries

49

have seen large portion of their gross domestic product comprised increasingly of information-related products and services. This includes computer software, sound recordings, films, and the like. International computer networks have evolved into one of the primary tools of virtually every sector of the world economy. Both "new economy" e-commerce businesses and "old economy" brick and mortar operations are now largely dependent on such networks for any number of their core business functions, from providing secure reliable customer service, to conducting billing, payment, or other financial transactions, or to interface with employees, suppliers, consumers, and business partners on a global scale.

Communications technologies have substantially shortened the time to market in virtually every sector of the economy. Companies around the world are increasingly forced to share critical proprietary information with customers, suppliers, contractors, consultants, and strategic partners during the early stages of product development.

In the face of the rapid development of computer and telecommunications technology, it is imperative that the business community at all levels, from the chief executive officer to the sales force, have an understanding of the security issues associated with international networking and the legal ramifications of security breaches. Whereas perimeter controls such as firewalls were the primary form of network security in the mid-1990s, companies now must balance the business risk with the need to share information freely in order to expedite production. For example, merchants conducting business in the online environment must face not only the emerging technological attacks such as hacking and infrastructure failures, but also the traditional fraud schemes that have plagued the industry since the inception of credit card transactions. As corporations continue to expand their global reach through complex integrated networks, the identification of points of compromise and methods of exploitation becomes an increasingly difficult task. The cellular telephone industry is a primary example of an industry that was faced with a significant information security vulnerability, in the form of cellular cloning activity, which threatened to reduce the integrity of the wireless system. Identification of the source of information security compromise incidents is increasingly difficult in light of the evolution of wireless communication technologies. From external attacks to abuse by internal employees, companies have a difficult task in the protection of data vital to corporate interests. As businesses become more dependent on their interfaces to global networks as the backbone for their businesses, there will be greater and greater risks to their businesses.

There are many reasons why these risks have been created. They include:

• Global economic competition where economic espionage can be conducted with little risk of being caught

- Increase in local area networks (LANs) and wide area networks (WANs) and client-server systems – all of which rely more on the users to protect the systems and information than a professional staff of systems personnel
- The focus on customer service by management and network staff as the highest priority – with technical staff being unfamiliar with their security role
- Security technology will always continue to be a step or two behind the attackers
- Lack of management support to provide better security as a higher priority.[4]

An environment that is open to everyone is not secure, whereas an environment that is closed to everyone is highly secure but less useful. A number of trends in business today tend toward less security. For example, competitive strategies emphasize openness to interactions with potential customers and suppliers. Such strategies also offer potential adversaries a greater chance of success because increasing ease of access often facilitates the penetration of security protections.

As another example, many businesses today emphasize decentralized management that pushes decision-making authority toward the customer and away from the corporate hierarchy. Yet security often is approached from a centralized perspective. For example, access controls are necessarily hierarchical (and thus centralized) if they are to be maintained uniformly.

Many businesses rely increasingly on highly mobile individuals. When key employees were tied to one physical location, it made sense to base security on physical presence (e.g., to have a user present a photo ID card to an operator at the central computer center). Today, mobile computing and communications are common, with not even a physical wire to ensure the person claiming to be an authorized user is accessing a computer from an authorized location or to prevent passive eavesdropping on unencrypted transmission with a radio scanner.

The amount of downtime has edged up, with more companies facing outages for longer periods. In 2001, 28% of U.S. companies suffered no downtime from attacks, whereas in 2003 only 16% avoided downtime. About 45% of companies were back up within 8 hours, a number similar to 2002. However, 39% had downtime of 8 hours or more – a 13% increase from 2002.[5]

Much of the improvement in combating attacks came from smaller companies getting their IT security in order with relatively quick fixes such as adding firewalls and antivirus tools. Larger companies, the preferred targets for hackers, fared worse than smaller companies. Only one-fourth of businesses with more than $500 million in annual sales escaped without security breaches in 2002, and 43% indicate that they suffered downtime that lasted more than 8 hours.[6]

For many companies, security and control over their operations and assets are vital to their success, and thus reporting breaches in that security is potentially damaging to future business. As one commentator noted, who wants to do business with a company whose unstable network security is being splashed across the front page? For example, Citibank's reward for reporting the $10 million stolen from its allegedly secure computer network was seeing its top twenty customers wooed by rival banks, all claiming their computer systems were more secure. Companies are also reluctant to report such thefts because they can spawn unwanted attention from the Securities and Exchange Commission and shareholder derivative suits. Probably the greatest reason why trade secret theft is not prosecuted more often is the failure of victim companies to report such thefts to government authorities. Companies are reluctant to report such crimes because of concern over a loss of public trust and public image.

Gaining Strategic Advantage Through Economic Intelligence

Globalization, increasing competition, and the growing importance of intellectual property have heightened temptations to steal corporate secrets, both by domestic employees and foreign spies.[7] The desire of states to possess the most modern industries and technologies possible is not an unreasonable one. Modernized states have a better understanding of the overall economic development, self-sufficiency, and political autonomy than do undeveloped states.[8] To become more modernized, states with lesser-developed economies are tempted to import foreign technologies by whatever means are available, including economic espionage. Successful nations, as well as Third World countries and former communist states, who do not have the financial resources to buy or build themselves quickly to prosperity, are stealing technological, scientific, and commercial secrets from others.[9,10]

A wide range of companies operating internationally are threatened by foreign information collection efforts. No business is immune from economic espionage. Companies around the world have become more vulnerable to trade secret theft for several reasons. First, the end of the Cold War made available intelligence resources that were previously devoted to securing military technology.[11] Second, disagreements between countries within the Western alliance are no longer of major strategic importance.[12] Third, intangible property,[13] which is often easier to steal than tangible property, has become more common.[14] Fourth, more employees have access to trade secrets than in the past.[15] Fifth, employees have greater opportunities to gain from knowledge of trade secrets, either by changing jobs or by becoming self-employed. Sixth, computer hackers have the ability to steal information from corporate computer systems thousands of miles away. Finally, advances in communications have made collection of trade secrets easier.[16]

A New Niche for Government Spies

Nations have been reshaping their intelligence agencies and investigative resources to be more responsive to the competitive and global needs of businesses.[17] However, this global economic environment fosters a powerful incentive for corporations, individuals, and foreign governments to use improper and illegal means to gain the competitive advantage and market share necessary to survive and prosper.[18] Furthermore, as technology advances, the methods for stealing corporate trade secrets and proprietary information are becoming highly sophisticated, less expensive, and easier to implement.

A nation's economic status makes up a large part of its national security.[19] This economic status is dependent on a nation's ability to compete effectively in the world market. Because of this, economic competition "must be more carefully balanced with traditional military and intelligence concerns in determining policy to protect national security."[20,21] Lawmakers are increasingly resorting to criminal codes to create and implement economic and social policies.

Because of the threat of economic espionage, many countries make economic security a priority, enacting laws that purport to deter the intelligence gatherers.[22] Prior to the end of the Cold War, many international relationships were defined according to military alliances. These relationships are changing significantly due to a shifting international focus from a military to an economic outlook, and allies now see one another as competitors in the global economy.[23] Under this new arrangement, industrialized countries striving to maintain their standards of living, and developing nations eager to improve such standards, face enormous pressure to succeed. The competing nations will pursue any and all means that bear the potential to ensure their productivity and economic security. When economic objectives begin to play a more dominant role in defining national security, the interest in economic espionage expands. The end result for today's society is that economic espionage is the front line of a new world economic war.[24]

Nations also commit economic espionage because it is an area in which many of them are capable of success. Many countries already have the ability to carry out economic espionage because they have sufficient funds and apparatus to do so. A U.S. Congressional Intelligence Committee Report in 1994 stated that "reports obtained since 1990 indicate that economic espionage is becoming increasingly central to the operations of many of the world's intelligence services and is absorbing larger portions of their staffing and budget."[25] In addition, many countries use their leftover Cold War spying apparatus, such as giant computer databases, scanners for eavesdropping, spy satellites, and bugs and wiretaps, to conduct economic espionage activities.[26] Peter Schweizer pointed out, "that so many states practice economic espionage is a testament to how profitable it is believed to be."[27] Some countries gain financial profit as well as technology from economic espionage. In Australia, for example, economic espionage is estimated to be worth $2 billion per year.[28] France acquired a $2 billion deal with India for airplanes because of the economic espionage activities of the Direction Generale de la Securite Exterieure.[29,30]

Getting the means of production is often more important for some countries than acquiring the actual technology.[31] The manufacture of a particular product, ballbearings for example, may not be a secret, but the means by which it is done takes years to develop. Countries that steal this information are therefore able to cut down the amount of time it would take to develop effective manufacturing processes on their own. In sum, the supported philosophy is that it is quick and cheap to steal – crime pays.[32] Economic espionage appeals to these states because it saves them the time and financial resources they would have spent to develop the technologies on their own.[33]

Nations that are actively pursuing economic and technological intelligence do it for three reasons: (1) to strengthen their industrial base, (2) to sell or trade the information with other countries, and (3) to obtain alternative sources of arms and intelligence.[34] The struggle among nations for a global economic advantage has forged a consensus in the United States that there is a definite need for economic intelligence activities.[35]

Race for Competitive Intelligence

A front line is no longer the one that divides East and West, but the one defined by technological innovations. Innovation, a significant factor in economic growth, requires a substantial investment of time, money, and human resources.[36] The battle line lies in research and development. The generals are being replaced with chief executive officers (CEOs) and the bottom line is not ideological, but financial. Some multinational companies are increasingly treating business like an economic war. Resources designed and previously used exclusively for military intelligence gathering are now being expanded to gather intelligence on mergers, investments, and other financial transactions. Those who develop a competitive advantage over their rivals stand to make millions from their innovations. That profit is enough for some to seek an unwarranted advantage of their own by indulging in corporate espionage as a quick-fix solution to their creative deficiencies and their inability to remain competitive in their field.

In the United States, intellectual property is an increasingly important part of the economy. For example, it is estimated that such misappropriation of trade secrets is costing American corporations billions of dollars annually. In 1996, the U.S. creative industries accounted for 3.65% of the gross domestic product, which is equivalent to $278.4 billion.[37]

The security of these trade secrets is essential to maintaining the vitality of the economy. The exploits of companies such as Toshiba, Procter & Gamble, ABB, Microsoft, Nike, and Frito-Lay are frequently highlighted in the business press. With ever-increasing diligence, these organizations are monitoring and investigating their competitors. They are deploying vast resources to beat their current or future competition both domestic or international. Alert companies such as Sony, have a competitor-focused business strategy and armies of employees sensitized to the competitive intelligence theme. These successful and stable organizations have tirelessly interwoven the philosophies and practices of competitive intelligence into their marketing, research and development, production, and human resources systems for years.

Global Risk and Cost of Economic Espionage

When economic objectives begin to play a more dominant role in defining national security, the interest in economic espionage expands. The end result for today's society is that economic espionage is the front line of a new world economic war. The increasing value of trade secrets in the global economy and the simultaneous proliferation of technology have increased the opportunities and methods for conducting economic espionage.

Generally, any country that competes in the world market has a motivation to spy on its foreign competitors.[38] Economic espionage, however, is most prevalent in the world's most economically competitive nations and regions, including the United States, Asia, and Western Europe. Economic espionage helps nations to maintain economic and technological competitiveness[39] and to gain an edge on a competitor because it helps to provide technologically limited countries with the modern devices they need.[40] If companies lose valuable secrets to industrial espionage, they cannot profit by using their competitive advantage.[41] In turn, if they are unable to recoup their investments in research and development, they lose their motivation to innovate and bring new products or services to consumers. The consequences include higher prices charged to consumers,[42] as well as a decrease in new technologies, creative inventions, and improvements.[43] Furthermore, the very concept of privacy "is threatened when industrial espionage is condoned or is made profitable."[44]

The same technologies that connect and empower corporations can expose their vital proprietary information to unwanted discovery and revelation, presenting alluring and sometimes irresistible opportunities for unscrupulous competitors, disgruntled employees, or malicious snoops.

According to the American Society of Industrial Security (ASIS), "the Internet and associated technologies are perceived as significant threats to every company's ability to protect the confidentiality of their proprietary information."[45,46] Further, as the Senate Judiciary Committee in the United States noted:

> What State law there is protects proprietary economic information only haphazardly. The majority of States have some form of civil remedy for the theft of [proprietary] information – either adopting some version of the Uniform Trade Secrets Act, acknowledging a tort for the misappropriation of the information, or enforcing various contractual arrangements dealing with trade secrets. These civil remedies, however, often are insufficient. Many companies chose to forgo civil suits because the thief is essentially judgement proof – a young engineer who has few resources – or too difficult to pursue – a sophisticated foreign company or government. In addition, companies often do not have the resources or time to bring the suit. They also frequently do not have the investigative resources to pursue the case. Even if a company does bring suit, the civil penalties often are absorbed by the offender as a cost of doing business and the stolen information retained for continued use. Only a few States have any form of criminal law dealing with the theft of this type of information. Most such laws are only misdemeanors, and they are rarely used by State prosecutors.[47]

Facing these challenges, responsible companies are devoting corporate attention and resources to the reaction and maintenance of effective information security regimes. Nevertheless, each technological security innovation contains the seeds of new circumvention, making it difficult for even the most vigilant company to avoid the damaging impact of a major computer intrusion. Businesses have long been concerned about the tension between openness and security.

Today, an item of trade secret information (e.g., computer source code, a biochemical formula, technical schematics) can be as valuable to a company as an entire factory was even several years ago. Computers now make it extremely easy to surreptitiously copy and transfer this valuable trade secret information. An employee can now download trade secret information from the company's computer on a diskette, take it home and scan the information on the hard drive of a home computer, and then upload it to the Internet where it can be transmitted within minutes to any part of the world. The receiving party, in turn, can do the same thing within minutes. Within days, a U.S. company can lose complete control over its trade secret rights forever.[48]

In the aftermath of September 11, 2001, security has become a critical concern in the operating environment for global business. Mainstreaming the security function is imperative if management is to rise to the challenge posed by recent events. This means that senior executives must become knowledgable about security issues in order to fulfill their responsibilities to their employees, customers, shareholders, and communities. The crisis that began on September 11 has raised the status of corporate security management to a core business function. What has changed? The simple answer might be "everything." However, from a business planning and implementation perspective, the specific factors include

- Domestic security in the territorial United States can no longer be assumed.
- War is being waged by, and against, nonstate actors.
- The potential scale of disaster has expanded from single buildings to entire business districts.
- Biological weapons are now a reality.
- Major disruptions in transportation systems and supply chains have occurred.
- Major disruptions in telecommunications and mail systems have occurred.
- Information management systems and the Internet are potentially vulnerable.
- Employees, customers, and communities have become extraordinarily sensitive to security issues.

What are the implications? Security is now everybody's business. The risks are clearly much greater than before – they are also much more difficult to anticipate, quantify, and plan for. Companies must now recognize that maintaining security is a core mission and a broadly based responsibility.

The complexities involved in responding to this problem were succinctly noted by the Canadian delegation to an early effort by the Organization for Economic Cooperation and Development (OECD) to confront computer crime:

> There are two critical challenges to Western society in respect of information. The first relates to the ability to devise new legal, economic and social arrangements that will ensure both the creation and the effective and profitable utilization of new information and technology. The second challenge for a liberal society is to protect its basic political and human values from unwise applications, withdrawals or restrictions of that new knowledge.[49]

Meeting the challenge will likely require increased cooperation among governmental, private, and international entities. However, the response need not necessarily be bound up entirely in new national or international legal norms:

> [W]e should not overestimate the capacity of the law to define and regulate every aspect of life in the information age. We know that attempts to create any kind of 'curtains" are not effective, and possibilities for control and

restriction will apparently continue to diminish in the future. In this context, education and promotion of ethics acquire a renewed significance. . . .[50]

Many scholars and reporters attempt to estimate economic espionage's financial burdens to society. Such costs are difficult to determine, due to the fact that international industry is generally reluctant to discuss them. A significant amount of economic espionage and trade secret theft goes undetected.[51] Victims of trade secret thefts are often faced with a dilemma when deciding whether to report the matter to law enforcement authorities. Generally, victims do not want the thief to go unpunished, but are concerned that if they report the matter, the trade secret will be disclosed during discovery or during the criminal trial. No company wants to admit it has suffered significant financial loss from foreign spies, as noted earlier, especially when it depends on shareholder support that may discontinue if shareholders believe the company is faltering.[52]

An exception to this was IBM, when it reported and discussed its losses. In 1992, IBM Vice President Marshall Phelps told a U.S. Congressional committee that his company suffered billions of dollars in losses due to theft of proprietary information.[53] This calculation supports the estimates of economists who claim that individual companies and firms lose billions of dollars annually through economic espionage.

A survey released by American Society of Industrial Security (ASIS) noted a 323% increase in economic espionage between 1992 and 1996.[54] A 1993 survey found that the number of thefts of proprietary information had increased 260% since 1985; those involving foreign governments increased fourfold.[55] A 1988 National Institute of Justice study found that 48% of high-tech companies surveyed had been the victim of trade secrets theft.[56] Of 1,300 companies surveyed by ASIS, more than 1,100 had confirmed incidents of economic espionage, whereas 550 had suspected incidents of espionage but were unable to prove them.[57] ASIS conducted an intellectual property loss survey of Fortune 1000 companies and 300 fastest growing companies. Despite just a 12% response rate, responding companies recorded $44 billion in known and suspected losses over a 17-month period during 1997. ASIS found that foreign nationals were identified in 21% of incidents involving intellectual property loss where the nationality of the perpetrators was known.[58] In 1994, seventy-four U.S. companies reported a total of 446 incidents of suspected targeting by foreign governments, either domestically or abroad.[59] In early 1996, the FBI was investigating approximately 800 cases of economic espionage, double the figure from 1994. Different sources estimated the monetary loss to U.S. industry resulting from economic espionage activities to be between $1.8 billion and $100 billion per year.[60] Estimates of losses from economic espionage in the United States range from $2 billion to $260 billion per year.[61] Including overseas operations of American corporations, the estimates rise to $400 billion per year. The number of jobs lost as a result of such activities was estimated to be between 1 million and 6 million.[62]

In 1996, the Office of Science and Technology Policy estimated that 6 million U.S. jobs had been lost in the first 6 years of the 1990s due to economic espionage. However, it is difficult to assess the dollar loss as a result of economic espionage and the theft of trade secrets. The U.S. intelligence community has not systematically evaluated the costs.

Another study sponsored by ASIS estimated that Fortune 1000 companies alone lost more than $45 billion from theft of trade secrets in 1999[63] and, in 2000, American companies lost in excess of $1 trillion overall.[64] ASIS put the loss to the American economy from economic espionage at $300 billion a year – triple what it was a few years ago. Other studies suggest that espionage costs U.S.-based businesses more than $200 billion annually in intellectual property losses, in addition to at least several tens of billions of dollars in related damages. The business community estimates that, in calendar year 2000, economic espionage cost from $100 billion to $250 billion in lost sales. More than 1,000 documented incidents of economic espionage transpired in 2001, and major companies reported at least 500 suspected episodes.[65]

The cost of industrial espionage is staggering stated a report to the U.S. Congress in 2001. The National Counterintelligence Executive claimed economic espionage could be costing the nation's business community up to $250 billion a year once lost sales are taken into account.[66] As noted earlier, the greatest loss to U.S. companies involves information concerning manufacturing processes and research development.[67]

According to the 2002 Computer Crime and Security Survey, 90% of respondents – mostly large companies and government agencies – experienced computer security breaches in 2001. About 80% of respondents acknowledged financial losses because of those breaches, according to the survey by the Computer Security Institute (CSI) and the FBI. The survey also found that more respondents – 74% – cited their Internet connection as a frequent point of attack, rather than internal network systems. Although more companies are reporting such intrusions to law enforcement, the number remains low at about 34%.[68]

Many companies are getting more skittish about revealing information technology security flaws, in large part to avoid becoming a more visible target for hackers. About one in five companies stated that they would report a security breach to government authorities. Almost one-half – 47% – stated that they would not tell anyone outside the company.[69] According to some security experts, it is nearly impossible to thwart a corporate spy from swiping computer disks or e-mailing trade secrets overseas.[70]

In addition, individual companies that are considered American icons could be targeted for industrial or economic espionage operations designed to ruin the company economically or cause its customers to feel uneasy about doing business with them online or otherwise. According to a February 2002 study by the University of Texas in Dallas, a compromised company tends to lose approximately 2.1% of its market value within 2 days after disclosing an Internet security breach.[71] In response, organizations are wrestling with the challenge of managing secure access to information and applications scattered across a range of computing systems, as well as how to provide access to a growing number of users, all without diminishing security or exposing sensitive information.[72]

Quantifying the Risks

Quantifying the risks is difficult because we simply do not have the data. Most of what we know is anecdotal, and what statistics we have are difficult to generalize. In summary, cyberattacks are very common on the Internet. Corporations are broken into regularly, usually by hackers who have no motivation other than simple bragging rights. There is considerable petty vandalism on the Internet, and sometimes that vandalism becomes large-scale and systemwide. Crime is rising on the Internet, both individual fraud and corporate crime. We know that this is occurring because surveys, corporate studies, and anecdotal evidence confirm it. However, we just do not know the exact numbers.[73]

For the past 8 years, the CSI has conducted an Annual Computer Crime Survey of U.S. corporations, government agencies, and other organizations.[74] The details are a bit numbing, but the general trends are that most networks are repeatedly and successfully attacked in a variety of ways, the monetary losses are considerable, and there is not much that technology can do to prevent it. In particular, the 2003 survey found the following:

- Fifty-six percent of respondents reported "unauthorized use of computer systems" in the last year; 29% said that they had no such unauthorized uses, and 15% said that they did not know. The number of incidents was all over the map, and the number of insider versus outsider incidents was roughly equal. Seventy-eight percent of respondents reported their Internet connection was a frequent point of attack (this has been steadily rising over the past 6 years), 18% reported remote dial-in as a frequent point of attack (this has been declining), and 30% reported internal systems as a frequent point of attack (also declining).
- The types of attack range from telecommunications fraud to laptop theft to sabotage. Thirty-six percent experienced a system penetration, and 42% a denial-of-service attack. Twenty-one percent reported theft of proprietary information and 15% financial fraud. Twenty-one percent reported sabotage. Twenty-five percent had their web sites hacked (another 22% did not know), and 23% had their web sites hacked ten or more times (36%

of the web site hacks resulted in vandalism, 35% in denial of service, and 6% included theft of transaction information).

- One interesting thing highlighted by this survey is that all these attacks occurred despite the widespread deployment of security technologies: 98% have firewalls, 73% an intrusion detection system, 92% access control of some sort, and 49% digital IDs. It seems that these much-touted security products provide only partial security against attackers.

Unfortunately, the CSI data are based on voluntary responses to surveys. The data only include information about attacks that the companies knew about, and only those attacks that they are willing to admit to in a survey. Undoubtedly, the real numbers of attacks are much higher. Further, the people who complete the CSI survey are those experienced in security; companies who are much less security-savvy are not included in this survey. These companies undoubtedly experience even more successful attacks and even higher losses.

Another source of data is the Honeynet Project. This is an academic research project that measures actual computer attacks on the Internet. According to their statistics published in 2001, a random computer on the Internet is scanned dozens of times a day.[75] The average life expectancy of a default installation of a Linux Red Hat 6.2 server – that is, the time before someone successfully hacks it – is less than 72 hours. A common home user setup, with Windows 98 and file sharing enabled, was successfully hacked five times in 4 days. Systems are subject to hostile vulnerability scans dozens of times a day, and the fastest time for a server being hacked was 15 minutes after connecting to the network.

Nearly all experts agree that the theft of America's economic secrets is growing. U.S. intelligence officials estimate that more than fifty countries – many of them, as previously mentioned, traditional allies of the United States – are actively engaged in economic espionage against American businesses.[76]

The monetary losses from the theft of corporate secrets are difficult to estimate. U.S. intelligence agencies have not studied in-depth the losses due to economic espionage. Private sector surveys have been criticized for being based on small, unrepresentative samples that have emphasized domestic holdings. Companies often prefer not to disclose that they have been the victims of industrial or economic espionage.[77] An admission can embarrass the company, lower stock prices, scare away investors and customers,[78] and reduce market share.[79] There is not likely to be a corresponding gain from revealing the misappropriation. An even greater problem is that most misappropriations are probably undetected.

In spite of the difficulties of determining exact costs of economic espionage, two notions are clear, the fact that intelligence agencies spend billions of dollars each year in their espionage efforts, and counterintelligence agencies spend billions of dollars each year trying to thwart those efforts.[80] In addition to direct financial loss, companies face other damages resulting from economic espionage, such as loss of jobs and contracts.[81]

Information Is Power

In an age where power stems from wealth, there is an ever-increasing fear that acquisition of economic information will lead to the breakdown of international security, with economic foes of today becoming military foes of tomorrow. Society therefore lives in fear of economic espionage. Economic espionage can further destroy the incentive to innovate. Innovation, a significant factor in economic growth, requires a substantial investment of time, money, and human resources.[82] If companies lose valuable secrets to industrial espionage, they cannot profit by using their competitive advantage.[83] In turn, if they are unable to recoup their investments in research and development, they lose their motivation to innovate and bring new products or services to consumers. The consequences include higher prices charged to consumers[84] as well as a decrease in new technologies, creative inventions, and improvements.[85] No one wants to create new ideas if there is a strong likelihood that the ideas will be stolen, used, and sold by competitors. Not only will competitors take credit for ideas that belong to the original creators, but they will also profit from them financially, while the original creator will be left with nothing. This greatly discourages creativity. As long as countries continue to conduct economic espionage activities, there will be serious implications for the world economy.

At the core of this issue is the rapidly escalating financial value of research and its results. For more than two decades, since a 1980 law encouraged scientists to patent discoveries from federally financed studies, universities and researchers have pushed with increasing intensity to commercialize their work. For example, in 2000, American universities collected more than $1 billion in licensing fees, according to a survey from the Association of University Technology Managers. The institutions reported more than 10,800 discoveries and had more than 3,270 patents issued by the U.S. Patent Office.[86] The circumstances can be even murkier when the theft is not the intent. The realities are that with the financial stakes so high, behavior that might once have been standard operating procedure – such as taking research materials home at night – might be construed as an attempt to steal the material and the intellectual property that undergirds it.[87] The EEA was enacted to increase the value of information.[88] The worth of products depends more on ideas than the materials from which products are made. Richard Heffernon and Dan Swartwood estimated in 1996 that about $24 billion in corporate intellectual property is stolen each year.[89] Passage of the EEA was also triggered by a perception that state and federal schemes were inadequate to stem the mounting problem of trade secret theft.[90]

Do They Know What You Know

Foreign collection continues to focus on U.S. proprietary economic and technical information and products. Further, programs associated with dual-use technologies, those that can be used for both military and civilian applications, are consistent targets for both foreign government and foreign commercially sponsored collection activity.

A 1996 Defense Investigative Service (DIS) summary of foreign contacts indicated that numerous foreign countries displayed some type of suspicious interest in one or more of the eighteen technology categories listed in the Military Critical Technology List (MCTL), which is published by the Department of Defense. These major technology categories include

- Aeronautics systems
- Armaments and energetic materials
- Chemical and biological systems
- Directed and kinetic energy systems
- Electronics
- Ground systems
- Guidance, navigation, and vehicle control
- Information systems
- Information warfare
- Manufacturing and fabrication
- Marine systems
- Materials
- Nuclear systems
- Power systems
- Sensors and lasers
- Signature control
- Space systems
- Weapons effects and countermeasures

The majority of the technologies included in the MCTL are dual use. As a result, the loss or compromise of proprietary or embargoed information concerning these technologies can affect both the economic and national security of the United States.

According to the Department of Energy (DOE), foreign researchers have gained fully sanctioned access to numerous sensitive technologies during preapproved visits and assignments to DOE facilities.[91]

Renaissance Software

In the early part of the 1990s, Marc Goldberg and Jean Safar, both French nationals, were arrested for trying to sell proprietary computer source codes of their employer, Renaissance Software.[92] Both men were working with the company under an official French government program that allowed citizens to opt out of required military service if they agreed to work at American high-tech companies.

Science Applications, Inc.

In 1992, Ronald Hoffman was caught selling software to Japanese industrial firms.[93] He had obtained the software through his position as a project manager for Science Applications, Inc., which had developed the programs under a secret contract with the Strategic Defense Initiative. Hoffman had been selling confidential information to Japanese companies since 1985.

British Petroleum

British Petroleum (BP) received a tip that a Taiwanese competitor was seeking to procure equipment from U.S. suppliers to build a $100 million chemical plant in Taiwan using BP's proprietary chemical process technology for acetic acid. BP had spent millions of dollars on a research program and years of effort to develop and commercialize this process, which gave it a leading position in the global marketplace.[94] BP brought a court action in the United States and eventually traced the technology theft to a former licensing executive. The executive admitted that he had sold BP secrets to the Taiwanese company, but denied that he had taken the secret documents from BP. He claimed instead that he purchased them in Moscow from an agent of the Russian government in a "technology bazaar" in the early 1990s. BP previously licensed the technology to the Soviet government, which built a plant using the BP process in Russia.[95] BP won, obtaining money damages and an injunction against the former employee and a settlement with the Taiwanese company. The case was a testament of how the trade secret litigation landscape has changed, sometimes involving international corporate espionage more elaborate than a Robert Ludlum spy novel.[96]

Supervision, Inc.

In November 2001, FBI and U.S. Customs agents were waiting at the San Francisco Airport when Fei Ye and Ming "Andy" Zhong checked in for their

1:30 P.M. United Airlines flight to China. In their luggage, agents found documents labeled "Transmeta Corporation – Confidential and Proprietary" and "Sun Proprietary Need-to-Know." Investigators were acting on a tip from Sun Li, one of their partners in a startup called Supervision Inc. The company received $2 million in funding from the local Chinese governments of Hanzhou and Guanzhou to develop a next-generation computer chip, according to court records. According to Li, Ye had told his partners that he had stolen trade secrets and proprietary information from current and former employers. Ye had worked for Transmeta Corporation, Sun Microsystems, Trident Microsystems, and NEC Electronics Corporation. Zhong had worked for Transmeta and Trident.[97]

In January 2003, Ye, 36, of Cupertino, and Zhong, 35, of San Jose, California, were indicted on ten counts, including conspiracy, economic espionage, ad possession of stolen trade secrets.[98] Lawyers for Ye and Zhong contend that the documents were not trade secrets and were background information for the engineers. Zhong said he was shocked when the FBI stopped him at the airport. "It was like a movie," said Zhong. "Basically, I think I'm an average Joe, and those things happen to 007."[99]

Lax Attitudes

The best-known example of lax attitudes in more recent years on guarding secrets ironically comes from the U.S. government, when the former CIA Director John Deutsche took the nation's most highly classified secrets to his home on a laptop computer and left the computer on his kitchen table, open to access by nongovernment personnel, including his foreign maid. There are also reported instances of State Department employees who lost their laptops, containing classified information, in airports.

The same lax attitude and insensitivity to secrets is relatively common in the business world. A senior marketing executive was traveling on an airplane and noticed an individual seated in front of him diligently creating a marketing plan on his computer. Without straining his eyes, the marketing executive immediately recognized the plan on the computer screen as one belonging to his most significant direct competitor. Without moving from his seat, he had a bird's-eye view of his competitor's future marketing plan.

There are a variety of situations in which confidential information is inadvertently communicated: a casual conversation outside the office, a job interview in which a prospective employee highlights his or her job accomplishments, a confidential project in which consultants and temporary workers are hired without restrictions to maintain secrecy, and discovery provided in response to lawsuits or confidential information unwittingly disclosed in filings required by regulatory agencies.

The Nature of Employer–Employee Relationships in Today's Global Economy

Since the mid-1970s, a growing number of federal and state courts in the United States have wrestled with employers' concerns regarding the disclosure of trade secrets in an attempt to develop a coherent approach to the doctrine of inevitable misappropriation. Unfortunately, the result has been an inconsistent patchwork of legal standards. For example, a former executive of Borland International, a software company, was accused of e-mailing trade secrets to a competitor, which happened to be his new employer, before he quit Borland. Criminal charges were filed but eventually dropped, and the civil dispute was quietly settled.[100]

In *Frasier v. Nationwide Insurance*,[101] Nationwide searched its file server and located e-mail communications that revealed its employee, Richard Frasier, had e-mailed correspondence critical of Nationwide's business practices to a competitor. Soon after discovering this, Nationwide terminated Frasier. Frasier sued, alleging that Nationwide had unlawfully intercepted his e-mail from storage in violation of stored communication laws.[102] The federal district court for the Eastern District of Pennsylvania rejected both contentions, first, because there was no "interception" and, second, because the employer had lawfully accessed its own equipment and "stored" e-mail to obtain the information.[103]

There is no question that the nature of the relationship between employers and employees has dramatically changed in recent years.[104] The turmoil of downsizing and restructuring, and the intensity of global competition, have changed the nature of the employer–employee relationship.[105] With more employees switching their employers at a greater pace than in the past, there has been a dramatic increase in ex-employees departing with their employers' trade secrets. Employees no longer have to photocopy documents surreptitiously; they can simply download reams of data to disk, CD, or DVD, or even e-mail the information to a competitor with the click of a mouse. A career with a single company has become the exception, not the norm.[106]

Today's employees also often have greater access to their company's secrets than in the past.[107] Thus, employees have greater opportunities to benefit from the knowledge of trade secrets, either by becoming self-employed or changing jobs.[108,109] Employees can become disgruntled with their current employers, pursue better offers, and valuable information ends up going out the door.[110]

Employers have argued that under certain conditions, employees who leave an employer to work for a competitor will inevitably disclose or use their former employers' trade secrets in the course of their new employment. This argument is known as "inevitable misappropriation." These employer-plaintiffs have brought suit under common law as well as state law versions of the Uniform Trade Secrets Act (UTSA).[111]

In her article, Katherine V. W. Stone analyzes the shifting expectations of loyalties behind employment-based trade secret law. According to Stone, nineteenth-century employers adopted mechanisms that served to bind employees to companies. Loyalty was encouraged through hierarchical vertical labor structures that provided for step-by-step progress up a career ladder within companies and rewarded loyalty. Training was assumed under the umbrella of the company itself, and promotion took place in orderly fashion. Most important, there was often an implied promise of job security.

Stone argues that a new psychological contract, which emerged in the late 1970s, has recently altered employment practices. The labor shortage of the U.S. postwar boom years, which encouraged lifetime employment, was replaced by free trade and highly competitive international business markets that demanded agile hiring to meet needs. In addition, companies retreated from investing in the layered managerial structures required to organize internal labor markets. Rather, the skills required for the new information economy demanded flexible individuals who brought experience from elsewhere. Large corporations no longer held out the implied promise of lifelong employment. Instead, employment relationships became contingent and the relationship marked by employees migrating from one opportunity to another with different employers. In lieu of job security, employees were provided with training in order to ensure their employability. Employers gain by having an increasingly flexible, highly skilled workforce; employees gain through the investments companies make in their human capital.

Such a new psychological contract has important implications for the question of who owns trade secrets after the termination of employment. In addition to the express contracts of covenants not to compete, which might define postemployment relations, there are also implied psychological contracts full of subtle exchanges of productivity for training, of flexible employment with the risk of termination for the accumulation of skills that might make an ex-employee employable by another enterprise.

American criminal law provides that corporations may be held liable for the acts of their agents or employees acting, at least in part, on the corporation's behalf. Under the doctrine of collective knowledge, the requisite intent to commit the crime can be imputed to a corporation, even if no single employee violated the law, because the prosecution can establish sufficient intent by piecing together the acts of a group of employees or agents. Consequently, the disgruntled employee is the most difficult kind of threat to protect against. It may be difficult to stop the knowledgeable, malicious former information technology employee who is intent on causing damage or stealing data.[112]

Fortunately, the EEA's legislative history indicates that it was not intended to prevent a person from using general business knowledge to compete with a former employer.[113] For example, it provides that employees "who change employers or start their own [company] should be able to apply their talents without fear of prosecution."[114] Moreover, "it is not enough to say that a person has accumulated experience and knowledge during the course of his or her employ" and that the individual is inappropriately using such knowledge.[115,116] However, the enhanced property rights in trade secrets and the threat of criminal sanctions could produce unintended consequences that undermine public policies encouraging competition, employee mobility, and the effective use of information products.

Reverse Engineering

Reverse engineering is generally defined as "a method of industrial engineering in which one begins with a known finished product and works backward to divine the processes and specifications involved in the product's development and manufacture."[117] It can also involve "looking at or testing a lawfully acquired product in order to determine its content."[118,119]

The purpose of intellectual property protection is to provide incentives to invest to advance the collective knowledge. Therefore, the law recognizes exceptions that allow for the study of, and improvement upon discoveries that have been committed to the public domain, in all realms of intellectual property protection.[120] Reverse engineering is one of these exceptions. Reverse engineering is the process of studying an item in hopes of obtaining a detailed understanding of the way in which it works.[121] Reverse engineering is used to create duplicate or superior products without the benefit of having the plans for the original item.

It is important, however, to understand that reverse engineering is not just a scheme to allow copying under the guise of research.[122] Reverse engineering, although it may involve copying, entails a detailed study of the item in question. Even in cases where the end product is a near duplicate of the original item, the purpose of the reverse engineering activities must have been to understand the item sufficiently to allow the accused party to redesign the product without resorting to step-by-step replication.[123] Because, as in the case of computer chips, any differences between the original and the new product may be infinitesimal, courts typically rely on the existence of a paper trail to prove that the product was reverse engineered, rather than simply copied.[124]

Depending on the nature of the item under study, reverse engineering may take many forms. For mechanical devices such as turbines or cargo containers, reverse engineering may consist of taking measurements, making detailed sketches, or disassembling the device.[125] In the case of computer chips, the process involves stripping away each layer of the chip to study the structure of the layer. To ensure the reverse engineering process is accurate, a duplicate may be made.

Protecting Trade Secrets from Dumpster Divers and Other Snoops

The U.S. economic welfare depends on increased efficiency, productivity, and technological advancement gained through the development and implementation of new processes, products, and services.[126] Concern for promoting scientific progress by protecting inventions and other forms of intellectual property is so deeply rooted in American jurisprudence that the framers of the U.S. Constitution included patenting as one of Congress's enumerated powers.[127] Corporate trade secrets and proprietary information represent the most valuable economic and business resource for gaining competitive advantage and market share in the U.S. free market economy.[128] Corporations put their faith in trade secret law, which has its foundation in common law and equity.[129] A company that can keep a secret can continue to profit from its rivals' inability to duplicate the company's process or formula.[130] Well-known and publicized is Coca-Cola's success in keeping its formula stashed in an Atlanta bank vault for nearly 100 years. Kentucky Fried Chicken hides its recipe of eleven herbs and spices in a time capsule guarded day and night at a secret location.

The U.S. criminal law addresses the growing importance and significance of protecting trade secrets and proprietary information. In more recent years, U.S. corporations have become concerned about the misappropriation of trade secrets.[131] Civil trade secret litigation has grown enormously since the mid-1980s, and trade secret law has become more popular among legal practitioners.[132] In light of these concerns, corporations may find that the EEA is well suited for pursuing disgruntled employees who steal or attempt to steal the company's trade secrets. Although such a defendant will likely have few resources with which to reimburse the company, prosecution will send a strong message to current and prospective employees that the company will not tolerate trade secret theft.

Recognizing the value of their trade secrets, corporations are increasingly seeking criminal sanctions to protect their private information.[133] In May 2000, a grand jury in Detroit indicted a senior vice president of General Motors, who had accepted a position with Volkswagen, on various charges for stealing trade secrets.[134] In January 2001, the recording industry threatened a Princeton professor with criminal charges.[135] The tactic led the professor to forego release of the research he and others had done, and thwarted a discussion of the results. In July 2001, the FBI arrested a Russian computer software designer for writing a program that enabled consumers to circumvent an encryption device.[136] The program did not infringe any copyright, but it did violate a federal law that makes it a crime to design software that might be used to infringe a copyright.

Although these disputes implicate a host of legal doctrines, common threads tie the stories together. The disputes involve intangible objects – songs, photos, and confidential or secret business information – that are all, at bottom, based on knowledge or information. Most basically, the stories highlight a persistent and perhaps irreconcilable problem, that is, how to protect interests in information without reducing too much the public's access to that information. Although failing to protect such interests may discourage innovation, limited public access may ultimately reduce production of new knowledge and ideas.

The American economy is increasingly integrated with the world's economy. More and more, U.S. companies develop products and ideas domestically, and produce or manufacture them overseas. This means that the U.S. economy and the success of many companies are increasingly dependent on ideas and other intangible assets, rather than industrial facilities and manufacturing ability. Protecting these intangible assets, therefore, whether in the form of patents, trademarks, copyrights, or trade secrets (known collectively as intellectual property or IP), is a major concern for businesses. As noted in the previous chapters, theft of trade secrets is as old as business itself. However, with huge sums to be made stealing the latest technology, the past decade has witnessed a dramatic upswing in the theft of proprietary information from corporate America.[137] Trade secret theft may be the largest obstacle faced by the United States in its worldwide business.[138] The increase in trade secret theft has place the technologies of U.S. companies, ranging from simple textile formulas to complex defense technology, at great risk. Pricing data, customer lists, information on product development, basic research, sales figures, and marketing plans appear to be the most coveted items.[139]

Facts Fight Fiction in Security Circles

The ever-expanding global information infrastructure underpins the global economy. Both business and government must adjust to a borderless world of unrestricted transactions and communications.

Many major infrastructure industries, particularly telecommunications and electricity, are being affected by deregulation and are restructuring. Organizations have harnessed information technology to accelerate their delivery of goods and services, improve the efficiency of their processes, and shed excess inventory and unused reserve capacity. Many businesses are so tightly balanced in their "just-in-time" processes that recovery from even a minor disruption would prove difficult.

Technology and change produce better service at lower cost, new markets, and more efficient processes. As a result, we depend more than ever on infrastructure services. However, at the same time, market forces result in a diffusion of accountability and responsibility, less research and development investment, and a reduction in reserve capacity. Today's infrastructure processes may be more efficient, but they lack the redundant characteristics that gave their predecessors more resilience.

In today's economy, it becomes more critical for companies to secure their information databases to avoid the millions of dollars lost annually to cybercrime and information theft. For many companies, information is the most important resource available. Many executives only realize the value of their corporation's secrets when these secrets are stolen and disclosed to a competitor, resulting in huge economic losses.[140] Companies must manage critical economic information in such a way as to reduce the possibility of a security breach. Corporate management must recognize the value of proprietary information and undertake physical steps to safeguard knowledge as a bank protects bullion on deposit.

The increasing strategic value of technology in all industries, even those traditionally perceived as low-tech, puts a premium on corporate security. Yet, the collapse of corporate loyalty, even in the executive suite, and the accelerating traffic of employees among competitors means an ever-increasing potential for the transfer of information of all kinds.

In more recent years, corporations and governments have rushed to construct network firewalls, add antivirus software, and set up intrusion detector systems, but none of those security tools can stop the determined insider from stealing company secrets or diverting funds or stock.[141] Yet, more than one-third of all corporate computer crime is the result of unauthorized access by insiders, according to the 2002 survey by the CSI and FBI.[142] Although the percentage of computer crime committed by insiders has fallen as the attacks from outside hackers via the Internet has grown, the CSI warns "the insider threat is still very real and very costly."[143] Some of the major U.S. companies such as General Motors, Fruit of the Loom, Avery Dennison Corporation, Disney, and scores of others have become embroiled in high-profile cases of corporate espionage, many with an international dimension. Such cases are now an increasingly common feature of the high-tech, information-age economy.[144] In this environment, companies need to think differently about their most valuable information resources.

Competitiveness and Legal Collection
Versus Espionage and Economic Crime

GATHERING AND USING information to advantage is the underlying theory of business intelligence systems. These systems attempt to bring to business the information gathering and analyzing methods of government intelligence agencies, much in the same way that military strategic planning tactics shifted into business practice after World War II. The difference is that the tool for gathering and analyzing information and distributing it to the proper decision makers is not a network of spies, but a LAN of personal computers. This approach combines pieces of data from multiple disparate sources and creates the key nuggets that comprise "intelligence." The data can come from structured (e.g., databases) or unstructured (e-mail, web pages, broadcasts, and other dissemination media) sources, and can originate as text, video/image/icons, and even as auditory or other "signal" data streams.

What Is Competitive Intelligence?

Structural analysis of industries, commonly known as the Harvard Business School[1] method, investigates industry competition through the study of rivalry among competitor firms, bargaining relationships between buyers and suppliers, substitutability of products and services, and potential new entrants to competition. The sources of competitive advantage are analyzed by investigating the nature of rivalry within the industry, including the number of firms and their market shares, the pace of growth in the industry, the extent of product or service differentiation, and the barriers to entry and exit. The analysis of entry barriers examines variables such as product differentiation and brand identification, capital requirements, access to distribution channels, scale economies, learning and experience curves, government regulation, and proprietary product knowledge or technology.

It is the last of these that is of special interests to the study of competition based on intellectual property.

Competitive intelligence (CI) is "a systematic and ethical program for gathering, analyzing and managing information that can affect a company's plans, decisions, and operations." After gathering and analyzing this research, one should be able to understand a competitor and its environment, strategies, capabilities and operations, and long-term goals.[2] On a global basis, CI is in use on every industrialized continent. CI practitioners are found in virtually every form of enterprise, including educational and nonprofit entities. CI gathering differs from industrial espionage, at least in theory, in that it is meant to consist of legal and ethical activities.

CI consists of two facets. First, the use of public sources to develop data (raw facts) on competition, competitors, and the market environment. Second, the transformation, by analysis, of that data into information (usable results) to support business decisions. Understanding CI today requires an understanding of what is meant by "public." If the term is to be taken in its broadest sense, it encompasses more than studies that the U.S. Department of Labor releases or what is reported in *The New York Times*. In CI, "public" is not equivalent to published. It is significantly broader in concept. Here, "public" means all information that can legally and ethically be identified, located, and then accessed. This ranges from a document filed by a competitor as part of a local zoning application to the text of a press release issued by a competitor's marketing consultant describing the client's proposed marketing strategy, while the marketing firm extols the specifics of its contributions to the design of a new product and the related opening of a new plant. It includes the webcast discussions between senior management and securities analysts, as well as the call notes created by the organization's own sales force. It is the common principle of the use and analysis of publicly available information to assist in the effective management of a company that links the variations of CI.

Thousands of companies have set up CI operations around the world. There is a professional association in Alexandria, Virginia, the Society of Competitive Intelligence Professionals (SCIP), which has about 7,100 members. SCIP has established a code of ethics to guide the CI community.[3] Drug and chemical makers, aerospace manufacturers, and defense contractors make up big parts of SCIP's membership.

There are generally two types of sensitive business information. One is intellectual property, which consists of ideas, concepts, and inventions, including product recipes or formulas. The second type is operation information, such as detailed production and marketing data, including things such as the production volume of a particular manufacturing facility, its market share, the changing compositions and locations of production, and the like.

The vast majority of business and competitive information may be obtained legally and ethically from newspaper articles, trade publications, Securities & Exchange Commission (SEC) filings, specialized databases, and materials readily available at trade shows.

Not all economic and financial data collection by competitors or representatives of foreign powers is illegal. Abundant data are available from such open sources as newspapers, the electronic media, books, and the Internet, which are examples of legal collection methods. Sensitive or restricted data include financial information, manufacturing processes, customer lists, and other information not normally shared with those outside a business. Commercial databases, trade and scientific journals, computer bulletin boards, openly available U.S. government data, and corporate publications are just some of the readily available sources of information on employees, companies, new products, and new manufacturing techniques. The use of the Freedom of Information Act (FOIA) has become quite popular with foreign governments and corporations. Not wanting to alert U.S. counterintelligence agencies, some foreign governments seek open-source material covertly.[4]

Economic intelligence gathering – usually based on open sources – is both legitimate and indispensable, especially considering the wealth of information now available via the Internet. Activities involving the acquisition of information by theft, bribery, or coercion are illegal and, hence, properly termed *espionage*.[5] The Internet has made the gathering of competitive business intelligence considerably easier and more effective. Clues to competitors' intellectual property development and strategic plans beckon from private sector and government web sites, news groups, chat rooms, and other public gathering spots of the information age.[6]

Often, a competitor's economic edge depends on its ability to stay one step ahead of its competitors. Rapid changes in technology are tempting many companies to acquire trade secrets in unscrupulous ways, thus circumventing the huge costs of independent development. More sophisticated global communications – cell phones, voice message, e-mail, and transmission of data over the Internet – make this type of espionage easier than before.[7]

The Modern Art of Competitive Intelligence

Why engage in CI? There can be great commercial advantage to getting a particular product into the market first, to producing an equivalent product at lower cost, or securing patent or other rights before a competitor does. As mentioned earlier, the advantages are so substantial that they have led to the generation of an entire industry of CI professionals. It borrows tools and methods from strategic planning, which takes a broad view of the market and how a particular company hopes to position itself.

In 2002, *Business Week* reported that 90% of large companies have CI staff and that many large U.S. businesses spend more than a $1 million annually on CI. Also, according to *Business Week,* corporations find it most necessary and beneficial to do CI during recessionary times. This function at times is outsourced to law firms that are knowledgeable about all levels of a corporation's business.[8] Now, with businesses more complex and the economic climate so uncertain, corporations are becoming far more sophisticated at scrutinizing the competition.

CI relies on techniques such as recruitment, tactical surveillance, profiling of corporate personnel, information assurance, and elicitation training to destabilize a competitor's ability to maintain or gain market share. According to John Nolan, a former U.S. government intelligence official, competing organizations are keen on profiling business leaders and others that influence the market. CI involves legal methods of data collection and analysis, some of which were mentioned earlier. This practice is different from corporate espionage – the theft of trade secrets through illegal means such as wiretaps, bribery, and cyberintrusions. Still, some intelligence gatherers step over the ethical line. There is a fine line between the collection, through open sources of information, of economic treads for policy-making purposes and the covert theft of proprietary business information for dissemination to competing corporations.[9]

CI, as practiced today, may be divided into four different yet overlapping types:

1. *Strategy-Oriented Competitive Intelligence.* This CI role means providing higher levels of management with information on the competitive, economic, legal, and political environments in which an organization and its competitors operate now and in the future. It may also involve developing CI on candidates for potential mergers and acquisitions, as well as for alliances and partnerships. Most CI practiced in the 1980s and early 1990s, including much of what fell into the category known then as "business intelligence," can be considered as strategy-oriented CI.
2. *Tactics-Oriented Competitive Intelligence.* In a real sense, tactics-oriented CI is a child of the computer age. It encompasses much of what has previously been called "market" or "sales and marketing" intelligence. Firms increasingly are tracking what is going on "in the trenches," that is, where competitors face off for customers and consumers with tactics-oriented CI. In turn, according to a *Competitive Intelligence Review* article by John Cain, this type of CI permits organizations to fine-tune marketing efforts, including field-force support, to respond faster.
3. *Technology-Oriented Competitive Intelligence.* Technology-oriented CI encompasses much of what has been referred to as technology intelligence or competitive technical intelligence. Technology-oriented CI, supporting

technology strategies as well as research and development (R & D), has become a growth area within CI.

4. *Target-Oriented Competitive Intelligence.* It is most often used when CI efforts are best focused on a small number of competitors that a firm faces in several market niches. It encompasses elements of what is sometimes called "business intelligence" or "competitor intelligence."

Business Counterintelligence

Likewise, business counterintelligence is the set of proactive measures taken by a business to identify and neutralize actual and potential disclosures of intellectual property assets through employees (including former employees, temporary employees, consultants, and others with temporal legitimate access to company information), or by means of another company or government's CI program.

For example, the FBI initiated an Economic Counterintelligence Program in 1994 that serves in a defensive role by protecting U.S. national security. Kenneth Geide, the head of the Economic Counterintelligence Unit at the time, explained that one of the methods that foreign governments often use is to hide their economic collection activities within their legitimate activities.[10]

Competitive Intelligence Is Not Corporate Espionage

Such intelligence gathering is so easy, it is almost criminal, but when is it criminal? CI or corporate intelligence becomes illegal espionage when it involves the theft of proprietary information, materials, or trade secrets. The distinction becomes difficult to ascertain given the potential to draw lines on ethical and legal grounds. In reality, practitioners are unlicensed, and the lines separating CI activities from those more commonly associated with unlawful industrial espionage are blurred.

In the United States, the answer lies, among other things, in the EEA of 1996. As outlined in Appendix A, the act defines trade secrets broadly and protects them with two central provisions. The first, Section 1831, applies only to individuals and entities sponsored by foreign governments. The second provision, Section 1832, criminalizes economic espionage, regardless of who benefits. The U.S. DOJ takes these matters seriously. A whole host of cases have been brought under EEA that provide more evidence of the DOJ's mounting efforts to criminalize intellectual property disputes. Appendix C provides a list of cases that have been prosecuted as of December 2003. How does an individual, a company, or its corporate officers avoid being caught in the crosshairs of the EEA?

Unfortunately, CI and its historical variants have caused, and will continue to cause, confusion. Competitive advantage may be deemed as an unfair advantage if the methods employed to obtain information fall outside the legal boundaries.

As with government intelligence operations, corporate analysis sometimes borders on the clandestine. But competitive intelligence professionals and many CEOs insist that effective intelligence gathering can be done both legally and ethically. They say the potential benefits are so great that operating without a CI capability is like entering the boxing ring with one hand tied behind your back. In fact, most academic business programs incorporate seminars or courses on topics related to business intelligence into their curriculum. These courses are designed to explore economic espionage and methods to protect an organization's assets. SCIP's Code of Ethics, for instance, asks members to follow all laws, to properly identify themselves when gathering information, and to respect requests for confidentiality. Many organizations have even more stringent guidelines.

CI is not (nor should not be) James Bond-type spying or unlawful corporate espionage. It does not involve the use of phone taps or computer hacking, or the payment of bribes.[11] For example, a detailed report from the Occupational Safety and Health Administration – available under the Freedom of Information Act – can provide extraordinary amounts of information about the inside of a plant, including the numbers of people working on the production line, the products coming through, and the actual tools or machinery being used.[12]

There are no agreed-upon definitions of economic or industrial espionage as mentioned in earlier chapters. For example, the U.S. Attorney General defined economic espionage as "the unlawful or clandestine targeting or acquisition of sensitive financial, trade, or economic policy information, proprietary economic information, or critical technologies." This definition excludes the collection of open and legally available information that constitutes a significant majority of economic collection. Aggressive intelligence collection that is entirely open and legal may harm a nation's industry, but is not considered illegal espionage. However, it can help foreign intelligence services identify information gaps and in some cases, may be a precursor to economic espionage. In the modern, competitive business world, billions are spent on the research and development of products and ideas. In addition, millions are spent on CI information gathering.

Corporate Spy Wars

Corporations, no less than countries, have been gathering information about one another for ages. Among nations, it is called spying and may involve sophisticated techniques, a lot of money, specially trained personnel, and undercover methods. Businesses spying on other businesses is nothing new. Companies have done it for decades – from "shoppers" hired to compare prices at discount giants Kmart and Wal-Mart to the top floors of global conglomerates in New York City.[13]

As alluded to earlier, massive amounts of corporate spying are accomplished with increasing ease through advances in communication such as the Internet, satellites, and cellular phones. Computer hackers access proprietary information from corporate computer systems and decode encrypted message from offices located in other countries.[14] Computer hacking and telecommunication interceptions are common, especially where systems are not fully protected against such instructions.[15] Easy targets are cellular and cordless telephones. Hacking and interceptions can provide much information to intelligence gatherers, including trade secrets and other forms of competitive information.[16] In one case, it was suspected that a host government was intercepting telephone conversations between an executive abroad and his Canadian company headquarters. Canadian executives discussed detailed negotiation information, including a specific minimum bid. This minimum bid was the immediate counteroffer put forward by the host company the following day.

Domestic companies also face potential theft of trade secrets by American employees looking to sell information to foreign competitors. Kodak experienced this situation when a 28-year engineering veteran retired, started his own consulting company and, according to Kodak, sold confidential documents, blueprints, and records to Minnesota Mining and Manufacturing Corporation (3M).[17] The following examples illustrate some of the most common means of economic intelligence gathering.

Maytag

In late 1993, Maytag announced that it was planning to develop a more energy-efficient and environmentally friendly washing machine known as a "front loader" or "horizontal axis" washer.[18] Although Maytag announced its intention to develop the new washer, it did not disclose details about how the washer would function. Maytag spent tens of millions of dollars to develop, manufacture, and market this new line of washers and made strenuous efforts to protect its investment.

Maytag's competitors have reportedly engaged in CI in an effort to obtain more information about these "front loader" washing machines.[19] Maytag was besieged by spies using a variety of methods to gather information. It has received phone calls from "college students" asking for information about the new washer for "term papers" that they were writing. One Maytag marketing executive received a phone call from someone who falsely claimed to be a fellow Maytag employee from another unit requesting the names of people in Maytag's front loader division.[20] On another occasion, a man who claimed to be from the local waterworks appeared at the door of two residents of Newton, Iowa. He requested permission to measure their laundry room, but abandoned his request when the homeowner began asking questions. The homeowner happened to be one of the local townspeople testing a model of the new machine.

To protect its investment in the development of this new product (estimated at $50,000,000), Maytag held "secrecy seminars" for its employees giving advice on how to detect and deal with suspicious callers. The cover of the company newsletter asks, "Who is really on the line?" and warns of "modem pirates." Maytag workers received orange telephone stickers that read, "Loose lips sink ships." Maytag claims to be aware of several attempts to breach its security and confirmed that an unnamed major competitor has hired a firm to find out everything it could about Maytag.

Maytag estimates that these modem pirates are inflicting billions of dollars worth of damage each year on American companies in missed sales, wasted research and development costs, and trade secrets lost to competitors. However, even Maytag admits to having conducted a little CI of its own.[21] For example, Maytag executives admit that they knew all about the recently introduced machine by its competitor, Frigidaire, before the machine first appeared in stores.

Qualcomm

In September 2000, Irwin Jacobs, founder and chairman of Qualcomm, Inc., gave a speech in a hotel to the Society of American Business Editors and Writers in Irvine, California, and stepped away from the podium talking with members of the audience. He soon discovered that his laptop computer was gone. Although local police considered it to have been a commonplace theft of a $4,000 piece of equipment, Jacobs told *The Wall Street Journal* that the information on the portable's hard drive could have been far more valuable to foreign governments. Jacob's laptop was protected by nothing more than a basic Windows password.[22]

Microsoft

In October 2000, Microsoft Corporation discovered that for 3 months someone had been breaking into the corporate network and accessing the source code of products under development. It is not known how many other documents were also accessible to the hacker, but those items could have included contracts, e-mail, marketing documents, and other key components of the company's business strategy and operations.

Microsoft officials are certain that this break-in was an act of industrial espionage. The incident was a reminder that breaking into networks has become a useful tool for illegally cutting corners. Obviously, the protection was not ironclad, but Microsoft's security team is considered top-notch and few corporations have more resources or greater incentive to maintain the integrity of their networks.[23]

Spy in the Gray Flannel Suit

Unlike their shadowy images in Hollywood films, the spies are not skulking about in trench coats. The new breed of corporate operatives blend into business settings. They are well educated in engineering, finance, marketing, and the sciences. They are trained in interviewing techniques that draw out valuable information. Many are knowledgeable about computer hacking and computer forensics. Some intelligence gatherers pose as technicians and repair persons to get to confidential information.[24] Others volunteer for positions that get them close to sensitive information. Some have even been known to pose as documentary camera crew members to gain access. Others roam corporate campuses and trade shows, using state-of-the-art spying tools, such as $10,000 laser microphones that pick up indoor conversations from 100 yards away by recording the sound vibrations on windows.[25]

There is no specific person who qualifies as an intelligence gatherer. However, some of the more common international snoops include competitors, vendors, investigators, business intelligence consultants, the press, labor negotiators, and government agencies.[26] Some countries hire individuals, rather than large organizations or intelligence agencies, to do their spying for them. When students study abroad, some governments ask them to acquire economic and technical information about their host countries. Common perpetrators are graduate students who serve professors as research assistants free of charge. In research positions, the foreign graduate students gain access to the professor's research, learning technological applications that they can then relay to their home governments. Foreign intelligence agencies sometimes hire information brokers and freelance spies. Freelance spies are attractive to intelligence agencies because they often specialize in certain fields and allow the agencies to insulate themselves from counterintelligence.[27] Others have been known to hire teams of individuals to enter foreign companies and steal ideas.[28]

Foreign corporations and nations also try to recruit employees of the same ethnicity, appealing to their love of the native homeland. Or they may set up small companies or consulting firms that work closely with a particular nation's businesses, quietly pilfering patents and documents over the years.

Moles

A foreign government's best source of information is an employee of the target company, often called a "mole." "Moles" are spies that are put into seemingly legitimate positions in a competitor's company. Such "moles" have been known to take documents from offices and hotel rooms. They routinely infiltrate businesses in disguise to obtain access to secret information. Graduate students are also used to infiltrate research plants, universities, and businesses.[29] Many intelligence gatherers rely on trusted workers within companies or organizations to provide them with proprietary and classified information.[30] These employees' value lies in their direct and legitimate access to desired information. Counterintelligence agents report that recruitment of moles is relatively easy in the United States. Intelligence collectors target both high-ranking employees and support staff. Intelligence agencies favor international scientific conferences, trade shows, and air shows for recruiting moles because these events draw many scientists and engineers.

A study by the ASIS concluded that "trusted insiders pose the greatest risk" to the divulgence of trade secrets. Lower-ranking employees, such as secretaries, computer operators, or maintenance workers, are regularly recruited because they often have desirable access to information and are easily manipulated by intelligence agencies due to their lower pay and status within their respective companies.[31] With few exceptions, all real-life James Bonds get their information exactly the same way.[32] According to the 1999 survey sponsored by the ASIS International and PricewaterhouseCoopers, onsite contract employees and original equipment manufacturers are perceived by firms to represent the greatest threat to corporate proprietary information.

Espionage and Other Illegal Operations

Traditional clandestine espionage methods, such as agent recruitment, U.S. volunteers and co-optees, surreptitious entry, theft, SIGINT intercept, computer penetration, and other specialized technical operations, continue to be used by foreign intelligence services targeting U.S. interests. Foreign governments increasingly use sophisticated data gathering techniques. The most effective means of economic espionage are specialized technical operations. These include breaking into computers, intercepting communications, and decoding encrypted messages. The increasing use of satellites, microwaves, and cellular phones makes interception easy and detection difficult.[33] Japan's Ministry of International Trade and Industry allegedly listens to the phone lines of American firms in Japan under an agreement with the Japanese national phone company.[34] Debriefing citizens after foreign travel is popular in some countries. Travelers are asked for any information acquired during their trips abroad. The debriefing sessions are considered offensive to some travelers, whereas others accept them as part of traveling abroad.[35]

Practitioners of economic and industrial espionage seldom use one method of collection; rather, they combine a number of collection techniques into a concerted collection effort that combines legal and illegal, traditional, and more innovative methods.[36] Foreign governments employ traditional espionage methods, as well as specialized economic collection methods, to pilfer trade secrets. For example, former heads of the CIA and the FBI have stated that the French and Russian intelligence services now use the same methods to spy on U.S. corporations as they used to spy on each other during the Cold War.[37]

Consistent with traditional espionage operations, significant foreign intelligence collection efforts are often conducted legally and openly as mentioned previously. These collection efforts often serve as precursors to economic espionage.

Collection Methods

Intelligence gatherers may break into their competitors' offices outright and steal the information they want. Many incident reports describe stolen laptop computers, disks, and confidential files. For example, "one common method of stealing laptops at airports is for the thief's accomplice to get into line at the x-ray machine just in front of the victim. While the accomplice slowly empties his pockets of keys and loose change, the thief takes your laptops off the conveyor on the other side of the machine and spirits it away."[38] In addition, hotel rooms and safes are regular targets. Some spies bribe hotel operators to provide access to the hotel rooms, which is known as a "bag op." During bag ops, gatherers search unattended luggage and confiscate or photograph anything they think may be valuable to them.[39] In one instance, the former chief of the French intelligence service admitted in 1991 that his agency made it a habit to spy on U.S. business executives traveling to France by bugging first-class seats on Air France and breaking into hotel rooms to search attaché cases.[40] Another method is dumpster diving, which is part of a larger industrial espionage problem. Also known as trash trawling, waste archaeology, and trashing, dumpster diving is the act of rummaging through a competitor's garbage to obtain information. Some believe it is the number one method of business and personal espionage.[41] Dumpster diving is one of the easiest and safest ways of gathering confidential information,[42] and yields secrets ranging from corporate executives' travel itineraries to descriptions of company merger plans.[43] The predatory nature of dumpster diving is demonstrated by the case of an international shipping company that got started by dumpster diving for the telex spools of an established company, then used customer lists on the spools to lure away clients.[44] Some companies even specialize in combing trash for valuable items and information,[45] and may privately contract with trash collectors to obtain "recycled" computer paper and whatever is printed on it. Although dumpster diving may not always yield trade secrets directly, sophisticated corporate spies employ trash searches as part of larger collection campaigns. As the value of intangible information rises exponentially, so too does the sophistication of modern-day spies.

Information available through electronic databases continues to expand as the number of databases and electronic bulletin board systems available to the public continues to grow dramatically. Bulletin board systems, some of which track sensitive U.S. government activities or provide information on proprietary activities performed by government contractors, have grown rapidly on the Internet.

In addition to traditional espionage and other illegal activities, foreign governments, instrumentalities, and agents gather economic intelligence via numerous other methods. These methods involve legitimate practices that do not constitute illicit activity. Although foreign governments and their entities have been known to turn legitimate transactions and business relationships into clandestine collection opportunities, often the overt collection of economic information is practiced for legitimate purposes. Even though some of these legal activities may be a precursor to clandestine or illegal collection, they do not of themselves constitute evidence of illegal activity.

There are numerous ways in which countries carry out economic espionage, and many of these methods require little effort on the part of the perpetrators.[46] Foreigners seeking to acquire U.S. proprietary economic and industrial information often engage in the following types of illegal activities.

Theft of Trade Secrets and Critical Technologies

U.S. businessmen traveling overseas are increasingly becoming targets of foreign collection activities. There are numerous examples of briefcases or laptop computers showing evidence of unauthorized access after being left unattended in hotel rooms. In addition, there is evidence of travelers being photographed during business meetings in foreign countries for future targeting. Business class seats on airlines, offices, hotel rooms, and restaurants are regularly bugged and tapped by spies. In a specific incident, a European airline bugged its entire business class section, while spies posed as flight attendants.[47]

Although most industry associations with foreign entities are in fact economically advantageous to the United States, a DIS summary of 1996 suspicious contacts that were reported by defense contractors, indicated that foreign entities employ a variety of legitimate collection methods in attempting to acquire U.S. proprietary economic information. Despite the legitimate nature of these collection practices, they may be an important element in a broader, directed intelligence collection effort. Last, the legitimate collection of economic information, in addition to clandestine methods that constitute economic espionage, depicts the broad scope of a successful foreign economic intelligence collection program.

Open-Source Collection

The openness of American society and the wealth of technical, scientific, political, and economic information available through the open media provide U.S. adversaries with a vast amount of detailed, accurate, and timely information. The use of open-source information as an intelligence source has a number of benefits. It is relatively cheap to obtain, legal in the majority of instances, and makes up the greatest volume of information accessible to an intelligence collector. Because of these benefits, open source information has increasingly been exploited by many foreign entities, to include foreign intelligence services in an attempt to target the United States.[48]

Defense industry reporting continues to reflect increasing trends of foreign collection activity. As reported by DIS, foreign intelligence services and foreign private industries, which may or may not be sponsored by a foreign government, employ the following legal collection methods.

Unsolicited Requests for Information

According to DIS, the most frequently reported method of operation used by foreign entities is the unsolicited request for information. This method is simple, low cost, nonthreatening and low risk. A reported majority of suspicious unsolicited requests for information involved data covered under the International Traffic in Arms Regulations that could not be lawfully exported without a license. A growing number of incidents involve mail, fax, phone, and Internet requests from a foreign entity to a cleared contractor.

According to the Defense Security Service (DSS), in 2000, these kinds of suspicious activities accounted for 41% of total reported collection efforts. Not surprisingly, there has been a dramatic rise in the use of the Internet for these kinds of collection activities. DSS reported that the use of the Internet by foreign entities collecting U.S. technology and technical information accounted for 27% of all suspicious contacts.

Solicitation and Marketing Services

Foreign collectors have also employed the use of marketing surveys to solicit information that often exceeds generally accepted terms – surveys may solicit proprietary information concerning corporate affiliations, market projections, pricing policies, purchasing practices, and types and amounts of U.S. government contracts. One of the most popular tactics used to gain access to U.S. research and development facilities is to have foreign scientists submit unsolicited employment applications. In 2000, facilities that were the targets of this kind of solicitation were working on such technologies as electrooptics, ballistics, and astrophysics. Other approaches included offers of software support, internships, and proposals to act as sales or purchasing agents. In addition, of growing importance is the greater use of foreign research facilities and software development companies located outside the United States to work on commercial projects related to protected programs. Any time direct control of a process or a product is relinquished, the technology associated with it is susceptible to possible exploitation.[49]

Foreign individuals with technical backgrounds may be solicited by, or may themselves seek to, market their services to research facilities, academic institutions, and even cleared defense contractors. In addition, U.S. technical experts may be requested by foreign entities to visit a foreign country and share their technical expertise. Usually associated with alleged employment opportunities, there is also an increasing trend involving "headhunters" who solicit information from targeted employees. In these instances, such solicitation may be a ploy to access and gather desired information.

Acquisition of Export-Controlled Technologies, Joint Ventures, and Front Companies

Joint ventures, joint research, and exchange agreements potentially offer significant collection opportunities for foreign entities. Joint efforts place foreign personnel in close proximity to U.S. personnel and afford potential access to science and technology (S&T) programs and information. Through joint venture negotiations, U.S. contractors may reveal unnecessarily large amounts of technical data as part of the bidding process. In addition, a number of governments use front companies to gather intelligence and provide cover for intelligence operations.

This is of special concern when foreign employees are in place for long periods of time. Some examples of suspicious activity in joint ventures include foreign workers seeking access to areas or information outside the purview of their work agreement, enticing U.S. companies to provide large quantities of technical data as part of the bidding process, and foreign organizations sending more representatives than reasonably necessary for particular projects.[50]

The unlawful acquisition of export controlled technologies by foreign collectors remains a considerable concern. Methods of operation employed to circumvent the export control process include using front companies within the United States and overseas, illegally transporting products to an undisclosed end user by using false end user certificates, and purchasing products that have been modified during the manufacturing processes to meet export-controlled specifications.

Acquisition of Technology and Companies

Foreign corporations use corporate mergers and acquisitions on very rare occasions to collect intelligence on competitors. For instance, in 1988, several French companies, in conjunction with Airbus, attempted to purchase a subcontractor of Boeing Company.[51] If the acquisition had succeeded, Airbus would have known an enormous amount about [Boeing Company's] production processes, capabilities, costs, specifications, and future plans.

However, acquisitions were greatly on the rise in 2000. This is the latest manifestation of an increased trend to acquire sensitive technologies through purchase. According to DSS reporting, 88% of all reported suspicious acquisition activities involved third parties. Third parties are not the actual entities acquiring the technology, but are the ultimate end users. Third-party acquisitions are often an indicator of a possible technology transfer or diversion because, when the ultimate recipients are determined, they are often countries that are on embargoed lists for the acquired items. One method that is commonly used involves setting up a freight forwarder, that is, a cooperating U.S.-based company that will provide the ultimate foreign recipient with a U.S. address to subvert U.S. export control laws.[52]

Exploitation of Visits to U.S. Companies, Commercial Markets, and Technology Transfers

To acquire technology, some governments use graduate students studying or researching in the United States. For example, the weak link that could compromise national security, according to authorities, is "dual use" technology – information or equipment that has a civilian use as well as a military application. For example, the U.S. Navy spent millions of dollars to develop Terfenol-D in the early 1980s, and intelligence experts estimate that the People's Republic of China (PRC) has devoted extensive resources to try to steal it.[53]

Those who have worked with this exotic material call it almost magical. Until recently, Etrema was the only U.S. company authorized by the Navy to work with Terfenol-D, following its development at the DOE's Ames Laboratory. According to scientists and engineers, Terfenol-D is a technology of the future with many commercial and industrial uses. However, the Navy has its own uses for Terfenol-D, including high-tech sonar devices in U.S. submarines to detect and track enemy vessels.[54]

Yet, a burgeoning demand from commercial markets for the material has caused Terfenol-D to be classified as a "dual-use technology." Because the Department of the Navy invented it, the Department of Defense (DoD) is allowed to say who can use it. So, in order for a U.S. company to export a product that contains even a tiny amount of Terfenol-D, that company must have permission from the DoD in the form of an export license. Even if such a license is granted, the DoD places strict limits on the exporter to ensure absolute control of the material. Although possession of some of the material would not by itself reveal the process, the DoD wanted to limit any opportunity for a potentially hostile government to get close inspection of the substance.[55]

Despite the U.S. government's best efforts to keep secret the process that creates Terfenol-D, the PRC was able to obtain enough information to develop a crude version according to some U.S. officials. China was able to obtain information about the secret process by placing "students at Iowa State University to work in and around the Ames Laboratory."[56]

Government officials are oconcerned that technology transfers are occurring in the context of academic exchanges between scientists and students working to solve scientific problems. It is during such "problem-solving discussions" that students from China or elsewhere are able to gain information that they take back "to their home countries and advance technologies there that often wind up in weapons systems."[57]

During the past several years, efforts continued by foreigners to exploit their visits to U.S. facilities. Inappropriate conduct during visits was the second most frequently reported modus operandi (MO) associated with foreign collection activity. Once in a facility, collectors may attempt to manipulate the visit to satisfy their collection requirements. For example, visitors may ask questions or request information that is outside the scope of the approved visit. Unchecked, this MO usually results in the loss of technology, and is therefore considered to be a damaging form of collection activity. Some examples of exploitation techniques include the following:

- Wandering around facilities unescorted, bringing unauthorized cameras and/or recording devices into cleared facilities, or pressing their hosts for additional accesses or information
- Adding last-minute and/or unannounced persons as part of the visit
- Arriving unannounced and seeking access by asking to see an employee belonging to the same organization as the visitor
- Hiding true agendas, for example, by trying to shift conversations to topics not agreed upon in advance
- Misrepresenting a visitor's importance or technical competency to secure visit approval[58]

Intelligence agencies may recruit students before, during, or after studying abroad. Some countries allows students to study abroad and gather foreign business and technological data instead of performing compulsory
military service. For example, the Japanese government has ordered some
Japanese graduate students in the United States to report on scientific developments or face having their scholarships terminated. China's conduct
is perhaps even more brazen. They are suspected of routinely sending vis-
iting scholars, business delegates, and students to the United States in an
orchestrated effort to infiltrate companies and eventually bring back valuable information and trade secrets to China.[59] Predictably, Chinese officials
consistently deny charges of economic espionage. Dismissing such allegations as untrue, a spokesperson for the Chinese embassy in Washington
has declared that "all of China's relations with other countries have been
conducted in compliance with international norms and the laws of those
countries." Although China is only one of many nations suspected of spying
on the United States, U.S. officials are so worried about the loss of intellectual property to Chinese agents that they have raised this concern in regards
to China's efforts to join the World Trade Organization (WTO).[60]

Co-Opting of Former Employees and Cultural Commonalties

Foreign intelligence services and government-sponsored entities continue
to use traditional clandestine espionage methods to collect U.S. trade secrets and critical technologies. These methods include agent recruitment,
U.S. volunteers, and co-optees.[61] Incidents involving the co-opting of former employees who had access to sensitive proprietary or classified S&T
information remains a potential counterintelligence concern. Frequently,
foreign collectors will exploit cultural commonalties to establish rapport
with their target. As a result, foreign collectors specifically target foreign
employees working for U.S. companies. Likewise, U.S. defense contractor
employees working overseas may be particularly vulnerable to foreign offers
of employment as their contracts expire.

Conferences

International exhibits, conventions, and seminars are rich targeting opportunities for foreign collectors. These functions directly link programs and
technologies to knowledgeable personnel. International seminar audiences
often include leading scientists and technical experts, who pose more of a
threat than intelligence officers due to their level of technical understanding and ability to exploit immediately the intelligence they collect. At these
venues, foreign collectors target U.S. scientists and businessmen to gain
insights into U.S. products and capabilities. Consequently, U.S. defense

industry reporting indicates that collection activity at these events is usually expected, is commonplace, and most often involves overt open source intelligence gathering.

The counterintelligence community reporting indicates that, during seminars, foreign entities attempt subtle approaches such as sitting next to a potential target and initiating casual conversation. This activity often serves as a starting point for later exploitation. Membership lists of international business and/or technical societies are increasingly used to identify potential U.S. targets. One of the most common targeting techniques is to use collectors who have common cultural backgrounds with the target such as origin of birth, religion, or language.[62] For example, the counterintelligence community has increasingly sought to make the private sector aware of the foreign collection threat and has conducted threat awareness briefings prior to such international symposia. Specific examples include counterintelligence and security awareness briefings for U.S. industry representatives who planned to attend or support the Paris and Fainborough International Air Shows.

Internet Activity (Cyberattack and Exploitation)

This category addresses cyberattack and exploitation via Internet-based requests for information. The majority of Internet endeavors are foreign probes searching for potential weaknesses in systems for exploitation. One example was a network attack that, over the period of a day, involved several hundred attempts to use multiple passwords to illegally obtain access to a cleared defense facility's network. Fortunately, the facility had an appropriate level of protection in place to repel this attack. This example reflects the extent to which intelligence collectors are attempting to use the Internet to gain access to sensitive or proprietary information.[63]

Who Is Spying on American Industry?

It is a known fact that virtually every traditional espionage method used during war is employed in today's business world. The openness of American government, industry, and society makes information fluid and accessible.[64] The United States has the most sought-after technology and many of the best research facilities in the world; no other country produces as much intellectual property as the United States.[65] In addition, few industrial spies in the United States were ever arrested.

Economic espionage directed at the U.S. government is focused on a few key areas. According to the FBI, over the past several years foreign governments have sought the following information: U.S. economic, trade, and financial agreements; U.S. trade developments and policies; U.S. national debt levels; U.S. tax and monetary policies; foreign aid programs and export credits; technology transfer and munitions control regulations; U.S. energy policies and critical materials stockpiles data; U.S. commodity policies; and proposed legislation affecting foreign firms operating in the United States.

Some estimate that "seventy foreign governments regularly eavesdrop on U.S. corporate communications being transmitted on telephone systems overseas."[66] Many governments use surveillance and surreptitious entry as effective and inexpensive means of intelligence. Agents have stolen papers, computers, and computer disks from company offices and from the hotel rooms of executives traveling abroad. The following sections demonstrate some examples of international economic espionage activities.

People's Republic of China

Two businessmen, one a Chinese national who is the president of a Beijing-based firm, and the other a naturalized Canadian citizen, pleaded guilty to charges of illegally exporting fiberoptic gyroscopes to the PRC without the required State Department permits. Export of these gyroscopes to the PRC is prohibited. The two men bought the gyroscopes from a Massachusetts company and planned to export them to the PRC via a Canadian subsidiary of the Beijing-based firm. The gyroscopes can be used in missile and aircraft guidance systems as well as smart bombs.

Two naturalized U.S. citizens were convicted of conspiring to illegally export weapons parts to their native China. They used their exporting company to purchase surplus U.S. missile, aircraft, radar, and tank parts from the Defense Reutilization and Marketing Service and then ship them to the PRC. The exported items were on the U.S. Munitions List that prohibited them from being shipped without a license from the State Department.

Two Chinese scientists and a naturalized U.S. citizen who was born in China were arrested for stealing product designs from a major U.S. telecommunications firm and passing them to a Chinese government-owned company in Beijing. Both Chinese scientists had received technical degrees from U.S. universities before being employed by the U.S. firm.

A Chinese company based in Orlando, Florida, was charged with illegally exporting radiation-hardened integrated circuits to Chinese missile and satellite manufacturers in the PRC without the required Department of Commerce licenses. The affidavit prepared by the Department of Commerce described three illegal diversions of the missile microchips. According to weapons proliferation specialists, the microchips have military applications and could be used by the Chinese military to improve their long-range missile-targeting capabilities.

A naturalized Chinese national was arrested for attempting to smuggle a defense-grade Radiance high-speed (HS) infrared camera to the PRC. Since the Radiance HS camera is on the U.S. Munitions List, companies must file with the Department of State to legally export such items. The camera was destined for the Chinese State Ship Building Corporation, a state-owned conglomerate of fifty-eight companies that is based in Beijing and Shanghai.[67]

Pakistan

U.S. Customs Service agents arrested two Pakistani brothers and charged them with conspiring to smuggle sophisticated cameras for military intelligence gathering to a Pakistani government laboratory. One of the brothers was a naturalized U.S. citizen, whereas the other, a Pakistani citizen, had recently completed requirements for a master's degree in engineering at a U.S. university. A U.S. aerospace company alerted the U.S. Customs Service to the suspicious activities of the brothers after they attempted to purchase the cameras despite being denied an export license by the State Department.

A British citizen pleaded guilty to violating the Arms Export Control Act by trying to ship night-vision goggles and blueprints for C-I 30 aircraft to Pakistan. He was acting on behalf of a firm located in Islamabad. The C-130 aircraft is used for a variety of military purposes, including troop transport, surveillance, and gunships.[68]

Iran

A 20-month federal investigation culminated in the arrest by the U.S. Customs Service of a naturalized Canadian from Iran and a Malaysian citizen for conspiring to illegally export aircraft parts for the F-14 Tomcat, F-S Tiger, and F-4 Phantom to the Iranian Air Force. In addition, a naturalized U.S. citizen from Iran pleaded guilty to violating the Arms Export Control Act by trying to smuggle F-14 parts into Iran.[69]

Guarding Secrets

As mentioned earlier, because of the threat of economic espionage, many countries make economic security a priority, enacting laws that purport to deter would-be intelligence gatherers.[70] Although laws in individual countries may help protect economic secrets of the country's nationals, such laws do not solve the problem of economic espionage internationally. Part of the trouble may stem from the history that some states do not respect the intellectual property rights of other states. Historically, patent law in some nations encouraged economic espionage abroad as seen per earlier examples. For example, one of the earliest patent laws, developed in France, gave "to whomsoever shall be the first to bring to France a foreign industry the same advantages as if he were inventor of it." France has since amended its patent law to exclude such encouragement, but the fact that it once existed only supports the idea that when a nation's economy is threatened, ethics will not necessarily keep it from protecting itself in any way possible.[71]

The number of countries engaging in economic espionage against U.S. corporations is staggering. An FBI's study of 173 countries found that 100 had spent money to acquire U.S. technology,[72] and that 57 of those had engaged in covert operations against U.S. corporations. According to the former CIA Director Robert Gates, "governments in Asia, Europe, the Middle East and, to a lesser degree, Latin America – nearly 20 governments overall – are involved in intelligence activities that are detrimental to our economic interests."[73] A 1996 declassified CIA report on national security threats listed countries that are extensively engaged in economic espionage against the United States; among them were France, Israel, China, Russia, Iran, and Cuba.[74] Notably absent from the list was Japan, a country viewed by many as possessing one of the most brazen and efficient intelligence services worldwide.[75] The CIA report concluded, however, that Japanese efforts are largely limited to legal data gathering and hiring "well-placed" consultants.

Yet, according to a survey, the worst offenders are Asian governments, with western European governments following closely.[76,77] Other offenders can be found in various businesses throughout the United States, as indicated in a 1997 survey by the Futures Group, "[a] full 82 percent of companies with annual revenues of more than $10 billion have an organized intelligence unit."[78] However, economic espionage is not carried out exclusively by the first world powers. "Countries that heretofore have not been considered intelligence threats account for much of the economic collection currently being investigated by law enforcement communities."[79] In general, any nation that competes in the world market and has enough motivation to spy will engage in economic espionage.[80]

The significance surrounding the classes of parties involved in economic espionage is twofold. First, friendly and allied nations commit espionage against one another. In the world of economic espionage, there are no true friendly relations, largely due to the fact that countries that engage in the activity are vying for a rung on the global market ladder.[81] As the former French intelligence chief Pierre Marion pointed out, "it is an elementary blunder to think we're allies when it comes to business, it's war."[82] Second, developing nations are heavily involved in the trade due to more recent political developments, especially the decline of communism. Formerly communist states must quickly catch up with the West, and economic espionage often provides an avenue to do just that. Without communism, intelligence agents from Eastern bloc countries are unemployed and available in the open market.[83] The involvement of Eastern bloc agents is threatening because their intelligence activities are not restricted by traditional notions of international business ethics.[84] Therefore, such agents may go to any lengths to acquire the information they seek.

Primary Targets

The primary targets of foreign intelligence agencies are high-technology and defense-related industries; however, even nontechnology-intensive industries are at risk of theft.[85] The industries targeted by foreign agents tend to be of strategic interest to the United States for three reasons: (1) they produce classified products for the government, (2) they provide products used in both the military and the private sector, and (3) they are critical to maintaining economic security. The most frequently targeted industries include aerospace, biotechnology, telecommunications, computer hardware and software, transportation technology, defense and armaments technology, automobiles, energy research, semiconductors, advanced materials, basic research, and lasers.[86] Intelligence agents seek not only technology, but also proprietary business information from their targeted industries. Pricing data, customer lists, product development data, basic research, sales figures, and marketing plans are stolen more often than advanced technology.[87] Foreign governments also seek development plans, propriety information reports, personnel data contract bids, manufacturing cost analyses, propriety software, and strategic planning.[88]

The Cox Report

In 1999, the U.S. House of Representatives released the Report of the Select Committee on U.S. National Security and Military/Commercial Concerns with the People's Republic of China. Otherwise known as the "Cox Report," it detailed PRC espionage against U.S. military technology. The report lists "rare-earth metals" and "special-function materials" as "exotic materials" that are "the key areas of military concern" about PRC espionage targets. The report also states that "professional intelligence agents from the Ministry of State Security (MSS) and Military Intelligence Department (MID) account for a relatively small share of the PRC's foreign science and technology collection." Rather, the report explains, "the bulk of such information is gathered by various nonprofessionals, including PRC students, scientists, researchers and other visitors to the West."[89]

A graduate student from the PRC who is known to have worked on a secret military project in China should not be doing research at a U.S. university with defense research projects, according to national security specialists familiar with the way the PRC conducts espionage. And especially not on a high-tech material related to that on which he or she focused in Beijing. "The MSS recruits students" as espionage agents, reported John Fialka in his 1997 sworn testimony before the Joint Economic Committee Hearings on Economic Espionage, Technology Transfers and National Security. With as many as 50,000 Chinese nationals entering the United States each year, the agencies tasked with being on the lookout for espionage cannot handle the workload. "While the FBI makes an effort to watch foreign students and businessmen, China's flood has simply overwhelmed the bureau," noted Fialka.[90]

China's so-called Sixteen Character Policy, codified in 1997, calls for "blurring of the lines between state and commercial entities, and military and commercial interests," according to the report. Fialka noted that "in this game China is a dragon with two heads." That is, its commercial companies often are part of the PRC's military research, development, and procurement. The Cox Report states the "main aim for the civilian economy [in China] is to support the building of modern military weapons and to support the aims of the People's Liberation Army (PLA)."[91]

In another incident in July 2002, according to federal law enforcement authorities, security officials at Hancock International Airport in Syracuse, New York, found more than 100 vials, test tubes, and petri dishes containing an unknown biological substance in the carry-on luggage of a former Cornell University postdoctoral researcher and his family. They were preparing to board a flight to China via Detroit. The researcher, Qianqiang Yin, was charged with stealing biological materials and attempting to transport them to China.[92]

Incidents such as these highlight the expanding scope of economic espionage. The need to address this will only increase in the future.

Tensions Between Security and Openness

THE U.S. INFORMATION and communications infrastructure sector generates more revenue than most nations produce. Far more than any other nation, the potential of new technologies has enabled the United States to reshape its governmental and commercial processes. All countries that make use of computer technology and especially those connected to the Internet are vulnerable, although the level to which the United States has incorporated new technologies and the highly networked nature of its infrastructure makes it the most vulnerable.[1]

Some experts have questioned whether such an open and flexible global information infrastructure is still in the best interests of the United States and the world in light of the growing threats from information warfare, information terrorism, and cybercrime. One must keep in mind this state of the world in assessing the efficacy of any proposed international agreement that portends to address the serious and far-reaching effects of information warfare, information terrorism, and cybercrime.

Growing Vulnerability in the Information Age

President Clinton chose his commencement address to the 1998 graduating class of the U.S. Naval Academy as a forum for highlighting the escalating threat posed by information warfare, information terrorism, and cybercrime:

> Our security is challenged increasingly by nontraditional threats from adversaries, both old and new, not only hostile regimes, but also international criminals and terrorists who cannot defeat us in traditional theaters of battle, but search instead for new ways to attack by exploiting new technologies and the world's increasing openness.[2]

Disruption of any infrastructure is always inconvenient and can be costly and even life-threatening. Major disruptions could lead to major losses and affect national security, the economy, and the public good. Mutual dependence and the interconnectedness made possible by the information and communications infrastructure lead to the possibility that our infrastructures may be vulnerable in ways they never have been before. Intentional exploitation of these new vulnerabilities could have severe consequences for our economy, security, and way of life.

Technologies and techniques that have fueled major improvements in the performance of our infrastructures can also be used to disrupt them. The United States, where close to one-half of all computer capacity and 60% of Internet assets reside, is at once the world's most advanced and most dependent user of information technology. More than any other country, the United States relies on a set of increasingly accessible and technologically reliable infrastructures, which in turn have a growing collective dependence on domestic and global networks. This provides great opportunity, but it also presents new vulnerabilities that can be exploited. It heightens risk of

Profile of Electric Power System

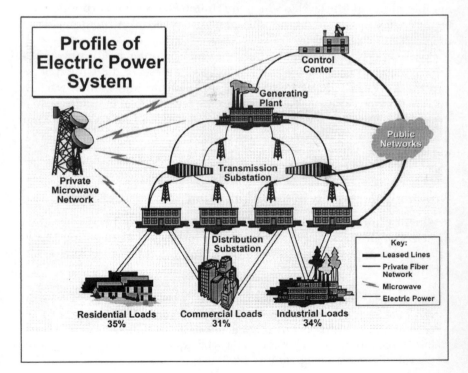

cascading technological failure, and therefore of cascading disruption in the flow of essential goods and services. Computerized interaction within and among infrastructures has become so complex that it may be possible to do harm in ways we cannot yet conceive.

A New and Challenging Environment

Alvin and Heidi Toffler pointed out in their book, *The Third Wave*, that the history of the world can largely be portrayed as three waves.[3] The first was the agricultural wave, the second was the industrial wave, and the third is the information wave. Not all countries have progressed to this third wave or even the second, nor is any country necessarily characterized by only one wave. The recognition that parts of the world have progressed into the third wave, however, calls for new thinking, new paradigms, and innovation.

Our dependence on information and communications technologies has created new vulnerabilities, which we are only beginning to understand. In addition to the possible disruption of information and communications, nations in the third wave also face the possibility that someone will be able to actually mount an attack against other kinds of infrastructures because of their dependence on computers and telecommunications.

Interdependence New Risks and Vulnerabilities

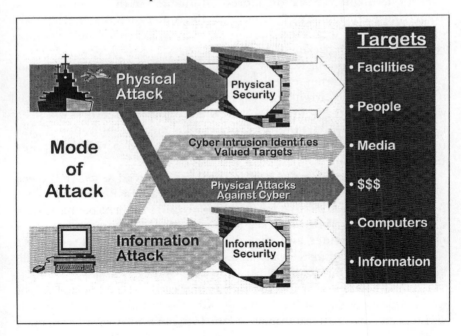

Information and Communications

All critical infrastructures are increasingly dependent on information and communications. The most important impact and vulnerability for this sector is the increasing interdependency of the public telecommunication network (PTN) and the Internet. The Internet depends heavily on the PTN. The PTN, in turn, depends on electrical power for operations and on telephone lines and fiberoptic cables that often run along transportation routes. The PTN is increasingly software driven, and managed and maintained through computer networks. Deregulation of the telecommunications industry will increase the number of access points, increasing opportunities for attack.

The Internet

The Internet is a global network of networks interconnected via routers that use a common set of protocols to provide communications among users. Internet communications are based on connectionless data transport. In other words, the IP does not establish a circuit between communicating parties during the lifetime of the communication. Instead, each message is divided into small packets of data that contain routing information in a packet header. Routers forward the packets to other routers closer to the packet's destinations based on address information in the packet headers. To maximize efficient use of the network, the routers may send each packet of a message over a different path to its destination, where the message is reassembled as the packets arrive.

The Internet and the PTN are not mutually exclusive because significant portions of the Internet, especially its backbone and user access links, rely on PTN facilities. Current trends suggest that the PTN and the Internet will merge in the years ahead: By 2010, many of today's networks will likely be absorbed or replaced by a successor public telecommunications infrastructure capable of providing integrated voice, data, video, private line, and Internet-based services.

The Internet originated in 1968 by the then Advanced Research Projects Agency (ARPA), now known as the Defense Advanced Research Projects Agency. The project was to determine how to build resilient computer networks that could survive physical attacks or malfunctions in portions of the network. The ARPAnet, as it was called, was not designed as a secure network, but depended for security on a small number of users who generally knew and trusted one another.

Commercialization of the Internet in the early 1990s, boosted by the world wide web, caused incredible growth. Government and the private sector began to seize the advantages of the Internet as an alternative to other unclassified means of communication. The Internet continues to expand globally at a rapid pace.

Key Factors in the Current State of Internet Security

Threats to the Internet are of primary concern because we are becoming increasingly dependent on it for communications. This includes government and military communications, commerce, remote control and monitoring of systems, and a host of other uses. In addition, the Internet is inherently insecure.

The Internet: Multiple Points of Access Yield Multiple Points of Vulnerability

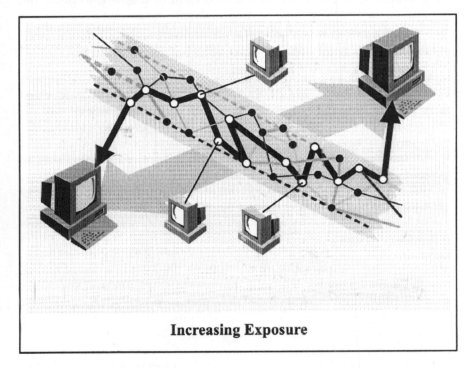

Increasing Exposure

The current state of Internet security is the result of many factors. A change in any one of these can change the level of Internet security and survivability. Because of the dramatically lower cost of communication and ease of connecting to the Internet, use of the Internet is replacing other forms of electronic communication. As critical infrastructure operators strive to improve their efficiency and lower costs, they are connecting formerly isolated systems to the Internet to facilitate remote maintenance functions and improve coordination across distributed systems. Operations of the critical infrastructures are becoming increasingly dependent on the Internet and, therefore, are vulnerable to Internet-based attacks.[4]

Most threatening of all is the link between cyberspace and physical space. Supervisory control and data acquisition systems and other forms of networked computer systems have for years been used to control power grids, gas and oil distribution pipelines, water treatment and distribution systems, hydroelectric and flood control dams, oil and chemical refineries, and other physical systems. Increasingly, these control systems are being connected to communications links and networks to reduce operational costs by supporting remote maintenance, remote control, and remote update functions. These computer-controlled and network-connected systems are potential targets of individuals bent on causing massive disruption and physical damage. This is not just theory; actual attacks have caused major operational problems. For example, attacks against wastewater treatment systems in Australia led to the release of hundreds of thousands of gallons of sludge.[5]

As the technology is being distributed, the management of the technology is often distributed as well. In these cases, system administration and management often fall on people who do not have the training, skill, resources, or interest needed to operate their systems securely.[6] The rush to the Internet, coupled with a lack of understanding, is leading to the exposure of sensitive data and risk to critical systems. Just one naive user with an easy-to-guess password increases an organization's risk.[7]

There is little evidence of improvement in the security features of most products. Developers are not devoting sufficient effort to apply lessons learned about the sources of vulnerabilities. The Computer Emergency and Response Team Coordination Center (CERT/CC) routinely receives reports of new vulnerabilities. In 1995, CERT received an average of 35 new reports each quarter, 140 for the year. By 2002, the number of annual reports received had skyrocketed to more than 4,000. Technology evolves so rapidly that vendors concentrate on time to market, often minimizing that time by placing a low priority on security features. Until their customers demand products that are more secure, the situation is unlikely to change.[8]

When vendors release patches or upgrades to solve security problems, organizations' systems often are not upgraded because it may be too time-consuming, too complex, or just at too low a priority for the system administration staff to handle. With increased complexity comes the introduction of more vulnerabilities. Because managers often do not fully understand the risks, they neither give security a high enough priority nor assign adequate resources. The problem is made worse by the fact that the demand for system administrators with strong security skills far exceeds the supply.[9]

Engineering for ease of use is not being matched by engineering for ease of secure administration. Today's software products, workstations, and personal computers bring the power of the computer to increasing numbers of people who use that power to perform their work more efficiently and effectively. Products are so easy to use that people with little technical knowledge or skill can install and operate them on their desktop computers. Unfortunately, it is difficult to configure and operate many of these products securely. This gap leads to increasing numbers of vulnerable systems.[10]

As we face the complex and rapidly changing world of the Internet, comprehensive solutions are lacking. Among security-conscious organizations, there is increased reliance on quick and easy solutions, such as firewalls and encryption. These organizations are lulled into a false sense of security and become less vigilant, but single solutions applied once are neither foolproof nor adequate. Solutions must be combined, and the security situation must be constantly monitored as technology changes and new exploitation techniques are discovered.[11]

Information Theft and Computer Crimes

"No area of criminal activity is more on the cutting edge or has greater global implications than crime involving technology and computers,"[12] so stated former Attorney General Janet Reno in an address to an elite group of experts from the G-8 countries convened to discuss transnational organized crime. Unfortunately, the way in which such crimes are committed has largely frustrated efforts to investigate and prosecute such crimes. Cyberattacks are cheap, easy to launch, difficult to trace, and hard to prosecute. Cyberattackers are using the connectivity to exploit widespread vulnerabilities in systems to conduct criminal activities, compromise information, and launch denial-of-service attacks that seriously disrupt legitimate operations.

Reported attacks against Internet systems are almost doubling each year and attack technology will evolve to support attacks that are even more virulent and damaging. Our current solutions are not keeping pace with the increased strength and speed of attacks, and our information infrastructures are at risk. Although some attacks require technical knowledge – the equivalent to that of a college graduate who majored in computer science – many other successful attacks are carried out by technically unsophisticated intruders. Technically competent intruders duplicate and share their programs and information at little cost, thus enabling novice intruders to do the same damage as the experts. In addition to being easy and cheap, Internet attacks can be quick. In a matter of seconds, intruders can break into a system; hide evidence of the break-in; install their programs, leaving a "back door" so they can easily return to the now-compromised system; and begin launching attacks at other sites.[13]

Attackers can lie about their identity and location on the network. Information on the Internet is transmitted in packets, each containing information about the origin and destination. Senders provide their return address, but they can lie about it. Most of the Internet is designed merely to forward packets one step closer to their destination with no attempt to make a record of their source. There is not even a "postmark" to indicate generally where a packet originated. It requires close cooperation among sites and up-to-date equipment to trace malicious packets during an attack. Moreover, the Internet is designed to allow packets to flow easily across geographic, administrative, and political boundaries. Consequently, cooperation in tracing a single attack may involve multiple organizations and jurisdictions, most of which are not directly affected by the attack and may have little incentive to invest time and resources in the effort. This means that it is easy for an adversary to use a foreign site to launch attacks at U.S. systems. The attacker enjoys the added safety of the need for international cooperation in order to trace the attack, compounded by impediments to legal investigations. We have seen U.S.-based attacks on U.S. sites gain this safety by first breaking into one or more non-U.S. sites before coming back to attack the desired target in the United States.[14]

Accurate statistics on the extent of this phenomenon have proven elusive[15] because of the difficulty in adequately defining computer crimes.[16] The statistics are also untrustworthy due to victims' failures to report incidents because of (1) fear of losing customer confidence[17] and (2) lack of detection. The aggregate annual losses to businesses and governments, however, are estimated to be in the billions of dollars.[18]

The fastest-growing computer-related crime is theft, and the most common object stolen is information. Thieves often target intellectual properties that include things like a new product patent, new product description, market program plans, a list of customers, and similar information. Previously thieves obtained such properties through employees, photocopying documents, and burglaries. Now the MO has changed and thieves would prefer stealing from the computers because it provides extensive access to more usable information.[19]

In the summer of 1996, hackers attached the worldwide web site of the U.S. DOJ, replacing official information with adult pictures, a photo of Hitler, and a swastika. Months later hackers gained entry to the CIA's web site, relabeling it "The Central Stupidity Agency." In December of 1996, the Defense Department shut down eighty sites on the global computer network after hackers inserted a sexually explicit video clip on the Air Force web site.[20] More recently, assessments by the House Government Reform Committee's Subcommittee on Technology revealed that the federal government does a poor job on security (see Appendix B).

Computer crime, also known as cybercrime, is a growing and increasingly costly phenomenon.[21] Computer crimes can be divided into three broad categories: (1) crimes where a computer is a tool, (2) crimes where a computer is the target, and (3) crimes where a computer is incidental.[22] In the first category, the computer is used as a tool to commit offenses. This group looks upon the computer as one of the instruments for committing crimes like fraud, embezzlement, and other related crimes. The second category contains crimes in which the computer itself or the stored information is the target.

First, a computer may be the "object" of a crime: The offender targets the computer itself. This encompasses theft of computer processor time and computerized services. Second, a computer may be the "subject" of a crime: A computer is the physical site of the crime, the source of, or reason for unique forms of asset loss. This includes the use of "viruses," "worms," "Trojan Horses," "logic bombs," and "sniffers." Third, a computer may be an "instrument" used to commit traditional crimes in a more complex manner. For example, a computer might be used to collect credit card information to make fraudulent purchases.

Computer theft offers distinct advantages to the cybercriminal. It allows the criminal to pilfer large amounts of money without having to face locked safes, foreign premises, or, most important, armed security guards. A heist can be done safely and efficiently through a few strokes on a computer keyboard. Moreover, although a gun offers a thief protection and control over his or her victims, a computer eliminates this need and supplements the thief's arsenal with anonymity and an unlimited range of victims. As one commentator accurately stated, "if I want to steal money, a computer is a much better tool than a handgun.... It would take me a long time to get $10 million with a handgun."[23]

As the Citibank heist[24] illustrates, a cybercriminal's reach is international and his or her crimes can often be committed without anyone knowing when it was done, how it was done, or who the culprit was. It is for these and other reasons that theft and fraud offenses committed with the aid of computers and other electronic media will soon become leading international crimes. There are no visa or passport requirements, no security checkpoints, and no physical barriers. Perhaps, most important, such crimes require little manpower and resources.[25]

Although the Citibank heist involved the stealing of U.S. currency, the modern-day criminal is now focusing his or her computer's attention on stealing something that is often more valuable, the corporate trade secret. The cybercrook has realized that stealing the next version of the Coca-Cola recipe or Windows software is worth more than a $10 million heist. More important, the trade secret – unlike the $10 million in cash – can be duplicated and downloaded without the true owner ever knowing that the trade secret has been stolen. The owner still has a copy; unfortunately, the cybercrook does, too.

High-Tech Thieves

Criminal groups who view computers as targets have been placed in three categories: (1) hackers, (2) those who break the systems to intentionally cause harm or mischief to data or programs, and (3) financially motivated offenders who use a "specialized skill" to steal or damage information contained in computer storage banks.[26] There is no "typical" computer-related crime and no "typical" motive for committing such crimes, although common motives including exhibiting technical expertise, highlighting weaknesses in computer security systems, punishment or retaliation, computer voyeurism, asserting a belief in open access to computer systems, or sabotage.[27] Computer criminals can be youthful hackers, disgruntled employees and company insiders, or international terrorists and spies. Because of the vast variety of computer-related crimes and motives, computer-related crimes are classified according to the computer's role in the particular crime.

Analysis of computer crimes suggests that threats of such crime generally come from employees. Studies reported on computer crimes have shown that primary threats come from full-time employees, followed by part-time and contract employees, and with computer hackers a close third. There is normally a close correlation between theft and access to computers, but the important thing to recognize is that as networking becomes widespread, access is also becoming easier.[28]

The Morris Case

Perhaps the most infamous Internet crime ever committed was the 1988 case of *United States v. Morris*.[29] Robert Tappan Morris was a 23-year-old first-year graduate student in Cornell University's computer science Ph.D. program who, through various jobs, had acquired significant computer experience. Morris was given an account on his school's computer and soon began work on a computer program, later known as the Internet "worm" or "virus." Morris intended to release the worm into university, government, and military computers around the country in order to demonstrate the inadequacies of current security measures on those computer networks. "The worm was supposed to occupy little computer operation time, and thus not interfere with normal use of those computers."[30]

After releasing his "harmless" worm, Morris soon discovered that it was actually infecting machines, ultimately causing computers at more than 6,000[31] educational institutions and military sites around the country to "crash" or cease functioning.[32] With the help of a friend, Morris then sent out an anonymous message instructing programmers how to kill the worm and prevent reinfection. However, "because the network route was clogged, the message did not get through until it was too late." Morris was found guilty of violating the Computer Fraud and Abuse Act, Section 1030(a)(5)(A), which prohibited intentional unauthorized access to federal computers. "He was sentenced to three years of probation, 400 hours of community service, a fine of $10,050, and the costs of his supervision."[33]

There is a common agreement that cybercrimes exist, but little overall agreement as to what they are other than they involve the use of the computers in some way. The term is most frequently used to describe either traditional or familiar forms of offending that use the Internet, or else to illustrate the more dramatic forms of offending via technological daring-do. Computer crime may be the subject of the biggest cover-up since Watergate. As such, it has proved difficult to give an accurate reliable overview of the extent of losses and the actual number of criminal offences.

Cybercrime – Computer Crime Defined

Although the term *computer crime* includes traditional crimes committed with a computer, it also includes novel, technologically specific offenses that arguably are not analogous to any noncomputer crimes. Computer crime represents the activity most likely to be confused with IW.[34] The phrase "computer crime" is itself a nebulous term covering a gamut of actions ranging from releasing a supposedly benign virus or hacking into computers to look at information,[35] to causing the computers that run the alarms at a chemical plant to malfunction. To further muddle the definition, many normal crimes are now committed with the assistance of computers.[36] The diversity of computer-related offenses, however, rendered any narrow definition untenable.

Although "computer crime" remains loosely defined, most industrialized countries have amended their legislation to address four needs created by computer crimes: (1) protection of privacy, (2) prosecution of economic crimes, (3) protection of intellectual property, and (4) procedural provisions to aid in the prosecution of computer crimes.[37] Worldwide, national governments are adopting computer-specific criminal codes that address unauthorized access and manipulation of data, similar to the Computer Fraud and Abuse Act of 1996 in the United States. Criminalization of copyright infringements are also gaining momentum around the world.[38]

Criminal actions that target or are facilitated through the use of computer systems are called *cybercrimes*. Cybercrime can be divided into two categories: (1) crimes that are "located" entirely in cyberspace and (2) crimes that have a physical component that merely are facilitated in cyberspace.

There has been a great deal of debate among experts on just what constitutes a computer crime or a computer-related crime. The term "computer crime" also includes intelligence collection activities, which is conducted by all advanced states.[39] Even after several years, there is no internationally recognized definition of this term. The head of the U.S. DOJ's Computer Crime unit echoed this sentiment and indicated that the term "computer crime" has no precise definition.[40]

In 1983, the OECD defined computer crime and computer-related crime as "any illegal, unethical, or unauthorized behavior involving automatic data-processing and/or transmission of data."[41] Including "unethical" behavior within the criminal definition without more amplification would likely be struck down as unconstitutionally vague.

Interestingly, the *United Nations Manual on Computer-Related Crime* stated that annoying behavior must be distinguished from criminal behavior in law.[42] Although such would seem to be a fairly noncontroversial statement, it seems considerably more contentious in the area of computer crime. For instance, a group of hackers, allegedly a Mexican group known as the zapatistas, intended to bring down a U.S. DoD site to bring attention to their cause. They chose as their MO the use of a computer to repeatedly "hit" the site in order to cause an overload and thereby render it inoperable, or cause it to crash outright. Obviously, trying to "hit" a site should not be a crime because that is the purpose of web sites. Even trying to repeatedly hit a site would not normally be thought of as criminal. Only the intentional overloading of a site would be criminal, which will involve line-drawing issues hinging on intent and possibly outcome, to the extent intent can be properly inferred from it.[43]

An early definition of computer crime proposed by the U.S. DOJ quite broadly included "any violations of criminal law that involve a knowledge of computer technology for their perpetration, investigation, or prosecution."[44] Such a definition would appear to reach too far because today's technologically oriented prosecutorial and investigative agencies employ computers to prosecute and investigate even mundane traditional crimes.[45] Some experts have suggested that DOJ's definition could encompass a series of crimes that have nothing to do with computers. For example, if an auto theft investigation required a detective to use "knowledge of computer technology" to investigate a vehicle's identification number in a state's department of motor vehicle database, under DOJ guidelines, auto theft could be classified as a computer crime. Although the example may stretch the boundaries of logic, it demonstrates the difficulties inherent in attempting to describe and classify computer criminality.[46]

Even though several individual states have attempted to define computer crimes or regulate within subfields of this area,[47] there have been only three significant international efforts – one by the OECD[48] and two by the Council of Europe (COE). Both the OECD and the COE define "computer crime," but leave it to individual states.[49] Nevertheless, both bodies put forth proposed standards to provide a common denominator for what should constitute computer crimes in each of their member nation-states.[50] It is instructive to assess and trace the development of these first international efforts to define computer crimes in order to obtain a better idea of how the law is developing in this area. All nations continue to struggle with defining computer crime and developing computer crime legislation that is applicable to both domestic and international audiences.[51]

Preparing for a New Cyberwar

The threat from computer crime and other information security breaches continues unabated and the financial toll is mounting at an alarming rate – with theft of proprietary information continuing to be the number one threat to information systems.[52] "Although there has never been accurate nationwide reporting of computer crime, it is clear from the reports which do exist . . . that computer crime is on the rise."[53] As a matter of fact, between January 1998 and December 1998, the CERT/CC[54] received "41,871 e-mail messages and 1,001 hotline calls reporting computer security incidents or requesting information."[55] In addition, they received 262 vulnerability reports and handled 3,734 computer security incidents, affecting more than 18,990 sites during this same period.[56]

With expanding computer-controlled infrastructure came an increase in the severity of computer hacker attacks.[57] Where a decade ago computers were relatively isolated and performed specialized tasks, today as mentioned earlier, computers control general, widespread systems that form the backbone of modern life.[58]

Computer crime is a global problem; many computer crimes are simply old-fashioned crimes of theft or fraud or vandalism, simply perpetrated in the electronic medium. Purely domestic solutions are inadequate because cyberspace has no geographic or political boundaries. Many computer systems can be easily and surreptitiously accessed through the global telecommunications network from anywhere in the world.[59] International financial institutions are common targets for computer fraud and embezzlement schemes.[60] The development of sophisticated computer technology has also enabled organized crime groups to bypass government detection and enter the international realm of drug trafficking and money laundering.[61] In addition, the specter of computer terrorism calls for an international strategy to preserve global security.

It seemed like a sequel to the 1983 movie "War Games." From the comfort of his own home, a hacker intentionally disabled one of NASA's communications uplinks to the Atlantis space shuttle, while another acquired "superuser" status, allowing a 24-year-old from Denver to control all of NASA's 118 computer systems and read all users' e-mail. Another hacker in Phoenix gained control of all U.S. water canals south of the Grand Canyon, whereas still another tapped into a local air traffic control system while toying with a municipal phone network.[62]

Unlike nuclear weapons, which require highly sophisticated parts and tightly regulated materials, information weapons consist of common programming commands arranged in a variety of ways to produce malicious code. This code can be delivered over the Internet, by conventional mail, fax, or phone in the exact same way that innocent commercial or personal communications are transmitted. Thus, information weapons are not subject to customs checks or other safeguards against international transport and, because of the volume of information transmitted in these ways, could not reasonably be so subjected. Testing of information weapons cannot be detected with seismographs or satellite sensors. Although the damage done by some information weapons might be readily apparent, studies indicate only an exceptionally small portion of users who are attacked by hackers are even aware of the attack.

Attackers include national intelligence organizations, information warriors, terrorists, criminals, industrial competitors, hackers, and aggrieved or disloyal insiders. Although insiders constitute the single largest known security threat to information and information systems, controlled testing indicates that large numbers of computer-based attacks go undetected, and that the unknown component of the threat may exceed the known component by orders of magnitude.

Adversaries can employ a variety of methods against the infrastructure, including traffic analysis, technical security attacks, physical attacks, and cyberattacks. Physical and cyberattacks pose the greatest risk. They have increased rapidly in sophistication and disruptive potential, while the infrastructure's vulnerability has grown. The availability of truck bombs, chemical agents, and biological agents has increased the disruptive potential of physical attacks. At the same time, the vulnerability of the information and communications (I&C) infrastructure to physical attack has increased.

Tools to remotely access, change, or destroy information in vulnerable systems and to control, damage, or shut down the systems themselves have become more sophisticated, easier to use, and more widely available. The U.S. DoD tests and exercises, together with the rising incidence of documented intrusions and cyber-related losses over recent years, indicate that networked computers are highly vulnerable to these techniques. A broad array of adversaries, including a sizable number of foreign governments, are currently capable of conducting cyberattacks.

The introduction of numerous third parties, including foreign companies, operating in partnership with U.S. companies or on their own, into every aspect of network operations will alter the trust relationship on which current network architecture is based. The security measures needed to compensate for the loss of trust will take years to develop. During this time, attacks to gain unauthorized access to sensitive data and functions will be easier to accomplish on a widespread basis than at any previous time in the history of telecommunications.

Today's level of threat and degree of vulnerability present two risks for national policy to address. The first is the cumulative risk generated by many small-scale attempts to steal information or money through cyberattack. The vulnerability of individuals and enterprises to cybertheft damages the nation's competitiveness. Losses undermine both the bottom line and public confidence in emerging information technology. For the I&C infrastructure to realize its full potential as a medium for commerce, government, and military operations, users must have confidence that transactions will be confidential and protected.

The numerous security vulnerabilities in today's I&C infrastructure afford little basis for such confidence, and the trends are not encouraging. In the meantime, the payoff for successful exploitation is increasing. With commerce growing exponentially over a medium with minimal protection, criminals and hackers can be expected to develop original and profitable new methods of operation. With larger and larger quantities of imperfectly protected information residing on networked systems, intelligence services and industrial competitors can be expected to find increasingly sophisticated ways to break in.

The second and more critical risk is that presented by cyberattacks and physical attacks intended to disrupt the U.S. I&C infrastructure and the critical societal functions that depend on it. With network elements increasingly interconnected and reliant on each other, cyberattacks simultaneously targeting multiple network functions would be highly difficult to defend against, particularly if combined with selected physical destruction of key facilities. The possibility that such disruption could cascade across a substantial part of the PTN cannot be ruled out. No one knows how the network would react under coordinated attack.

To address the risk posed by the mounting incidence of cybertheft and other small-scale attacks, national policy must encourage a cooperative approach to strengthening security. National and international policies must ensure that there is an effective national and international capability to detect and defend against large-scale attacks on the I&C infrastructure.

The ability to communicate with large numbers of hackers and the widespread availability of tools to carry out a break-in exacerbate the problem. Relatively unsophisticated computer users are now able to quickly accumulate premade tools and detailed instructions on how to anonymously attack a target.[63] This makes it easier to stay ahead of law enforcement.

Furthermore, the Internet was not designed with security in mind.[64] By promoting connectivity over security, users are able to travel through multiple computers all over the world. Tracing the hacker is difficult. Only one computer along the hacker's route need be insecure, lack adequate logs of users, or reside in an uncooperative foreign jurisdiction for law enforcement to fail in tracking the intruder.

Weapons of Mass Disruption

Tools To Do Harm

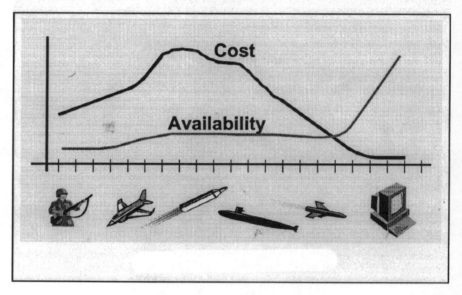

In the online world, we often face a problem with criminal actions that are not treated as crimes. Although our society does not tolerate people breaking into homes and businesses, we seem to have more tolerance for computer break-ins. Yet, breaking into computers is just as much a crime and both break-ins harm innocent people and weaken businesses.

In the last few years, we have realized that the issues posed by criminal hackers are real and costly. The "ILOVEYOU" virus of 2000 slowed down worldwide e-mail systems. The Ramen and Lion worms attacked Linux software to deface web sites and extract sensitive information such as passwords. The Code Red worm exploited Windows server software to infect servers and attack other web sites. The Trinoo attacks exploited vulnerabilities in the Solaris operating system to mount denial of service attacks against several prominent web sites. Estimated damage in these attacks runs into the billions of dollars.[65]

Cyberattacks, Information Theft, and Online Shakedown

Cyberattacks are frequently in the news, but far more go unreported. Each year the CSI and the FBI publish a study that demonstrates the number of companies that reportedly suffered some form of unauthorized computer intrusion. Each year, the percentage creeps closer to 100%. In a more recent study,[66] 92% of the companies surveyed reported that they suffered some form of attack to or misused computer systems during the 2002–2003 year. Some forms of disruptive practice are on the increase, and the estimated damage to business is usually estimated in the hundreds of millions or billions of dollars.

Potential cyberthreats and associated risks range from recreational hackers to terrorists to national teams of IW specialists. Insiders are repeatedly identified as the most worrisome threat. Other malefactors may make use of insiders, such as organized crime or a terrorist group suborning a willing insider or making use of an unwitting insider.

Many financial institutions have been contacted by cyberterrorists threatening to penetrate and destroy their computer systems unless they receive huge sums of money. Many banks around the world have been victimized and have paid millions of dollars as extortion money to keep their systems intact. Such cyberterrorism is becoming a matter of concern and exposes national security systems, banking or communication networks, and financial and commercial transactions to grave dangers.[67]

Five examples of new types of attack described below help illustrate the way commonplace cybertools can be used to do harm.

A Cyberattack on the Specific Database of an Owner/Operator

In the case of unauthorized entry into a network or system for the purpose of illegal financial transfers, stealing proprietary information, disrupting records, or merely "browsing," owners and operators have a responsibility for prudent and sufficient security systems, such as firewalls and passwords and qualified personnel to detect anomalies that indicate a successful entry, so further isolation or deflection measures can be taken to foil the attack.

A Cyberattack for the Purpose of Gaining Access to a Network

If a particular system or network is discovered to have low security standards and to be interconnected to other networks of interest to the attacker, the attacker will use the most weakly defended pathway to access the targeted system. Thus, operators need to consider establishing security standards for those with whom they are connected.

A Cyberattack for the Purpose of Espionage

Intellectual property is vulnerable to theft in entirely new ways. The threat may come from a witting or unwitting insider, an unscrupulous competitor, or the intelligence service of a foreign power. Competitive advantage may be lost without knowing it was even at risk. This is true in business as well as in government.

A Cyberattack for the Purpose of Shutting Down Service

Attacks by flooding communication lines have denied emergency service in some communities and shut down e-mail service to major users. Denial-of-service attacks are of concern to all institutions that depend on reliable communications.

Another form of computer attack is the distributed denial-of-service (DDoS) attack (commonly referred to as a DDoS attack). The DDoS attacker uses multiple compromised systems to attack a single target, thereby causing denial of service for users of the targeted system.[68] The flood of incoming requests to the target system essentially forces it to shut down, thereby denying service to legitimate users. DDoS threats have been escalating and future attacks may target routers, key hubs of the Internet's infrastructure, instead of individual web sites.[69] Denial-of-service attacks and viruses cause the most downtime to business applications, e-mail systems, and networks. In January 2003, CloudNine Communications, a UK Internet service provider, indicated that it had to close its doors after a series of denial-of-service attacks prevented its 2,500 customers from connecting to the Internet and cut access to the web sites of its hosting customers.[70]

A denial-of-service attack is an attack or intrusion designed for use against computers connected to the Internet, whereby one user can deny service to other legitimate users simply by flooding the site with so much useless traffic[71] that no other traffic can get in or out. In fact, the "hacker" is not necessarily trying to break into the system or steal data, but rather just prevent users from accessing their own network[72] for reasons only the hacker knows.[73] A denial-of-service attack is considered to take place only when access to a computer or network is intentionally blocked as a result of some malicious action.[74] Sharing information about the tools used in these attacks and techniques to deflect or defeat them is therefore of interest to a wide range of public and private institutions.

A Cyberattack for the Purpose of Introducing Harmful Instructions

An attacker can plant a virus or leave behind a program that will give the attacker critical information, such as passwords that can be used to log in to other networks. A virus may be transmitted within a LAN or passed on to an external network. "Logic bombs" and "Trojan horses" are designed, respectively, to destroy software at a preselected time and to enable future access. Given the rate of development of viruses, it is essential that all interconnected users adopt a high level of virus detection.

Vulnerability of the United States

The potential impact of failing to protect the intellectual property and information infrastructure on which this world-leading economy is increasingly dependent poses potentially serious risks. Almost all the Fortune 500 corporations have been penetrated electronically by cybercriminals. The FBI estimates that electronic crimes are running at about $10 billion a year. However, only 17% of the companies victimized report these intrusions to law enforcement agencies because their main concern is protecting consumer confidence and shareholder value.[75]

A spectrum of malicious actors can and do conduct attacks against the United States' critical information infrastructures. Of primary concern is the threat of organized cyberattacks capable of causing debilitating disruption to the nation's critical infrastructures, economy, or national security. The required technical sophistication to carry out such an attack is high, which may explain the lack of a debilitating attack to date.

Shared Responsibility

The government and private sector share substantially the same national information infrastructure. Both have been victims of unauthorized computer intrusions, theft, and disruption. The line separating threats that apply only to the private sector from those associated with traditional national security concerns must give way to a concept of shared threats. Shared threats demands a shared response, built from increased partnership between government and the owners and operators of our infrastructures.

In general, the private sector is best equipped and structured to respond to an evolving cyberthreat. There are specific instances, however, where federal government response is most appropriate. A government role in cybersecurity is warranted where high transaction costs or legal barriers lead to significant coordination problems.

Public–private engagement is key. This is true for several reasons. Public–private partnerships can usefully confront coordination problems and enhance information exchange and cooperation. Public–private engagement will take a variety of forms. It will address awareness, training, technological improvements, vulnerability remediation, and recovery operations.

Threat Spectrum

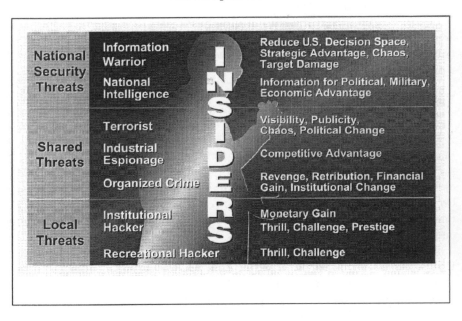

National Security Threats	Information Warrior	Reduce U.S. Decision Space, Strategic Advantage, Chaos, Target Damage
	National Intelligence	Information for Political, Military, Economic Advantage
Shared Threats	Terrorist	Visibility, Publicity, Chaos, Political Change
	Industrial Espionage	Competitive Advantage
	Organized Crime	Revenge, Retribution, Financial Gain, Institutional Change
Local Threats	Institutional Hacker	Monetary Gain / Thrill, Challenge, Prestige
	Recreational Hacker	Thrill, Challenge

Federal actions to secure cyberspace are warranted for purposes including forensics and attack attribution, protection of networks and systems critical to national security, indications and warnings, and protection against organized attacks capable of inflicting debilitating damage to the economy. Federal activities also should support research and technology development that will enable the private sector to better secure privately owned portions of the nation's infrastructure.

Domestic and International Legislative Responses

Does computer crime pose a serious threat to a nation's national security? More recent highly publicized computer virus attacks have shown that computer crime has become an increasing problem. Defining criminal phenomena is important because it allows police officers, detectives, prosecutors, and judges to speak intelligently about a given criminal offense. Furthermore, generally accepted definitions facilitate the aggregation of statistics, which law enforcement need to analyze to reveal previously undiscovered criminal threats and patterns.[76] The absence of a standard definition for computer crime, a lack of reliable criminal statistics on the problem, and significant underreporting pose problems for police agencies.[77]

Law enforcement organizations cannot determine exactly how many computer crimes occur each year. No agreed-upon national or international definition of terms, such as computer crime, high-tech crime, or information technology crime, exists. Thus, as a class of criminal activities, computer crime is unique in its position as a crime without a definition, which prevents police organizations from accurately assessing the nature and scope of the problem.[78]

Legislative bodies define criminal offenses in penal codes. Crimes such as murder, rape, and aggravated assault all suggest similar meanings to law enforcement professionals around the world. But what constitutes a computer crime? As mentioned earlier, the term covers a wide range of offenses. For example, if a commercial burglary occurs and a thief steals a computer, does this indicate a computer crime or merely another burglary? Does copying a friend's program disks constitute a computer crime? The answer to each of these questions varies among different jurisdictions.[79]

There is increasing cooperation between the United States and Europe in this area. In September 2000, the United States sponsored a meeting of the G8's Senior Law Enforcement Experts on Transnational Crime to discuss international intellectual property crime. The meeting focused on the involvement of organized criminal groups in counterfeiting and pirating merchandise, but the delegates also discussed the possibility of mutual legal assistance and extradition agreements in the area of intellectual property crime. The Lyon Group endorsed various recommendations, including sharing strategic intelligence concerning organized criminal groups and sponsoring an annual meeting on trends in intellectual property crime and member countries' enforcement activities.

Since the early 1990s, several international organizations, such as the United Nations, the OECD, the COE, the G-8, and Interpol, have worked to combat the problem of computer crime. Despite their efforts, no single definition of computer crime has emerged. Although many state and federal laws in the United States define terms, such as "unauthorized access to a computer system" and "computer sabotage," neither the federal nor any of the state penal codes provide a definition for the term computer crime.[80]

The U.S. DoD's Defense Information Systems Agency (DISA) completed an in-depth investigation on computer crime. From 1992 to 1995, DISA attacked their own DoD computer systems using software available on the Internet. Of the 38,000 attacks perpetrated, 96% of the successful attacks went undetected. Furthermore, of the detected attacks, only 27% were reported. Thus, approximately 1 in 140 attacks were both detected and reported, representing only 0.7% of the total. If the detection and reporting of computer crime is less than 1% in the nation's military systems, how often might these crimes go unreported when the intended victim is an individual or a small business owner?[81]

An annual report compiled by the CSI in San Francisco, California, and the FBI provides statistics on computer crime by surveying computer security practitioners. The anonymity provided to the survey respondents may contribute to the accuracy of their responses. The report does not directly poll law enforcement organizations about the number of computer crimes reported to police. No single governmental body maintains responsibility for asking police forces about the prevalence of computer crimes reported and investigated.[82]

An analysis of penal legislation in nearly fifty nations suggests that at least one-half of those countries surveyed had laws in place or legislation pending that prohibited crimes affecting the confidentiality, integrity, and availability of a computer. A variety of international organizations also support legislative efforts prohibiting computer crimes. Groups such as the United Nations, the G8, the COE, the OECD, and Interpol each have delineated confidentiality, integrity, and availability offenses as forming the minimum basis of proscribed computer crime behavior. The Council of Europe, the forty-one-nation body of which the United States is an observer, has been working on a draft treaty on cybercrime for several years. If adopted as currently drafted, the treaty would ensure that confidentiality, integrity, and availability offenses were outlawed in all signatory nations.

Cybercriminals have forced law enforcement agencies to learn to deal with complex computer issues to solve many of the crimes perpetrated today.[83] In the United States, to patrol the Internet and to enforce new Internet laws, the FBI established "computer crime teams" in each of its field offices.[84] To coordinate the efforts of each team, the Washington, DC field office has a National Computer Crime Squad, which both investigates and provides a national resource for computer crime issues.[85]

The Department of Homeland Security (DHS) was created in 2002. This new cabinet-level department unites twenty-two federal entities for the common purpose of improving the homeland security of the United States. The Secretary of DHS has important responsibilities in cyberspace security. The DHS guideline document outline an initial framework for both organizing and prioritizing efforts. It provides direction to the federal government departments and agencies that have roles in cyberspace security. It also identifies steps that state and local governments, private companies and organizations, and individual Americans can take to improve their collective cybersecurity. The documents highlight the role of public–private engagement. The document provides a framework for the contributions both public and private sectors can make to secure cyberspace. The dynamics of cyberspace will require adjustments and amendments to the strategy over time.

The DOJ also has a computer crime component, centralized in the Criminal Division.[86] In 1991, the Computer Crime Unit was established in the General Litigation and Legal Advice Section.[87] In 1996, it was transformed into the CCIPS section of the Criminal Division. It directly attacks cybercrime by litigating cases and providing litigation support for U.S. attorneys. In addition, CCIPS comments on proposed legislation and tries to coordinate both federal and international efforts to respond to computer crime and the tracking of computer criminals.[88]

In 1998, President Clinton by presidential directive established the National Infrastructure Protection Center (NIPC), in an effort to have a more comprehensive, joint effort between the Justice Department, the FBI, the DoD, and the private sector.[89] Led by FBI officials, the NIPC was established to provide early warning to private industry about imminent threats to their networks.[90] Although it has more than 100 workers, its 2000 budget was only $18.5 million, not enough to enable it to be effective.[91]

Various other computer security agencies exist, but they lack the ability and resources to prosecute cybercriminals. The Commerce Department, for example, has its own computer security agency, but it lacks any law enforcement powers. In addition, CERT only attempts to warn industry about potential security threats it sees. At the local levels, some efforts are in place. In each federal district, the U.S. Attorney's Office has designed an agent called the "Computer and Telecommunication Crime Coordinator."[92] At the state level, some states, such as Massachusetts and New York, have created "high-technology crime units," where state police and investigators pursue computer-related offenses.[93]

Prosecution and Enforcement Efforts

Because of the flood of new Internet crime cases, law enforcement at all levels is losing the battle. The government catches about 10% of those who break into government-controlled computers and far fewer of those who break into computers of private companies.[94] There are several reasons for this. Most significantly, because of the explosion in computer crimes, law enforcement simply does not have the resources or technical support to stop any significant number of cyberthieves. For example, the NIPC's caseload rose 300% from 200 investigations in 1996 to more than 800 in 1999. Also, the rise in the number of networked computers makes it much easier for hackers to penetrate and control vast numbers of computers with one break-in, rather than being forced to break in to each computer individually.[95] Finally, the trend toward computer networking has also provided more avenues for intruders to search for the "weakest link" in a large chain of potential access points, enabling a cleverly programmed computer to methodically test for vulnerabilities in a network.

Cybercrime can be a lucrative business. In 2001, the Internet Fraud Complaint Center (IFCC) received 49,711 complaints of Internet fraud. The 49,711 people were hit by cybercriminals for about $17 million, according to a report released by the IFCC. Those numbers only reflect crimes that are considered Internet fraud; other crimes such as child pornography, identity theft, and computer intrusion are immediately reported to other agencies.[96]

The first half of 2002 saw a 28% increase in Internet attacks, with more than 180,000 of them successful.[97] In a more recent study, the FBI and the CSI[98] reported that 90% of corporate and other respondents detected some type of computer breach in the prior year.[99] Although only 44% of these respondents specified a loss amount, the quantified losses from computer security breaches exceeded $455 million.[100] There were approximately 73,000 computer-related complaints referred to the Carnegie Mellon Software Engineering Institute from January 2002 to September 2002, a 237% increase over the same time period in 2001. Florida ranked no. 2 in the United State in 2002 behind California for the number of computer fraud complaints that were reported to the IFCC, a web site run in part by the FBI and the nonprofit National White Collar Crime Center. Roughly, 42.8% of the complaints received by the IFCC in 2001 were auction fraud, followed by nondelivered merchandise at 20.3%, Nigerian letter fraud at 15.5%, and credit/debit card fraud at 9.4%.[101]

Although their number has fallen, virus and worm attacks remain the most prevalent security breach, followed by denial-of-service attacks, which also trended down slightly, to 12% in 2002 from 15% in 2001's report. Many businesses felt the sting, with Code Red and Nimda worms infecting thousands of companies' Internet servers. The number of companies claiming less than $10,000 in damages is slightly lower, but those saying such breaches cost them between $10,001 and $100,000 rose to 13% in 2002 from 9% in 2001. In North America, about 6% of companies indicated that they lost more than $100,000, although more than one-third indicated that they did not know the financial damage. Companies that could boast no breach-related expenses fell to 21% from 26%.[102]

Obtaining the evidence to prosecute cybercrimes and information terrorism generally requires promptly trapping certain evidentiary data that may have been left by the suspect and also tracing the perpetrator back through the system to its source. Once the perpetrator breaks the connection with the computer being used as the target of the criminal activity, identifying the perpetrator becomes significantly more difficult, and in some cases impossible. The speed with which computer connections can be made and dropped usually requires action within seconds or minutes, not the hours or days that may be required for traditional search warrants, especially those sought in foreign jurisdictions. As such, perhaps the most important advantage to be gleaned by entering into a multilateral treaty on cybercrime would be mutual cooperation and assistance in the investigative process.

Of course, in today's largely interdependent world community, the general sentiment has been that cybercrime is not the first class of offenses to require international cooperation. Money laundering, insider trading, and the illegal smuggling of drugs, weapons, and technology have all led the United States to internationalize its criminal law enforcement efforts.[103] Indeed, the Drug Enforcement Agency, the FBI, the Customs Agency, the Secret Service, and the Commerce Department collectively operated out of 140 offices in fifty-one different foreign countries.

Interestingly, the Office of International Affairs (OIA) of the DOJ has taken the position that, "U.S. law enforcement agencies such as the FBI have worldwide investigative authority that would apply to investigations of crime carried out against or with the aid of computer systems."[104]

Most computer-detection techniques are time-consuming and costly. Because the Internet allows one to "travel" from one computer to another so easily, a clever hacker can cloak his or her identity by simply directing his or her path through one computer with inadequate tracking or logging devices.[105] For example, Wind River Systems, a publicly traded Internet company in Alameda, California, had its computers broken into by German hackers.[106] However, Wind River's technology manager could not determine what the hackers stole or even how the hackers were able to infiltrate the system.

Yet, even when the intruder is an insider, obtaining satisfactory evidence is often beyond the capability of law enforcement. In 1992, software company Borland International contacted the Santa Clara District Attorney's office because they suspected Eugene Wang, a former vice president, of transferring trade secrets to Symantec Corporation, a major competitor.[107] The District Attorney's Office was willing to prosecute, but told Borland that it did not have the resources or expertise to obtain proof. Borland International decided to subsidize the District Attorney's investigation; it paid for a private company to investigate and obtain proof leading to Wang's prosecution.

Furthermore, the private sector lacks confidence in government because companies view law enforcement agencies as intrusive and inflexible. Phil Karn, a well-known Internet researcher, explained that the Internet industry was rushing to develop software to locate, trace, and block denial-of-service attacks that recently crippled Yahoo! and a host of other popular web sites, in large part because it feared government intervention. Karn observed the following about the DOJ's efforts: "when the only tool you have is a hammer, the whole world starts to look like a nail."

Private industry also is reluctant to report intrusions because it sees the FBI as insensitive to business needs. An FBI agent in San Francisco indicated that executives fear calling authorities because they fear it will hinder their business, while the FBI investigates the computers. Alan Paller, research director of the Bethesda, Maryland-based Sans Institute, also confirms this: "They won't share because they're concerned that either their computers will be confiscated, or enough parts of the computers will be confiscated that their systems will have to stop."

Even when police already know of an attack, private companies frequently refuse to cooperate. In 1992, when Chemical Bank discovered a high-tech device called a "Van Eck"[108] aimed at its credit card processing plant in Manhattan, the bank turned down a police offer to help. Instead, they used jamming equipment to stop the thieves. According to their security consultant, "[We] just wanted the problem to go away."

Private companies also are not convinced that the FBI is attentive to their needs because they believe that the FBI has displayed a lack of sensitivity in the area of encryption regulation. Moreover, the FBI has urged Congress to place limits on the "strength" of computer data encryption available to private companies because strong levels of data encryption could limit the FBI's ability to intercept and decode the data communication it needs to stop terrorist plots.[109] The IT industry claims, however, that strong encryption is already widely available outside the United States, and is a vital element in protecting business and retail transactions over the Internet and in ensuring the privacy of e-mail. The FBI's opposition has made many companies suspicious that the FBI does not have their interests at heart. A network manager at MIT indicated that the FBI has "completely compromised itself on giving advice on security, because every time the FBI has weighed in on this issue, it's been to weaken it."

Other private companies distrust the FBI because the NIPC refuses to release the source code of programs it writes. When the NIPC released software it wrote to help companies monitor their networks, many companies rejected the software because it feared the FBI would use the software to spy on their companies. Qualcomm, Inc., for example, rejected the software because the FBI refused to allow Qualcomm to inspect the source code.

Some companies are reluctant to report because they want to employ the hacker instead. Morty Rosenfeld, for instance, was convicted in 1992 for stealing almost 200 credit reports from TRW. When he was released from prison, he was quickly hired by Panasonic to monitor security. Rosenfeld also gets free Internet access from his local service provider because they believe that it "is better to have them on your side than against you." Other hackers are also widely sought for their talents: Hacker Kevin Poulsen joined SecurityFocus.com, a provider of intelligence services for businesses;[110] Kevin Mitnick was employed by a college he broke into years before; and the hacker who briefly controlled the southern U.S. water canals was employed as a security consultant.

The majority of laws currently in place clearly were not written with the Internet in mind. The imperfections are believed to stem from the widespread perception that existing statutes are limited to "the ancient common-law paradigm of one's neighbor's livestock." For example, larceny statutes are premised on depriving someone of lawful possession. They therefore implicitly do not apply to information, because the victim retains possession as well as the thief. The problems, however, are less intractable than widely perceived and more easily correctable by altering existing statutes than by writing new ones.[111] Because the laws were written to protect physical property, not electronic property, cyberthieves and electronic vandals have been able to evade prosecution for their reckless or malicious acts.[112] The shift to a fast-moving, borderless electronic environment means that even small imperfections in the law, whether due to inadequate breadth or imprecise drafting, are likely to have disastrous consequences.

Legal Exposure and Cybercrime

Cybercrime is a far-reaching problem, often harming parties other than the company targeted by the attack. Employees, customers, business partners, investors, and others may be indirectly victimized by the same act of cybercrime. For a targeted company, the costs of cybercrime include not only the loss of business, but also the expense of defending against lawsuits brought by indirect victims seeking to recover their own related losses. Targeted companies in certain industries may also confront additional costs from cybercrime, including risk of governmental actions for failure to take adequate security precautions to prevent the harm to others.

Although few lawsuits in this context have emerged to date,[113] the incentives for bringing such claims are clear: Targeted companies are more easily identified than cybercriminals, they are much less likely to be judgment proof, and the party seeking to recover can almost always argue that the company could have taken some additional security measure that would have prevented the loss. These claims appear imminent, creating significant legal exposure for companies that have failed to develop and implement comprehensive cybersecurity plans.

Legal Avenues to Combat Cybercrime

The emergence of new technology generally provokes the creation of new laws.[114] The new technology threatens to disrupt social relations in two arenas.[115] The first concerns the possibility that some new technology will disrupt existing economic relations. The potential for conflicting signals over radio airwaves, for example, precipitated the creation of a licensing system for radio stations to determine who had the right to specific frequencies.[116] The technology for photographic reproduction brought about new laws of copyright to establish the legal rights of both those who owned this new technology and those whose images might be captured by the use of photography.[117] In both cases, new forms of value – radio frequencies and photographic images – had to be defined within the established system on property rights before these problems could be resolved.

The second problem concerns the potential for new technology to disrupt established economic patterns. For example, the steam locomotive reduced the powers of individual states to control and regulate economic relations within their borders. Technological innovation remains troublesome until it is firmly lodged within the established patterns of economic relationships and social authority.

There are a variety of civil and criminal legal weapons to help companies combat cybercrime, hacking, and the online shakedown. In addition to traditional common law claims of trespass, fraud, unfair trade practices, and theft of trade secrets, there are several federal laws that specifically contemplate and condemn computer-related crimes.[118]

Statutory Provisions in the United States

Law enforcement authorities have only more recently begun to respond to computer crime and crimes committed through the use of a computer.[119] The current U.S. legal structure presents a disjointed view of what is considered computer crime. Congress responded to the flood of computer and Internet crimes by passing the Computer Fraud and Abuse Act (CFAA),[120] which duplicated much of existing law, but left unaddressed several injustices that spurred the bill's passage.[121] The CFAA makes it unlawful for any person to access a protected computer "without authorization."[122] It also forbids a person who has a legitimate and authorized right of access from "exceeding the authorized access." If either type of access results in the person's obtaining information from the protected computer and the conduct involves interstate or foreign communication, then a violation of the CFAA is established. The CFAA also prohibits activities such as the dissemination of malicious software[123] and trafficking in stolen passwords. The CFAA allows any person who suffers damage or loss by reason of a violation of the statute to maintain a civil action to obtain compensatory damages and injunctive relief or other equitable relief.[124] The legislative flaws stem from Congress's erroneous belief that computers are fundamentally different from everything else. Statutes such as the CFAA represent clear attempts to respond to computer crime. Other statutes, such as the Mail Fraud and Copyright Statutes,[125] are used to prosecute normal crimes such as fraud and copyright violations if they are committed through the use of a computer. The statutes targeting computer criminals have been written with the intent of prosecuting individuals, not nation-states. The U.S. statutes also criminalize invasions of privacy that occur via information networks.[126]

In the United States, the "interruption of computer services to authorized users" involves a violation of a series of federal and state computer-related criminal laws that are designed to protect the authorized users of computer systems. Because most of these laws have only more recently been legislated and because few people have ever actually been charged with such violations, there is little history or case law in this area. However, as computer-related crimes continue to escalate, these statutes could prove to be a positive force in efforts to catch the electronic criminals of the future.

The chief problem with the U.S. Federal Mail and Wire Fraud Statutes – which prohibit any scheme involving the use of the mail or wires to obtain property by false pretenses – is the need to prove a "scheme to defraud." Because a trade secret thief often only copies information, he or she does not necessarily "defraud" the company permanently of the information. Moreover, much trade secret theft occurs without the use of the mail or wires.

Three principle federal statutes prohibit computer hacking and other unauthorized uses of computers and computerized information: CFAA, the Electronic Communications Privacy Act, and the EEA. Although none completely addresses the full range of computer crimes, most cybercrimes fall within the scope of one or all these laws.

The threat posed by cybercrime and information theft will require those who increasingly rely on computers and the Internet to become more vigilant. It will also require effective laws that can be used to prosecute those who attempt to disrupt cyberactivities. The legislatures of several nation-states have already passed computer crime laws of varying effectiveness. As cybercriminals have become progressively more sophisticated and internationalized, the ability of a single state to effectively prosecute those who attack it from and through other states has become increasingly complex. In today's highly networked world, states' borders pose no obstacles to cybercriminals, but do create hurdles for prosecutors and law enforcement.

The New Rule for Keeping Secrets – The Economic Espionage Act

ALTHOUGH THE dominance of technological developments has made trade secrets more valuable, warranting greater protection, the rise of globalization has made them harder to protect. Intellectual property – inventions and innovations in products and processes – has been the engine driving economic growth. Because controlling the use of inventions, innovations, and other business-enriching information is essential to competitive success, trade secrets have become increasingly valuable.

At the same time, globalization of the economic system has increased worldwide demand for these inventions and innovations. As demonstrated earlier, globalization, the decline in customer and employee loyalty, the availability of venture capital, and improved information flow all makes trade secrets less secure.

Legal Initiatives in the Earlier Days

In an 1868 U.S. case involving trade secret litigation, the Massachusetts Supreme Court stated: "it is the policy of the law, for the advantage of the public, to encourage and protect invention and commercial enterprise."[1] The principle articulated by the justice was that "if a man establishes a business and makes it valuable by his skill and attention, the good will of that business is recognized by the law as property." This case began the evolution of trade secret law in the United States, which has now been in existence for more than a century.

The U.S. Congress enacted the first criminal law protecting intellectual property in 1909.[2] The law covered only copyright violations and only at a minimal level. Since then, Congress has gradually and consistently expanded the role of federal law enforcement in this area, by imposing felony penalties for unlawfully reproducing or distributing motion pictures or sound recordings in 1982,[3] by broadening the protection to all types of copyrighted works in 1992,[4] by making a copyright violation a "specified unlawful activity" for money laundering in 1994,[5] by including copyright violations as predicate offenses under RICO in 1996,[6] and, most recently, in 1997, by passing the No Electronic Theft Act (NET), which criminalizes copyright infringement even in certain circumstances where the infringer does not act for commercial purpose or private financial gain.[7] Copyright infringement may now constitute a felony under federal law if ten copies of a copyrighted work or works with a total retail value of at least $2,500 or more are reproduced or distributed.[8]

In more recent years, Congress has also chosen to protect other forms of intellectual property with criminal sanctions. In addition to criminalizing trademark infringement in 1984, Congress in 1996 criminalized the theft of trade secrets by passing the EEA, which became effective on October 11, 1996.[9] In his remarks the day that the Senate passed the EEA, Senator Arlen Spector expressed concern "with the threat posed to American economic competitiveness in a global economy by the theft of intellectual property and trade secrets."[10]

International Initiatives for Protection of Intellectual Property

The Paris Convention

The Paris Convention[11] was the first international agreement protecting intellectual property. The Paris Convention requires signatory nations to extend to foreign nationals the same intellectual property protections that are provided to their own citizens. It has been revised by successive negotiations and has established the international standards for patents and trademarks.[12] It is the foremost industrial property law treaty and has extensive membership. Parties to the Paris Convention make up a union that protects industrial property. The union consists of several administrative bodies: the Assembly (the chief governing body under Article 13 of the convention), the Executive Committee (a smaller body elected from the Assembly under Article 14), and the International Bureau of the World Intellectual Property Organization (a body that performs the union's administrative tasks under Article 15). The Convention sets forth uniform rules by which member states must abide with respect to industrial property rights. The Paris Convention was designed to be flexible and allow signatory countries to have some discretion in implementing national legislation.[13] The Paris Convention does not, however, specifically address economic espionage. Article 10 on unfair competition only prohibits "any act of competition contrary to honest practices in industrial or commercial matters."[14]

World Intellectual Property Organization

The World Intellectual Property Organization (WIPO) was established by a convention at Stockholm in 1967. It administers international unions related to intellectual property, including the Paris Convention for the Protection of Industrial Property, first signed in the 1880s. Its main purpose is protecting the interests of intellectual property worldwide. More than 175 countries belong to WIPO. WIPO's intent is to build cooperation regarding intellectual property and to improve the administration and protection of industrial property and intellectual property.[15] The WIPO Convention defines intellectual property broadly to include rights related to any inventions, any industrial property and designs, protection against unfair competition, and "all other rights resulting from intellectual activity in the industrial, scientific, literary or artistic fields."[16]

General Agreement on Tariffs and Trade

On April 15, 1994, an agreement resulted from the Uruguay Round of GATT, establishing the WTO and promulgating several trade-related agreements.[17] The Trade-Related Aspects of Intellectual Property Rights Agreement (TRIPs Agreement), another product of the Uruguay Round, requires member countries to protect against acquisition, disclosure, or use of a party's trade secrets "in a manner contrary to honest commercial practices." Although the TRIPs Agreement specifically refers to "confidential information" rather than "trade secrets," it defines such information as having commercial value, not being in the pubic domain, and being subject to "reasonable steps under the circumstances" to maintain its secrecy.[18] The agreement allows for injunctions and damages, as well as provisional remedies to prevent infringement and to preserve evidence.

Trade-Related Aspects of Intellectual Property Agreement

The most extensive multilateral protection of intellectual property was established by the TRIPS Agreement.[19] It requires member countries to protect against acquisition, disclosure, or use of an individual party's undisclosed information. Specifically, it protects "confidential" information having commercial value. The TRIPS Agreement also protects trade secrets, not as individual intellectual property, but as a prohibition against unfair competition.[20] It also enhances IPRs through improved enforcement mechanisms and remedies. The TRIPS Agreement provides a broad exception, however, permitting members to adopt contrary national laws if necessary to protect "sectors of vital importance to their socio-economic and technological development...."[21] This exception may allow countries to avoid specific prohibitions against economic espionage.

The North American Free Trade Agreement

Another significant multilateral treaty protecting trade secrets is the North American Free Trade Agreement (NAFTA) between the United States, Canada, and Mexico.[22] NAFTA, which entered into effect on January 1, 1994, is significant because it is the first international agreement to expressly provide protection for trade secrets. Under Article 1711, trade secret protection of parties is perpetual, as long as the information remains secret and unknown to the general public. NAFTA also requires the U.S. government to maintain the secrecy of confidential data submitted to it. This provision helps to close a source of information to foreign governments and industrial spies who previously could explore U.S. government reports and records for information. However, under NAFTA, a misappropriation of proprietary information is only actionable if the acquiring party knew, or was grossly negligent in failing to know, its actions were illegal.[23]

U.N. Resolution 1236 and Resolution 2131

Two U.N. Resolutions indirectly relate to the problem of economic espionage. "Peaceful and Neighborly Relations Among States" is the title of Resolution 1236, passed in 1957.[24] It addresses the duty of nonintervention in other states' internal affairs and calls upon states to settle their disputes in a peaceful manner.

A second resolution, Resolution 2131, was passed in 1965 and is entitled the "Declaration on the Inadmissibility of Intervention in the Domestic Affairs of States and the Protection of Their Independence and Sovereignty" (the "Declaration on Inadmissibility"). It resolves that "no state has the right to intervene, directly or indirectly, for any reason whatever, in the internal or external affairs of any other State."[25] It condemns armed intervention as well as "all other forms of interference or attempted threats against the personality of the State or against its political, economic, and cultural elements." This resolution, however, probably was intended to deal more with economic sanctions than with theft of private commercial secrets.

Both resolutions could be construed as indirectly condemning economic espionage because a nation's economy is part of its internal affairs. Economic espionage, after all, is an activity by which one nation intervenes in another nation's economic affairs. These resolutions have been ineffective against economic espionage. Because these resolutions are persuasive and not binding materials, some states tend to ignore them. The end result is that, in spite of U.N. resolutions that are seemingly against it, economic espionage continues.

The Convention on Combating Bribery of Foreign Public Officials

Bribery of employees or government officials is a common way of conducting economic espionage.[26] More recently, multilateral efforts have sought to discourage this practice. The Convention on Combating Bribery of Foreign Public Officials in International Business Transactions (OECD Convention)[27] became effective in February 1999. This multinational treaty, which was formulated by the OECD,[28] obligates signatory countries to make bribery of foreign public officials a criminal act.[29] The U.S. Congress ratified and implemented the OECD Convention by adopting amendments to the 1977 Foreign Corrupt Practices Act.

Economic Espionage War and the European Union

The EU is one of the largest trading partners of the United States, and the EU's intellectual property laws directly impact the U.S. market.[30] The EU evolved from the Treaty Establishing the European Economic Community (the Rome Treaty),[31] which was enacted on March 25, 1957 to enhance economic coordination among western European nations. The Rome Treaty generally referred to the protection of industrial and commercial property, but did not create a central authority to protect IPRs. Without a central authority, member states were left to regulate their own national intellectual property laws subject to EU "guidance." Over time, however, the EU sought to directly protect IPRs through competition laws.[32] Under Article 36 of the Rome Treaty, the IPRs granted by any member state and are afforded the full force of law.[33]

Trade secrets are only indirectly recognized as an IPR in the EU.[34] Article 81(3)[35] of the Rome Treaty is the provision under which the EU has established most intellectual property regulations. EU regulations and directives indirectly recognize and protect "know-how" defined as "a package of non-patented practical information, resulting from experience and testing, which is secret, substantial and identified."[36] The three necessary elements of know-how are further defined as follows: "secret," which means that the know-how is not generally known or easily accessible; "substantial," which means that the know-how includes information that is indispensable for the manufacture of the contract products or the application of the contract processes; and "identified," which means that the know-how is described in a sufficiently comprehensive manner so as to make it possible to verify that it fulfills the criteria of secrecy and substantiality. In 1989, the EU granted an exemption from competition rule for pure know-how licensing agreements.[37] In 1996, this regulation was incorporated into the Technology Transfer Regulation[38] that exempts the licensing of patent and know-how and "ancillary provisions" regarding other IPRs.

U.S. Initiatives for Protection of Intellectual Property Assets

In the late 1980s and early 1990s, the United States found itself facing an increasingly weak competitive position as an industrial power. As explained earlier, it turned to a series of multilateral treaties, such as the TRIPS component of GATT, in order to police intellectual property piracy and to secure potential markets for its intellectual property assets. The United States also claimed that a strengthening of international IPRs would serve as an economic engine on a global basis.[39]

The United States was concerned with trademark, patent, and, especially, copyright. However, corporations were soon to adopt the idea that intellectual property might play a leading role in asserting their economic worth to investors. Consultants remind companies that their major assets often are not in real estate or industrial equipment, but in the knowledge required to run businesses. The Brookings Institute has estimated that 50% to 85% of the value of a business may reside in its intangible assets, including trademarks and trade secrets.[40]

Since the mid-1990s, intellectual property assets have become frequent topics for seminars.[41] Rust-belt industrial corporations[42] as well as information economy businesses turned to valuing their knowledge assets to attract investors. In part, the idea of trade secrets as assets was fostered by new start-ups, and especially biotechnology companies, which chose to create portfolios of trade secrets rather than pursue the much more expensive route of protection through patents.

Comprehensive Scheme to Protect Proprietary Economic Information

From its inception, the EEA has attracted attention in various circles and has resulted in multiple prosecutions. These cases provide initial insights into the operation of this law.

The EEA is the first federal criminal law in the United States designed to protect trade secrets. Although the title of the act suggests its primary purpose is the protection of the proprietary information of American companies against foreign theft, it also has a significant impact against the domestic theft of trade secrets. The EEA created two federal crimes: economic espionage and theft of trade secrets.[43] Under the EEA, economic espionage consists of stealing, copying, or receiving a trade secret with the intent of benefiting a foreign government or entity. The EEA also makes it a crime to attempt to conspire to commit espionage, if the defendant intended to benefit a foreign government. The statute not only specifically targets agents of foreign governments who steal trade secrets for the benefit of those governments; it also criminalizes the theft of trade secrets when there is no foreign government involvement. The type of benefit intended (e.g., theft for idealistic reasons rather than pecuniary motives) is irrelevant. For economic espionage, as defined by the EEA, one of the offenses must be committed knowing it will benefit a foreign government, foreign instrumentality, or foreign agent. Trade secret theft under the EEA requires a different intent: an intent to convert a trade secret to the economic benefit of anyone other than its rightful owner, knowing the conversion of the trade secret will injure the rightful owner. If the stealing of the trade secret is for the benefit of a foreign government, the U.S. prosecutor does not need to prove any other intent. If the theft was not for the benefit of a foreign government, the prosecutor must prove that the trade secret misappropriator intended to injure the owner of the trade secret and confer economic benefit on another, and that the person accused knew the consequences of his or her actions. Penalties for economic espionage include fines of up to half a million dollars and imprisonment up to 15 years[44] (see Appendix A).

The legislative history indicates that at the time the bill was under consideration, the FBI was "investigating reports and allegations of economic espionage activities conducted against the United States by individuals or organizations from 23 different countries."[45] Although the main selling point for this legislation was combating foreign "espionage," a survey found that foreigners had been identified in 21% of incidents involving intellectual property loss where the nationality of the perpetrators was known. In cases not involving a foreign government or a company, the perpetrator was an individual with a trusted relationship with the company, often an employee or former employee, retiree, contractor, vendor, supplier, consultant, or business partner.

Prior to the passage of this legislation, the U.S. espionage statutes and other federal criminal statutes did not cover many economic intelligence-gathering operations. Because no federal statutes directly addressed economic espionage or the protection of proprietary economic information in a thorough, systematic manner, investigators and prosecutors attempted to combat the problem by using existing laws. These other U.S. criminal laws were deemed inadequate to protect valued private company information from theft. In addition, the laws failed to provide confidentiality for the information in question during criminal and other legal proceedings.

If confidentiality is lost during legal proceedings, then the value of the information is greatly diminished.

Large gaps in trade secret law needed to be filled.[46] Companies failed to prosecute thefts of trade secrets due to fear of disclosing confidential information at trial, loss of public trust and image, and the inability of prosecutors to deal with foreign espionage.[47] Before the passage of the EEA in the United States, there was only one very limited federal statute that prohibited the theft of trade secrets.[48] There were also limited means of redress for companies that faced theft of their trade secrets and attempted to prosecute. Until the EEA was passed, no federal statute directly dealt with economic espionage or the misappropriation of trade secrets and intellectual property. That statute provides for criminal penalties for the unauthorized disclosure of trade secrets by a government employee.[49] However, due to the narrow applicability of this law, victims of espionage and trade secret theft were forced to resort to a variety of other statutes. Prosecutors often relied on the Interstate Transportation of Stolen Property Act (ITSP), Mail Fraud and Wire Fraud statutes, or various state laws based on either the Uniform Trade Secrets Act (UTSA) or Restatement of Torts.

Two major hearings were held to consider the need for federal legislation to prevent the theft of trade secrets as a result of economic espionage. The first, held on February 28, 1996, was a joint hearing before the Senate Select Committee on Intelligence and the Senate Judiciary Subcommittee on Terrorism, Technology, and Government Information.[50] The second hearing was held before the Subcommittee on Crime of the House Judiciary Committee on May 9, 1996.[51] The lead witness in both hearings was former FBI Director Louis J. Freeh. A number of industry leaders, primarily representing Silicon Valley and aerospace companies, supported Freeh's contention that federal legislation was necessary to combat the growing surge of economic espionage by both domestic and, especially, foreign agents and entities.[52]

The hearings documented the two major underpinnings of the legislation. First, foreign governments, through a variety of means, were actively involved in stealing critical technologies, data, and information from U.S. companies or the U.S. government for the economic benefit of their own industrial sectors. Second, federal laws then on the books were of limited use in prosecuting acts of economic espionage.

Hearings were held in 1996 on "business intelligence" to address the topic of economic espionage both as a crime and as a national security issue.[53] Trade association and business representatives spoke to highlight their concerns for a comprehensive federal effort to curb industrial espionage.[54] The inventor of MRI technology testified that both German and Japanese firms systematically spied on his company.[55] The former president of a defunct software business described how his firm had been driven out of the market after Chinese agents stole confidential software information. As a result of the perceived need for stronger measures against industrial espionage, the EEA was designed to criminalize the misappropriation of trade secrets and encourage and preserve investments in innovation.[56]

Prosecution of Trade Secret Theft Prior to EEA

Before the passage of the EEA, federal prosecutors sometimes were left to strained readings of existing statutes to establish criminal intellectual property theft cases. *United States v. Hancock*[57] illustrates this point. Mr. Hancock represented a California company and offered an AT&T engineer in Atlanta $10,000 to provide blueprints for a manufacturing device to be used to develop plants abroad. The engineer reported the attempted bribe to his superiors, and the company called in the FBI. Under the watchful eye of the FBI, the engineer agreed to negotiate a deal and carry the blueprints to California. The FBI arrested Mr. Hancock for the attempted theft upon delivery.

The government had difficulty in proving that the blueprints were "property" as defined by the statute, and the blueprints were never actually "stolen" because AT&T still had them. Ultimately, the prosecutor proceeded with the case as an interstate transportation in aid of racketeering, using a California commercial bribery statute as the predicate offense for the attempted racketeering. To say the least, this was a circuitous route to prosecute a case that today would fit within the EEA.[58]

Before the EEA, the government sometimes sought to prosecute trade secret theft under the National Stolen Property Act (NSPA).[59] However, the NSPA was drafted before computers, biotechnology, or copy machines existed, and a growing body of case law held that it could not cover intellectual property theft. State laws also were inadequate. Although many states had laws on the books concerning trade secret theft, few resources were devoted to prosecute corporate espionage. And civil lawsuits under state law are expensive and are frequently hampered by people who are "judgment proof" or beyond the jurisdiction of the state courts.[60]

The legislative history of the EEA shows the problems with prosecuting the theft of trade secrets under federal criminal law, which often led the U.S. Attorney's Office to decline matters that involved employees of U.S. corporations attempting to sell proprietary information to foreign governments. Legislators realized that the only practical way to protect critical U.S. corporate information from theft by foreign governments and unscrupulous competitors was to enact a single comprehensive federal law that could bring federal resources to bear against defendants who steal proprietary information.

The Legislative Intent

An analysis of the legislative history indicates that the EEA is not intended to apply to individuals who seek to capitalize on personal knowledge, skill, or abilities.[61] Moreover, the statute is not meant to be used to prosecute employees who change employers or start their own companies using general knowledge and skills. Rather, the goal of the EEA is to preserve fair competition by making sure that corporate spies do not illegally take the fruits of their employment in order to compete with their prior employer."[62]

Prosecution of Trade Secret Theft Under the EEA

Trade secret theft under the EEA does not require an intent to benefit a foreign government. Trade secret theft under the EEA involves three significant elements of proof.

First, a defendant must have intended to convert the trade secret for economic benefit of someone other than the owner. So a defendant must have a pecuniary goal on behalf of someone. In civil law, that requirement is not needed.[63] Second, the defendant must intend to injure the owner of the trade secret. It is sufficient that the defendant knew his or her actions would injure the owner. Again, this requirement is absent from traditional civil trade secret liability. Third, the secret must be related to or included in a product that is either produced for or used in interstate or foreign commerce[64] (see Appendix A).

Civil or Criminal

A civil statute may be particularly useless to small businesses that may not be able to afford a civil suit against a much larger competitor engaging in trade secret theft.[65] The civil statute is also fairly ineffective in curbing industrial espionage schemes implemented by foreign culprits. A corporation based in North Carolina, for example, is not likely to recover from one of its former engineers, a Korean citizen who has relocated to Korea after disclosing company secrets to a Korean company. Finally, a civil statute does not ensure the confidentiality of the information at issue will be preserved in the course of a trial. Without such guarantees, civil litigation can do more harm than good.

Consequently, legislative reform was needed to provide a stronger deterrent and to address the modern concerns of instant communication, a decrease in employee loyalty, a shift from an economy based on manufacturing to one based on intellectual property, and a shift of espionage resources by foreign countries to economic targets. As the U.S. Supreme Court noted years ago, "existing trade secret law provides far weaker protection in many respects than the patent law."[66] Therefore, it became increasingly clear that a federal criminal statute would better protect U.S. companies. A federal criminal statute would allow small businesses to ride the coattails of federal prosecutors who perform investigations, gather evidence, and build a record.

Civil laws also do not offer the same remedies as criminal sanctions. The UTSA[67] applies to civil disputes and various trade secret concepts, but only provides for damages and injunctive relief to punish violators. In contrast, the EEA includes criminal sanctions that raise the stakes well above the prospect of civil damages.[68]

What Is a Trade Secret?

As society advances into the information age, businesses are increasingly affected by issues of trade secret protection. For example, in the United States, this area of intellectual property law can impact a wide array of commercial activities.[69] Trade secret laws protect commercially beneficial secrets from wrongful misappropriation with one notable caveat: Trade secrets are only protectable if they are indeed treated as "secrets" by their owners.[70] Trade secret law serves as a system of regulation to encourage research, innovation, and development of new ideas of a useful nature.[71] Trade secrets are a key part of industrial power, representing assets that are a requirement for competitiveness in any given market.

It is not easy to define the term "trade secret." The improper and unethical procurement of information constituting a trade secret was addressed in 1939 when the original Restatement of Torts was drafted and published.[72] In the United States, the comments to Section 757 of The Restatement of Torts stated:[73]

> A trade secret may consist of any formula, pattern, device or compilation of information which is used in one's business and which gives him an opportunity to obtain an advantage over competitors who do not know or use it. It may be a formula for a chemical compound, a process of manufacturing, treating or preserving materials, a pattern for a machine or other device, or a list of customers. Generally, it relates to the production of goods, as, for example, a machine or formula for the production of an article. It may, however, relate to the sale of goods or to other operations in the business, such as a code for determining discounts, rebates or other concessions in a price list or catalogue.

The Restatement lists a set of factors that are important in determining whether a trade secret exists:

- The extent to which the information is known outside the business
- The extent to which it is known by employees and others involved in the business

- The extent of measures taken by the business to guard the secrecy of the information
- The value of the information to the business and its competitors
- The amount of effort or money expended by the business in developing the information
- The ease or difficulty by which the information could be properly acquired or duplicated by others[74]

For example, the prices that a company charges for its products are generally not trade secrets because this information can normally be obtained simply by making a few phone calls. However, where a company has a complex formula for setting prices, the formula may be a protected trade secret.[75]

Trade secrets do not necessarily have to be created within the company. For example, the report of an outside consultant regarding proposed product improvements might qualify as a trade secret. Many companies are tempted to label nearly all corporate documents as confidential, but this is generally not a good practice. When material marked "confidential" is routinely given to members of the public, the designation loses its credibility. Thus, the "confidential" label should be reserved for items that truly are kept secret.

The more modern[76] Restatement (Third) of Unfair Competition defines trade secrets as "any information that can be used in the operation of a business or other enterprise and that is sufficiently valuable and secret to afford an actual or potential economic advantage over others."[77] To qualify for trade secret protection, the item in question must truly be secret. A company who regularly disseminates the material through advertisements or web sites will be unable to establish trade secrets.[78]

It is possible for a trade secret to exist even when some of the elements are known by the public. When, for example, known chemical compounds are put together in carefully determined percentages to produce a new and desirable result, a trade secret has been created.[79] Customer lists may or may not be trade secrets, depending on the type of list and how it was compiled. For example, if the list is derived from canvassing a large number of prospective customers, and the list is the result of years of time and effort and the expenditure of a considerable sum of money, courts are more likely to grant trade secret protection. However, when the names of customers are readily ascertainable in the trade, courts are more likely to find that the lists are not trade secrets.[80]

Even if the names of customers are well known, the particular needs of customers are not. When a defendant can demonstrate that the customer needs can easily be obtained just by calling up the customers' respective purchasing managers, courts probably will reject the trade secret claim. However, when a company keeps a database of highly specialized and complex customer requirements, some courts may find that trade secrets exist.[81]

For an item to qualify as a trade secret under the EEA, the owner of the information must not only take "reasonable measures" to keep it secret, but it must also have value.[82] The act requires that the information must derive "independent economic value, actual or potential, from not being generally known to, and not being readily ascertainable through proper means by, the public."[83] There are three generally accepted methods used for appraising the value of a trade secret: (1) the market approach (which compares the sales price of similar assets to the assets being valued), (2) the cost approach (which uses replacement cost as the indicated of value), and (3) the income approach (which measures the value of anticipated future economic benefits to be derived from the use of the asset in question).[84,85]

In the past, the theft of trade secrets has been litigated in the civil, as opposed to criminal, forum.[86] Today, however, companies are becoming more and more vulnerable to the theft of their proprietary information by rogue nations and foreign competitors. Consequently, corporations, recognizing the value of their trade secrets, are increasingly seeking criminal and civil sanctions to protect their private information.[87]

Patents Versus Trade Secrets

It is important to recognize the difference between trade secrets and patents. Patents protect inventions.[88] To qualify for a patent, the device must meet the statutory requirements of novelty[89] and nonobviousness.[90] Under the novelty requirement, the patent applicant must show that he or she was the first in a WTO country to invent the claimed subject matter of the application without subsequently abandoning, suppressing, or concealing it.[91] The patent law also requires that the inventor promptly apply for patent protection. Consequently, if the device is publicly used in this country more than 1 year before the filing of the patent application, the invention will be considered to be part of the public domain and the patent will be denied.[92]

If a patent is granted, the owner has the right to exclude others from making the product, extending from the issue date to 20 years after the date of the initial application.[93] This also gives the patent holder the right to exclude others from using, selling, or importing any product covered by the patent. Infringers are subject to civil damages that may cover the patentee's lost profits or reasonable royalties for the product.[94] Willful infringement can result in treble damages. In determining infringement, the patent owner is held to the definitions of the property that were given in the "claims" portion of the approved patent application.[95] Items that are not within the patent claims generally will not be found to infringe the patent. Furthermore, the patent law does not provide criminal sanctions for infringing a patent.[96]

Uniform Trade Secrets Act

The UTSA requires three general elements to establish a trade secret: (1) the secret must possess actual or potential economic value, (2) the owner must take reasonable measures to guard secrecy and preserve confidentiality, and (3) the trade secret's information must not be capable of being acquired by competitors or the general public without undue difficulty or hardship.[97] Many states in the United States have adopted the UTSA. Although thirty-eight states and the District of Columbia have enacted trade secret statutes, often modeled after the UTSA, these state laws have not been effective, primarily because the resources need to prosecute trade secret cases are usually not available at the state government level.[98] Furthermore, because most states modified the UTSA when they drafted their own state laws, resulting in a lack of uniformity, the statutory framework provided by states is inefficient and unpredictable.[99] To complicate things further, states such as New York, Pennsylvania, and Texas have wholly adopted the Restatement approach to trade secret theft, ignoring the UTSA and contributing further to the creation of an unstable and unstructured statutory regime. As a result, companies do not know in advance of the trade secret theft which state's law will govern. In other words, company executives have no way of knowing where a stolen trade secret will be disclosed or where it will be used after disclosure, leaving executives unable to tailor confidentiality and compliance programs to a specific region or statutory regime. In most states, trade secret theft is not even a felony. Commentators agree that a uniform trade secret regime is much more useful to avoid these choice of law issues in litigation.[100] With modern technology resulting in a fountain of information, a uniform federal system of law designed to protect trade secrets is better suited to combat industrial espionage than fifty conflicting state legal systems. This argument is bolstered by the fact that international trade is a uniquely federal concern.[101]

The UTSA constituted the first attempt at comprehensive national legislation of trade secrets theft.[102] The UTSA defines misappropriation similarly to the Restatement, but provides examples of what "improper means" include, namely, "theft, bribery, misrepresentation, breach or inducement of a breach of duty to maintain secrecy, or espionage through electronic or other means."[103] The main advantage of the UTSA over the common law is that it allows an aggrieved party to use and recover from a third party that has accepted stolen information, which often turns out to be a foreign company with deeper pockets than the culprit.[104] The USTA also provides for civil remedies for the theft of trade secrets, including both injunctive relief and recovery of monetary damages. Although damages include lost profits, the cost of investment in research and development, loss of reputation in the business community, and loss of the value of the trade secret, many of the businesses engaging in these offenses view the potential damages as a necessary risk, the cost of doing business, and a way to gain an economic advantage over competitors. In other words, for many companies and individuals involved in stealing competitors' secrets, the penalties are not a deterrent.[105]

The UTSA defines the term "trade secret" and provides remedies for misappropriation.[106] *Trade secret* means information, including a formula, pattern, compilation, program, device, method, technique, or process that derives independent economic value, actual or potential, from not being generally known to, and not being readily ascertainable by proper means by other persons who can obtain economic value from its disclosure or use, and is the subject of efforts that are reasonable under the circumstances to maintain its secrecy.[107] *Improper means* include theft, bribery, misrepresentation, breach or inducement of a breach of a duty to maintain secrecy, or espionage through electronic or other means. *Misappropriation* means acquisition of a trade secret of another by a person who knows or has reason to know that the trade secret was acquired by improper means, or disclosure or use of a trade secret of another without express or implied consent, by a person who used improper means to acquire knowledge of the trade secret, or at the time of disclosure or use, knew or had reason to know that his or her knowledge of the trade secret was derived from or through a person who had used improper means to acquire it; acquired under circumstances giving rise to a duty to maintain its secrecy or limit its use; or derived from or through a person who owed a duty to the person seeking relief to maintain its secrecy or limit its use; or before a material change of his or her position, knew or had reason to know that it was a trade secret and the knowledge of it had been acquired by accident or mistake.[108]

A Trade Secret under EEA

The EEA defines trade secret broadly to include all forms and types of scientific or technical information. The term *trade secret* means all forms and types of financial, business, scientific, technical, economic, or engineering information, including patterns, plans, compilations, program devices, formulas, designs, prototypes, methods, techniques, processes, procedures, or codes, whether tangible or intangible, and whether or how stored, compiled, or memorialized physically, electronically, graphically, photographically, or in writing, if (1) the owner thereof has taken reasonable measures to keep such information secret; and (2) the information derives independent economic value, actual or potential, from not being generally known to, and not being readily ascertainable through proper means by, the public.[109,110]

If the owner of the trade secret makes reasonable efforts to keep the information secret, and the information is not generally known or readily ascertainable to the public, it meets the EEA's definition. Some people contend that this definition is too broad. Many state law provisions require that the trade secret remain generally unknown or ascertainable to competitors. Competitors obviously have greater knowledge and capability on a particular subject than the general public has, and that restricts many state definitions of a trade secret.[111]

To qualify under Section 1832, trade secrets must be "related to or included in a product that is produced for or placed in interstate or foreign commerce."[112] Because trade secrets must explicitly be embodied in a product in the stream of commerce, protection is limited if the trade secret relates to a rendering of services rather than a produced ware that contains or uses the secret. As noted by some commentators, "this means that the EEA arguably does not cover either 'negative know-how' or information discovered but not [currently] used by a company."[113]

The owner of the information must take "reasonable measures" to keep it secret.[114] According to the legislative history of the EEA, "if the owner fails to attempt to safeguard his or her proprietary information, no one can be rightfully accused of misappropriating it."[115] The critical question becomes: What constitutes a "reasonable measure" under the EEA? There is, of course, no definitive answer.[116] The drafters of the EEA stated that "what constitutes reasonable measures in one particular field of knowledge or industry may vary significantly from what is reasonable in another field or industry."[117] Although no "heroic or extreme measures" are necessary,[118] the owner of the material "must assess the value of the material it seeks to protect, the extent of a threat of the theft, and the ease of theft in determining how extensive their protective measures should be."[119,120]

The Territorial Reach of the EEA

The EEA has a very broad territorial reach,[121] extending beyond the borders of the United States. Section 1837 provides that the EEA applies not only to acts conducted entirely within the United States, but also to foreign schemes so long as any "act in furtherance of the offense was committed in the United States."[122] A trade secret theft involving the electronic transfer (by any means) of the secret through the United States on its way to another foreign locale would constitute a violation of the act.[123] Further, the EEA applies to foreign acts of trade secret theft if the defendant is a "natural person who is a citizen or permanent resident alien of the United States."[124] For example, "if a United States citizen residing abroad steals a Russian trade secret on behalf of the Chinese government, that act is in violation of the EEA even though there is no other connection between the misappropriation and the United States."[125,126]

The territorial reach of the EEA is intentionally broad and includes a provision that explicitly addresses "conduct outside the U.S." This provision rebuts "the general presumption against the extraterritoriality of U.S.

criminal laws" and makes "it clear that the Act is meant to apply to the specified conduct occurring beyond U.S. borders." It is designed to provide the Justice Department "with broad authority to prosecute international theft and will prevent willful evasion of liability for trade secret misappropriation by using the Internet or other means to transfer the trade secret information outside the country."[127]

Jurisdictional Hooks

The EEA has several jurisdictional hooks. The EEA applies to "conduct occurring outside the United States" if (1) the offender is a citizen or permanent resident alien of the United States, (2) the offender is an organization organized under the laws of the United States or any state or political subdivision of the United States, or (3) "an act in furtherance of the offense was committed in the United States."[128] The first two standards are easy to apply, but the third probably will produce diverging opinions of the proper jurisdictional scope of the EEA. For example, suppose a computer hacker in France uses IBM's computer network in New York to break into a company's system in Canada. Was an act "in furtherance of the offense" committed in the United States such that jurisdiction exists?

The jurisdictional puzzle is particularly perplexing because the Internet is not one computer "superhighway" and there is no centralized storage location for information, no central control point, and no singular communications channel.[129] Rather, the Internet is hundreds of thousands of computer networks linked together.

Examples of Economic Espionage Activities

When the EEA was signed into law in 1996, predictions varied widely over its potential impact. Some predicted a flood of new court cases, whereas others dismissed the event as much ado about nothing. The 8-year history shows that the pace of criminal prosecutions of intellectual property crimes continues to build. The cases illustrate that understanding trade secret law in the United States may be particularly important for foreigners from countries that do not have such broad criminal laws protecting intellectual property. In many cases, actions that are regarded merely as aggressive business practice in their home country may be flatly illegal in the United States.

First Trial under the EEA – Pin Yen Yang and Hwei Chen Yang

Although the legislative history of the statute clearly indicates that the EEA was created mainly to fight international spies who have shifted their resources toward economic intelligence since the end of the Cold War,[130] the first prosecution under the statute demonstrated that federal prosecutors will also be using the EEA for domestic cases involving strictly American interests.[131] David E. Green, the Principal Deputy Chief of the CCIPS of the Criminal Division of the U.S. DOJ, was the lead prosecutor on the first EEA case that went to a jury verdict in April 1999, *U.S. v. Four Pillars et al.*[132]

On September 5, 1997, Dr. Ten Hong Lee, an employee of the Avery Dennison Corporation in Concord, Ohio, was arrested when an FBI surveillance team captured him rummaging through a colleague's files, which contained confidential documents. The Yangs wanted to obtain Avery's trade secrets from the employee, who worked at Avery Dennison Corporation's facility in Concord, Ohio. After his arrest, Lee cooperated with officials to obtain the indictment of the chairman of Four Pillars, Pin Yen Yang and his daughter, Hwei Chen Yang, an employee of Four Pillars. Lee had reportedly received between $150,000 and $160,000 from Four Pillars–Pin Yen Yang for his involvement in causing the transfer of Avery Dennison Corporation's proprietary manufacturing information and research data over an 8-year period.[133] Pin Yen Yang and his daughter, Hwei Chen Yang, were arrested on September 4, 1997 at Cleveland's airport as they were about to embark on a trip to New York.

On October 1, 1997, a federal grand jury returned a twenty-one-count indictment charging Four Pillars, Pin Yen Yang, and Hwei Chen Yang with the theft and attempted theft of trade secrets, mail fraud, wire fraud, money laundering, and receipt of stolen property. Lee pled guilty to one count of wire fraud.

Mr. Yang, age 70 at the time, was the president of Four Pillars Enterprise Company, Ltd., of Taiwan. The company manufactures and sells pressure-sensitive products in Taiwan, Malaysia, the PRC, Singapore, and the United States.[134] Sally Yang, Mr. Yang's daughter, a Ph.D. chemist, was believed to have had a dual citizenship in the United States and Taiwan. Sally Yang was an officer of the company, which has more than 900 employees and annual revenues of more than $150 million.

The sting operation was prompted as a result of information given to Avery Dennison Corporation by a Four Pillars employee who sought employment with Avery Dennison Corporation. Federal prosecutors estimated that Avery Dennison Corporation's research and development costs to develop the information obtained by the Yangs were between $50 million and $60 million.

The Yangs were originally indicted on twenty-one counts of various charges. They did not testify at trial, and their attorney argued that Mr. Lee took Avery Dennison Corporation's trade secrets on his own and that the Yangs never ordered him to steal them. To bolster its case that the Yangs intentionally stole Avery Dennison Corporation's trade secrets, prosecutors played a tape that showed the Yangs clipping confidential markings off papers they had received from Lee.

By the end of the proceedings, nineteen of the twenty-one charges against the Yangs were dropped (e.g., the mail and wire fraud charges).[135] However, the two EEA charges (1832(a)(4) and (5)) remained, and after deliberating over 3 days for 18 hours, the jury convicted the Yangs on both charges.[136] Pin Yen Yang was sentenced to 6 months' home confinement and a $250,000 fine, and Hwei Chen Yang was fined $5,000 and received 1 year's probation.

Takashi Okamoto and Hiroaki Serizawa

A grand jury in Cleveland, Ohio, returned a four-count indictment against Takashi Okamoto and Hiroaki Serizawa on May 8, 2001, charging them with conspiracy to commit the following violations: two counts of violating the EEA, one count of interstate transportation of stolen property, and making false statements to the government. These are the first charges setting forth violations of the EEA in the United States. Serizawa, 39, at the time resided in Kansas City, Kansas, whereas Okamoto, 40, at the time was believed to reside in Japan.

The indictment charged that Okamoto, from in or about January 1997 to on or about July 26, 1999, was employed by the Lerner Research Institute of the Cleveland Clinic Foundation (CCF) to conduct research into the cause and potential treatment for Alzheimer's disease. Serizawa, from on or about December 16, 1996, was employed by the Kansas University Medical Center (KUMC) in Kansas City, Kansas. According to the indictment, Serizawa was a close friend and peer of Okamoto from the time they met in Boston, Massachusetts, in the mid-1990s. The first count of the indictment charged that Okamoto and Serizawa, from January 1998 to September 1999, conspired to misappropriate from the CCF certain genetic materials called dioxyribonucleic acid (DNA) and cell line reagents and constructs, which were developed by researchers employed by the CCF, with funding provided by the CCF and the National Institutes of Health, to study the genetic cause of and possible treatment for Alzheimer's disease. Alzheimer's disease affects an estimated 4 million people in the United States alone and is the most common cause of dementia.

The indictment charged that, as an object of this conspiracy, Okamoto and Serizawa, and others known to the grand jury, would and did confer a benefit upon Riken, an instrumentality of the government of Japan, by providing Riken with the DNA and cell line reagents and constructs that were misappropriated from the CCF. According to the indictment, the Institute of Physical and Chemical Research (Riken) was a quasipublic corporation located in Saitama-Ken, Japan, which received more than 94% of its operational funding from the Ministry of Science and Technology of the government of Japan. The Brain Science Institute of Riken was formed in 1997 as a specific initiative of the Ministry of Science and Technology to conduct research in the area of neuroscience, including research into the genetic cause of, and possible treatment for, Alzheimer's disease.

According to the indictment, in or about April 1999, Riken offered and defendant Okamoto accepted a position as a neuroscience researcher to begin in the fall of 1999. The indictment charged that from on or about the late evening hours of July 8, 1999, to on or about the early morning hours of July 9, 1999, Okamoto and a third co-conspirator known as "Dr. A" misappropriated DNA and cell line reagents and constructs from Laboratory 164, where Okamoto conducted research at the CCF. Also during this time, the indictment charged that Okamoto and Dr. A destroyed, sabotaged, and caused to be destroyed and sabotaged, the DNA and cell line reagents and constructs that they did not remove from Laboratory 164 at the CCF. The indictment further charged that, on or about July 10, 1999, Okamoto stored four boxes containing the stolen DNA and cell line reagents at the Cleveland, Ohio, home of "Dr. B," a colleague at the CCF, with whom Okamoto was residing temporarily. On or about July 12, 1999, Okamoto then retrieved the boxes of stolen DNA and cell line reagents and constructs from Dr. B's home and sent them from Cleveland, Ohio, by private interstate carrier to defendant Serizawa in Kansas City, Kansas. On or about July 26, 1999, defendant Okamoto resigned from his research position at the CCF and, on or about August 3, 1999, started his research position with Riken in Japan. Okamoto returned to the United States and, on or about August 16, 1999, retrieved the stolen DNA and cell line reagents and constructs from Serizawa's laboratory at KUMC, in Kansas City, Kansas. The indictment charged that, before Okamoto left for Japan, he and Serizawa filled small laboratory vials with tap water and made meaningless markings on the labels on the vials; Okamoto instructed Serizawa to provide these worthless vials to officials at the CCF in the event they came looking for the missing DNA and cell line reagents. The indictment charged that on or about August 17, 1999, Okamoto departed the United States for Japan and carried with him the stolen DNA and cell line constructs reagents. The last overt act charged in the conspiracy was that, in or about September 1999, Serizawa provided materially false, fictitious, and fraudulent statements in an interview with special agents of the FBI, who were investigating the theft of the DNA and cell line reagents from the CCF.

Count two charged that the defendants committed economic espionage by stealing trade secrets that were property of the CCF, specifically, ten DNA and cell line reagents developed through the efforts and research of researchers employed and funded by the CCF and by a grant from the National Institutes of Health. Count three also charged a violation of the EEA against Okamoto and Serizawa for, without authorization, altering and destroying trade secrets that were the property of CCF, specifically, DNA and cell line reagents developed through the efforts of researchers employed by and funded by the CCF and by a grant from the National Institutes of Health. The last count of the indictment charged Okamoto and Serizawa with Transporting, Transmitting and Transferring in Interstate and Foreign Commerce, DNA and cell line reagents developed through the efforts of researchers employed and funded by the CCF and by a grant from the National Institutes of Health, knowing that such goods were stolen, converted, and taken by fraudulent means.

This case was prosecuted by Robert E. Wallace, Senior Trial Attorney from the Internal Security Section, Criminal Division, U.S. DOJ, and Christian H. Stickan, Assistant U.S. Attorney for the Northern District of Ohio. The case was investigated by the FBI, in Cleveland, Ohio; Kansas City, Kansas; Boston, Massachusetts; and New York, New York, with the assistance of the U.S. Attorney's Office for the District of Kansas.

Harold Worden

Retired Eastman Kodak manager Harold Worden pleaded guilty in 1997 to selling trade secrets to Kodak officials who were working undercover, posing as Chinese agents.[137] He agreed to pass on Kodak's formulas, drawings, and blueprints to undercover agents.[138] Because he agreed to cooperate in a continuing investigation, he was able to negotiate a plea bargain, which resulted in a 1-year prison sentence, including 3 months of home confinement with a monitoring bracelet, and a fine of $30,000.[139] In sentencing him, U.S. District Judge Telesca denounced him for disclosing trade secrets to "not just any foreign national, but China," a longtime adversary of the United States with a poor human rights record.[140] The company alleged in its complaint that Strobl, a current employee, was selling the documents to Worden, who in turn found third-party buyers. When FBI agents conducted a search of Worden's home in Santee, South Carolina, they found nearly 40,000 documents, many of them related to Kodak trade secrets. Mr. Worden had taken early retirement from Kodak in 1992 after a 28-year career and opened a consulting business, Worden Enterprises, Inc. Worden allegedly had recruited about sixty former Kodak employees in order to obtain key documents containing proprietary trade secrets.[141] While Mr. Worden worked for Kodak, he was responsible for what was then referred to as the "401 machine," a piece of Kodak equipment that made film base. The base created by the machine was then lined with emulsions according to a formula that was one of Kodak's most closely guarded trade secrets, with comparable formula secrets being similarly guarded by competing photography companies. The characteristics of the formula in question greatly enhanced color resolution and sensitivity to air exposure, thereby affecting the total quality of a photograph's resolution. The plan to begin work on the "401 machine" was initiated in 1987 by Kodak, and Worden was among the few people within the company aware of the plans.

Between 1993 and 1995, Mr. Worden acted aggressively to expand his consulting firm, and, in mid-1995, he confided to a friend that he was suspicious that perhaps Kodak was concerned as to whether he may be selling its trade secrets.[142] At that time, Worden was unaware that Kodak employees were posing as representatives of a Chinese company from Shantou, China, and they asked Mr. Worden to provide information about his consulting service and his associates. Worden provided this information and later on July 18, 1995, he met individuals in New York City who claimed to be the Chinese officials with whom he had been corresponding and had agreed to have a follow-up meeting. The first meeting lasted for 4.5 hours, during which Worden discussed considerable confidential and secret information that related to Kodak's film processing equipment, especially the secret "401 machine." Just 4 days after the meeting, telephone calls were placed to Mr. Worden at his South Carolina home, to which he responded by sending a written communication to the alleged Chinese clients detailing the services that his firm would provide to build a new film manufacturing plant in China.

What makes the Worden case even more interesting is that through 1995, Kodak acted independently. It did not approach federal prosecutors until after the New York City meeting; subsequently, the FBI secured a search warrant, which was executed in May 1996, in South Carolina. This is when the agents took the previously mentioned documents, some of them marked confidential and some appearing to be copies of blueprints and drawings.

In August 1997, Worden pleaded guilty in the U.S. District Court to selling Kodak's trade secrets to competitors, and he received a 1-year prison sentence. At the sentencing hearing on November 13, 1997, the judge had some special remarks prepared for Mr. Worden regarding his criminal conduct. The remarks were particularly striking in that the judge indicated that his personal preference was for an upward departure from the Federal Sentencing Guidelines; however, he would accede to the lesser terms of the plea agreement as long as Worden agreed to completely cooperate with the investigation that was ongoing regarding damage done to the Kodak company.

In December 1997, Kodak concluded that putting Mr. Worden behind bars was not sufficient, and accordingly, the company filed a lawsuit against 3M and one of its Italian subsidiaries, and the Imation Corporation, which had purchased some of 3M's film-making secrets and assets during the time that Worden Enterprises, Inc., was actively selling Kodak trade secrets to them. When the lawsuit was filed, officials of 3M and Imation refused to comment on the allegations of federal racketeering laws that had been allegedly violated by and through Worden's company, especially issues regarding technology transfer of the development of the "401 machine."

Kai-Lo Hsu

Kai-Lo Hsu, a Taiwanese national, was a technical director for Taiwan's Yuen Foong Paper Company.[143] Chester Ho, also a Taiwanese national, was a biochemist and professor at Taiwan's National Chiao Tung University. These two individuals were arrested in June 1997 at the Four Seasons Hotel in Philadelphia as a result of an FBI sting operation.[144]

Hsu was allegedly trying to obtain secret information on how to make Taxol, a powerful anticancer drug manufactured by Bristol-Myers Squibb Company that grossed $800 million for Bristol-Myers in 1996, so his company could expand into pharmaceuticals.[145] One of Hsu's associates, Jessica Chou, on June 7, 1995, contacted an undercover FBI agent posing as a technology broker with the intent of purchasing secret information from a purportedly corrupt Bristol-Myers scientist. Ms. Chou worked as a mid-level manager for a Taiwanese company. She met with the "information broker" a number of times to discuss acquisition of information concerning the production and distribution of Taxol. This ultimately culminated in a meeting between a higher-ranking manager of the foreign company, a meeting in which the Taiwanese openly discussed their interest in acquiring the Taxol technology. Further, when told that it was unlikely that Bristol-Myers would part with such a valuable commodity freely, the foreign company representative acknowledged that the firm was ready to bribe employees to acquire the proprietary information that was needed.

A meeting was arranged in Philadelphia in June 1997, at which the government contended that representatives of the Taiwanese company attempted to illegally purchase the Taxol technology. Bristol-Myers had cooperated with prosecutors by providing real documents to make the sting operation look authentic. During the meeting, Hsu asked the agent to locate a Bristol-Myers employee willing to sell information on the anticancer drug. Bristol-Myers agreed to provide an employee to pose as a corrupt engineer. Defendants Hsu and Chester S. Ho, a biochemist and professor at a Taiwan university, examined scientific documents that contained some of the trade secrets and discussed the technology with the undercover agent and "corrupt" employee. Reportedly, about $400,000 in cash, stocks of a Taiwanese company, and royalties from the sale of the drug were offered for the information.[146]

Although the case was brought against foreign nationals, it was brought under section 1832 of the EEA (the domestic activity section), not section 1831 (the foreign activity section, which targets defendants working on behalf of a foreign government or instrumentality). Specifically, the indictment charged violations of sections 1832(a)(4) (the EEA's attempt provision) and

1832(a)(5) (the EEA's conspiracy provision). The indictment did not allege that the defendants ever received the secret Taxol information. Hence, the indictment was attempt and conspiracy based. Hsu was also indicted on six counts of wire fraud, one count of general conspiracy, two counts of foreign and interstate travel to facilitate commercial bribery, and one count of aiding and abetting.

On March 31, 1999, Hsu pled guilty to one count of conspiring to commit trade secret theft. He was sentenced to 2 years' probation and fined $10,000.[147] All other charges against him were dropped. In early 1999, the government dropped all charges against Chester Ho.[148] Chou, the person who allegedly sought out the secret Taxol information for Hsu, remains the subject of a federal arrest warrant.[149] It is believed that she now resides in Taiwan, but cannot be extradited because Taiwan does not have an extradition treaty with the United States.

Patrick and Daniel Worthing

On December 7, 1996, the first arrest under the EEA was made in Pittsburgh, Pennsylvania.[150] Patrick Worthing and his brother, Daniel, were arrested by FBI agents after agreeing to sell Pittsburgh Plate Glass (PPG) proprietary information for $1,000 to an FBI undercover agent posing as a representative of Owens-Corning. Patrick Worthing, a maintenance supervisor in Pittsburgh-based PPG Industries' fiberglass research center, contacted the CEO of Corning Glass, a competitor,[151] and offered to sell PPG's trade secrets, including computer disks, research, and blueprints. The Corning Glass executive promptly contacted PPG, which called the FBI.[152] An undercover operation was planned in which an agent, posing as a Corning employee, met with Worthing to exchange money for the trade secrets.

The government alleged that Worthing solicited Owens-Corning's CEO under an assumed name in a letter that stated: "Would it be of any profit to Owens-Corning to have the inside track on PPG?" The Owens-Corning executive, in turn, provided the letter to PPG executives, who then contacted the FBI. Both defendants were charged under 18 U.S.C. Section 1832. Patrick Worthing admitted to stealing documents, blueprints, photographs, and product samples from PPG. He pled guilty and was sentenced to 15 months in jail and 3 years of probation. His brother also pled guilty to conspiracy to violate the EEA, for which he received 5 years of probation.[153] PPG estimated that the stolen secrets were worth up to $20 million.

Hai Lin and Kai Xu

Two Chinese nationals working in high-level technical positions at Lucent Technologies, Inc., in Murray Hill, New Jersey, were charged on May 3, 2001 with conspiring to steal source code and software associated with an industry-leading Internet server developed exclusively by Lucent, and to transfer it to a Chinese state-owned company. The two Chinese nationals – both of whom were working at Lucent on business visas – and a third co-conspirator, a naturalized Chinese-American, sought to use the stolen technology to create the leading data networking company in the PRC – "the Cisco of China." Hai Lin, 30 at the time, of Scotch Plains, and Kai Xu, 33 at the time, of Somerset, New Jersey, were arrested at their homes by special agents of the FBI. Also arrested was Yong-Qing Cheng, 37 at the time, of East Brunswick, New Jersey, a naturalized American citizen and vice president of Village Networks, an optical networking vendor in Eatontown. Cheng was arrested at Village Networks. Simultaneous to the arrests, the FBI executed search warrants at the defendants' homes.

In the e-mails, the defendants and representatives of the Chinese-owned company allegedly planned the theft and transfer of Lucent's technology to create a server identical to Lucent's PathStar Access Server. Both men were experts in the source code, software, and entire design of Lucent's PathStar system – the highly advanced and profitable technology that Lin, Xu, and Cheng allegedly conspired to steal and transfer out of the United States.

Each of the defendants was charged with conspiracy to commit wire fraud. Charged in the same complaint was ComTriad Technologies, Inc., a New Jersey corporation that was founded in January 2000 by the defendants. Beginning with a July 2000 trip by Cheng to Beijing, ComTriad started negotiations for a joint venture with Datang Telecom Technology Company of Beijing, a company that is majority-owned by the Chinese government. Subsequent to that trip, according to the complaint, the defendants and representatives of Datang exchanged e-mail and visited in China and the United States to negotiate the joint venture. Ultimately, the Lucent technology – the PathStar source code and software – was stored in its entirety on a password-protected web site created by ComTriad and established with a web hosting company. The source code and software were stored on that web site – www.comtriad.com. The defendants transferred the data earlier in 2000 to Datang for use in developing a ComTriad system – the CLX 1000 – that was identical to Lucent's PathStar Access Server, according to the complaint.

The Datang–ComTriad joint venture, funded with $1.2 million from Datang, was named DTNET, and was approved by the Datang board of directors on or about October 28, 2000, according to intercepted e-mails described in the complaint. Datang was engaged in the development, manufacture, and sale of telecommunications products in the PRC, including computer hardware and software to facilitate voice transmissions over the Internet. The PathStar access system for transmitting voice communications over the Internet was recognized as a unique product in the industry, designed to facilitate low-cost voice and data services over the Internet. In the market for telephony and packet networking integration, the PathStar system commanded a 93% share, according to the complaint, and generated a revenue of approximately $100 million for Lucent in fiscal year 2000. Lin, Xu, Cheng, and ComTriad planned to go public in a joint venture with Datang through initial public offerings of stock in the United States and China.

Following their arrests, bail was set by U.S. Magistrate Judge Stanley R. Chesler in the amount of $900,000 (actually requiring the equivalent of $1.8 million in real estate equity). Cheng was released under a court ruling requiring only a $900,000 bail to be secured in full by real estate equity. Xu was released after posting a $900,000 bond secured by approximately $680,000 in real estate equity and the posting of $12,000 from one individual in a court escrow account. Also, as a further condition, Xu, his wife, and three others were to cosign and personally guarantee the $900,000 bond. Lin also had bail set at $900,000, to be secured by approximately $400,000 in real estate equity and two individuals posting $50,000 in a court escrow account. Lin, his wife, and two others would also be required to cosign and guarantee the $900,000 bond. Magistrate Judge Chesler further conditioned the release of each defendant on house arrest with electronic monitoring; confinement to the residence except, with prior approval of Pretrial Services, meetings with counsel or court appearances; the signing of an irrevocable waiver of extradition; and the surrender of passports by the defendants and their wives.

Several more criminal charges have been leveled against the two former Lucent employees for allegedly stealing the New Jersey company's trade secrets and turning them over to a Chinese company, according to the U.S. Attorney's Office in Newark. *United States v. Lin et al.*, No. 01-CR-00365, superseding indictment was issued on April 11, 2002. The superseding indictment filed in U.S. District Court for the District of New Jersey further details the alleged plan by Lin and Xu to steal the software and hardware for Lucent's PathStar Access Server. According to the prosecutors in this case, Lin and Xu were originally indicted for the trade secret theft on May 31, 2001. The new indictment alleges that Lin and Xu formed ComTraid Technologies, Inc., in New Jersey to market a product based on the stolen PathStar data. According to prosecutors, the indictment alleges that Lin and Xu demonstrated their new CLX-1000 product to a representative of Beijing-based Datang Telecom Technology Company in July 2000, and that the Chinese company gave the two defendants $500,000 to begin a joint marketing venture. Later, according to prosecutors, Lin and Xu tried to conceal their interest in ComTriad and the CLX-1000 to hide their former Lucent employment and relationship to the PathStar program. According to the new indictment, victims of the theft include companies that had licensed software to Lucent that was used in the PathStar program and was allegedly incorporated into the CLX-1000.[154]

Federal prosecutors identified those companies as Telnetworks, a subsidiary of Next Level Communications in Rohnert Park, California; Net-Plane Systems, Inc., a subsidiary of Dedham, Massachusetts-based Mindspeed Technologies, Inc.; Hughes Software Systems Ltd., a subsidiary of Hughes Network Systems, Inc., of Gurgaon, India; and Zia Tech Corp., a subsidiary of California-based Intel Corp.[155]

Mylene Chan

An employee of the SEC was forced to resign after it was discovered that she had sent sensitive data on American computer companies to China, according to U.S. officials.[156] Mylene Chan, a computer and online service analyst with the SEC for 10 months, left the commission in July 2002 after co-workers discovered she had compromised sensitive information by sending it to Shanghai. A co-worker in the computer office discovered that database files had been corrupted and that several e-mails to Miss Chan from China were discovered in a computer after she had used the database service. The case was covered up by the SEC and never reported to the FBI. Numerous U.S. companies whose proprietary information was handled by Miss Chan also were never informed that their information may have been compromised.[157]

Within the commission, a CTR is a confidential treatment request, secret reports provided by U.S. companies to the SEC that contain proprietary and other sensitive information that companies do not want disclosed to the public or to competitors. The confidential information contained in the reports includes financial data and other information about a public company's financial status and operations. According to SEC documents, the number of CTRs handled by the commission grew from about 540 in 1992 to more than 1,000 in 1996. The disclosure that the SEC shared sensitive corporate data with China is the latest problem for the commission that is charged with monitoring the securities industry. Several of the companies whose data were compromised are engaged in security-related work and are contractors for U.S. defense and intelligence agencies. The CTRs that Miss Chan handled during her employment included sensitive data from Acclaim Entertainment, which makes video game software for Sony, Nintendo, and Sega, and Interplay Entertainment, another major gaming software producer. Miss Chan also had access to security-related companies, including Verint Systems, which produces analytic software "for communications interception, digital video security and surveillance, and enterprise business intelligence," according to the Verint web site. She also had access to data from Citadel Security Software, which produces "security and privacy software" for computer networks, and Ion Networks, another computer security firm that does business with the government.[158,159]

Fei Ye and Ming Zhong

Two California men with ties to the PRC have been indicted for economic espionage by a San Jose, California, federal grand jury. The grand jury in Silicon Valley on December 4, 2002 indicted Fei Ye, 36 at the time, of Cupertino, and Ming Zhong, 35 at the time, of San Jose, California, for allegedly conspiring to steal computer chip trade secrets from Sun Microsystems, NEC Electronics, Trident Microsystems, and Transmeta.[160] Fei Ye and Ming Zhong were arrested November 23, 2001, at the San Francisco Airport while allegedly trying to smuggle trade secrets from Transmeta Corporation and Sun Microsystems in their luggage. Both men had worked for Transmeta and Trident Microsystems, and Ye had also worked at Sun and NEC Electronics Corporation. More trade secrets belonging to Sun, NEC, and Trident were allegedly found at Ye's home. Zhong also had trade secrets from Trident in his Transmeta office and residence, according to the indictment. Ye and Zhong were on their way to China, where the indictment alleged they were planning to use the stolen documents from the Silicon Valley companies to produce and sell microprocessors for Supervision Ltd., aka Hangzhou Zhongtian Microsystems Company Ltd., or Zhongtian Microsystems Corporation.

The indictment charges the thefts would benefit China's government because Supervision was involved in a joint venture to raise China's ability to develop superintegrated computer circuits and was working with the city of Hangzhou and Zejinang University, both instrumentalities of China, and was seeking funding from a Chinese government program. There is no allegation against China in the indictment. The counts against Ye and Zhong were one count of conspiracy in violation of 18 U.S.C. Sections 371, 1831(a)(5), and 1832 (a)(5); two counts of economic espionage in violation of 18 U.S.C. Section 1831(a)(3); two counts of foreign transportation of stolen property in violation of 18 U.S.C. Section 2314; and five counts of possession of stolen trade secrets in violation of 18 U.S.C. Section 1832(A)(3). The conspiracy and economic espionage counts carry the same maximum penalties, 15 years, and a fine of $500,000 (or twice the gross gain or loss, whichever is greatest) plus restitution where appropriate. The counts for possession of stolen trade secrets and foreign transportation of stolen property both carry maximum 10-year sentences and a fine of $250,000 (or twice the gross gain or loss, whichever is greater) plus restitution where appropriate.[161]

Igor Serebryany

A University of Chicago student was charged under federal EEA with distributing hundreds of secret documents over the Internet that could help television owners steal signals from a leading satellite TV provider. Igor Serebryany, 19 at the time, lived in Los Angeles.

Serebryany was accused of stealing blueprints of DirecTV, Inc.'s latest "P4 access card" technology, a device that prevents free access to digital television signals by the company's 11 million subscribers. The information on the design and architecture of the technology, which cost the company about $25 million to develop, allegedly was distributed by Serebryany to several Internet sites that cater to hackers. However, apparently no hackers were able to crack the code of the technology.[162]

Serebryany came across the information while working with his uncle, who was employed by a document-copying service, according to court documents. That firm in turn was hired by Jones Day – one of the nation's top law firms – which represented DirecTV in a civil dispute over what it claimed was misappropriation of company secrets. In September 2002, DirecTV sued NDS in federal court alleging fraud, breach of contract, and misappropriation of trade secrets. DirecTV at one point had contracted with NDS for its "smart" card technology, but has since moved its encryption technology in-house. According to court documents, DirecTV delivered about twenty-seven boxes of confidential material related to the case to the Jones Day law firm in August 2002. To help its lawyers manage all the documents, Jones Day hired an outsourcing firm, Uniscribe Professional Services of Norwalk, Connecticut, a company founded in 1998 that does imaging work for law firms, accounting firms, investment banks, universities, and museums. Because the documents were so sensitive, Uniscribe set up a special imaging center at the law firm's offices to which only a few people had access. One of those, according to court documents, was Michael Peker, Serebryany's uncle and a Uniscribe employee. Without the law firm's approval, Peker brought in his nephew and paid him to help with the workload after the firm ordered that the pace be increased, according to court documents.[163]

Serebryany, who was born in Ukraine, was released in January 2003 by a federal judge on a $100,000 bond put up by his parents. He was ordered not to use the Internet, but was given some e-mail access so he could keep up with his studies. It was not known what Serebryany is studying, although he has done work as a computer technician on the University of Chicago's Internet Project. The allegations against him carry penalties of up to 10 years in prison and a $250,000 fine.

Kenneth Branch and William Erskine

Federal officials in Los Angeles on June 25, 2003 charged two former Boeing Company managers with conspiring to steal Lockheed Martin trade secrets concerning a multibillion-dollar rocket program for the U.S. Air Force. In a criminal complaint filed on June 25 in U.S. District Court in Los Angeles,

Kenneth Branch and William Erskine were each charged with conspiracy, theft of trade secrets, and violating the Procurement Integrity Act. Branch, 64 at the time, and Erskine, 43 at the time, both residents of Cape Canaveral, Florida, are former managers of Boeing Company's Evolved Expendible Launch Vehicle (EELV) program, which was based in Huntington Beach, California, and had facilities in Cape Canaveral. The EELV is a rocket launch vehicle system, such as the Atlas or Delta rocket system, which is used for the transportation of commercial satellites into space. EELVs are also used to launch government satellites into space. Branch was a Lockheed Martin EELV engineer who in 1996 was recruited by Erskine, a Boeing Company EELV engineer, to bring proprietary Lockheed Martin EELV documents to Boeing Company. In exchange for the proprietary Lockheed Martin documents, Branch would receive employment at Boeing Company as well as a higher salary. Branch left Lockheed Martin in January 1997 and began working at Boeing Company on Boeing Company's EELV project.

In 1997, the Air Force announced that it wanted to procure EELV services from both Boeing Company and Lockheed Martin, and that it wanted both aerospace companies to invest their own money in the EELV program because there was a potential for substantial profits to be made by using EELVs to launch private communication satellites. The Air Force agreed to provide both Boeing Company and Lockheed Martin $500 million each for development costs associated with their respective EELV programs, and both Boeing Company and Lockheed Martin agreed to pay any additional development costs.

On July 20, 1998, Boeing Company and Lockheed Martin submitted bids for twenty-eight EELV contracts being awarded by the Air Force. The total value of the contracts was approximately $2 billion. On October 16, 1998, based largely on price and risk assessment, Boeing was awarded nineteen out of the twenty-eight contracts, and Lockheed Martin received the other nine EELV contracts.

In mid-June 1999, according to the affidavit, Erskine told another Boeing Company employee that "he had hired defendant Branch because defendant Branch, while still working at Lockheed Martin, came to defendant Erskine with an 'under-the-table' offer to hand over the entire Lockheed Martin EELV proposal presentation to aid in Erskine's proposal work in exchange for a position at Boeing if Boeing Company won the United Sates Air Force EELV contract award."

Later in June 1999, a Boeing Company attorney assigned to interview Branch and Erskine regarding allegations that they possessed proprietary Lockheed Martin documents conducted a search of Erskine's and Branch's offices and, according to the affidavit, found a variety of documents marked "Lockheed Martin Proprietary/Competition Sensitive" in their offices. In early August 1999, Branch and Erskine were terminated by Boeing

Company. Air Force personnel familiar with the EELV competitive-bidding process examined the Lockheed Martin documents recovered from Branch's and Erskine's workspaces at Boeing Company. The investigation determined that 141 documents, consisting of more than 3,800 pages, which appeared to belong to Lockheed Martin, were recovered from the workspaces of Branch and Erskine in June 1999; thirty-six of the documents were labeled "Lockheed Martin Proprietary or Competition Sensitive"; sixteen of the documents appeared to be related to the manufacturing cost of Lockheed Martin's EELV and, in the opinion of the U.S. Air Force EELV staff, possession of these proprietary documents by a competitor could have had a "medium" or moderate chance of affecting the outcome of a competitive bid; and seven of the documents appeared to be related to the manufacturing costs of the Lockheed Martin EELV and, in the opinion of the U.S. Air Force EELV staff, possession of these proprietary documents by a competitor could have had a "high" or significant chance of affecting the outcome of a competitive bid. The U.S. Air Force EELV analysts determined that, had they known that Boeing Company EELV personnel had possession of proprietary Lockheed Martin EELV documents in 1997, they would have immediately suspended the competition and conducted a thorough investigation into whether the procurement competition should be terminated.

If convicted of all three counts in the complaint, both Branch and Erskine face a maximum possible penalty of 15 years in federal prison and fines of up to $850,000. The charges against Branch and Erskine are the result of an investigation conducted by the Defense Criminal Investigative Service.

Robert R. Keppel

John McKay, U.S. Attorney for the Western District of Washington, and Charles Mandigo, Special Agent in Charge, FBI, announced that former Vancouver, Washington, resident Robert R. Keppel entered a guilty plea on August 23, 2002 to theft of trade secrets, in violation of Title 18, United States Code, Section 1832(a)(2).

Beginning sometime in January 2001, Robert R. Keppel began to purchase, from an individual in Pakistan, actual copies of the Microsoft MCSE and MCSD exams and answers, which that individual obtained by photographing and/or videotaping the actual tests at a site in Pakistan. Between July 2000 and October 17, 2001, Robert R. Keppel marketed numerous copies of MCSE and MCSD exams and answers via his web site, www.cheetsheets.com, selling them to persons throughout the United States, including persons residing in the Western District of Washington.

Microsoft Corporation has certification programs for network engineers, called Microsoft Certified Systems Engineer (MCSE) and Microsoft Certified

Solution Developer (MCSD), which involve passing approximately twenty-eight exams that test expertise in different Microsoft (MS) software areas. Many of these areas include MS operating systems, databases, and networking issues. MS has this certification program so that when a third-party user of their software hires an individual who is certified as a MCSE or MCSD, that individual will have a known level of expertise in order to properly administer the MS system. The MCSE and MCSD certifications are difficult to acquire, but once an individual has the certification, that individual is highly marketable to companies that use MS products, and just having the MCSE or MCSD certification usually raises salaries substantially. These exams are administered on Microsoft's behalf worldwide.

When the tests are administered, there are two separate "banner" pages that the test taker encounters before the test starts. These "banner" pages require the test taker to agree to certain terms regarding the test material, including an agreement not to copy or release the test material. By the terms of its contracts with the testing sites, MS does not allow the test material outside the testing locations for any reason. Consequently, the sale and distribution of Keppel's "cheat sheets" violated MS copyright and constituted a conversion of MS proprietary information for personal gain. MS's development costs for each test are approximately $100,000. In addition, when companies hire people who have obtained MCSE and MCSD certificates by cheating, but who, in fact, cannot install and maintain the systems correctly because they have neither experience nor expertise in the MS products commensurate with the certificates, those companies tend to blame the MS product and become reluctant to buy further products.

U.S. Bankcorp bank records reflect that there were three bank accounts and one credit card listed for Robert Keppel and Keen Interactive, including a personal checking account and a money market account, both in the name of Robert R. Keppel and a merchant account listed in the name of Keen Interactive. The U.S. Bank records reflect that among the Internet billing companies that were disbursing funds into the merchant account was Nova, a company that does billing for Visa and MasterCard. Nova records reflect that an account was opened by Robert R. Keppel, as owner of Keen Interactive, on or about July 6, 2000. Since the Nova account was opened, there was a total of approximately $756,633.03 deposited into the merchant account. All those funds constitute proceeds from the sale of MCSE and MCSD exams and answers, as well as other exams that were proprietary information belonging to Microsoft Corporation, Cisco, and other businesses, in violation of Title 18, United States Code, Section 1832(a)(2), and Section 2. In addition, during the time period covered by the Information, Robert R. Keppel caused numerous transfers of monies from the merchant bank account to Keppel's personal checking account and savings (money market) account. In total,

Keppel transferred $200,200 to his personal checking account and $167,000 to his money market account.

The U.S. Bank documents also reveal that, on September 14, 2001, Keppel opened a new merchant account number in the name of Cheet Sheets. The ensuing deposits into this account were from credit card receipts constituting proceeds from the sale of MCSE and MCSD exams and answers, as well as other exams that were proprietary information belonging to Microsoft Corporation, Cisco, and other businesses, in violation of Title 18, United States Code, Section 1832(a)(2), and Section 2.

On February 26, 2001, Keppel wrote a check number drawn on his money market account, to Lexus of Portland, in the amount of $38,703.40, for a new, white Lexus RX300. This vehicle was purchased with proceeds from Keppel's sale of trade secrets, in violation of Title 18, United States Code, Section 1832(a)(2) and Section 2.

On or about July 27, 2001, Keppel caused a wire transfer in the amount of $112,000, to be made from his U.S. Bank money market account to the credit of Premier Financial Services, in payment for a 1997 Ferrari 355 Spider. This vehicle was purchased with proceeds from Keppel's sale of trade secrets, in violation of Title 18, United States Code, Section 1832(a)(2) and Section 2.

As part of his plea agreement with the United States, Robert R. Keppel has agreed to forfeit his interest in the 2001 Lexus RX300 and the 1997 Ferrari 355 Spider referenced previously, and more than $56,000 seized from the various bank accounts referenced previously.

Jiangyu Zhu and Kayoko Kimbara

U.S. Attorney Michael J. Sullivan and Charles S. Prouty, Special Agent in Charge of the FBI in New England, announced on June 16, 2002 that Jiangyu Zhu, a/k/a "Jiang Yu Zhu," age 30 at the time, and Kayoko Kimbara, age 32 at the time, both residents of San Diego, California, were charged in a criminal complaint with conspiracy, theft of trade secrets, and interstate transportation of stolen property. The charges arose out of the alleged theft of certain trade secrets belonging to Harvard Medical School, including reagents made and used by Harvard Medical School to develop new immunosuppressive drugs to control organ rejection and also to study the genes that regulate calcineurin, an important signaling enzyme in the heart, brain, and immune systems. It is alleged that Zhu and Kimbara stole the trade secrets and then transported them from Boston, Massachusetts to San Antonio, Texas.

It is alleged that, on or about February 27, 1997 until on or about December 31, 1999, Zhu was employed as a research fellow in the Harvard laboratory, and that, on or about October 1, 1998 until on or about

December 31, 1999, Kimbara was also employed as a research fellow in the Harvard laboratory. According to the affidavit filed in support of the complaint, Zhu and Kimbara were working in Harvard Medical School's Department of Cell Biology (Harvard) as postdoctoral research fellows on a research project in a lab under the direction of a professor of cell biology at Harvard. The complaint alleged that using information, reagents, and technology developed by the Harvard professor and working under his direction, Zhu and Kimbara were involved in screening drugs, genes, and proteins to find new agents that would block calcineurin, an immune cell constituent that when activated can cause organ transplant rejection. Further research and analyses by Zhu and Kimbara from February 1999 through September 1999 showed that in addition to binding tightly to calcineurin, the two genes blocked the activity of calcineurin. These findings offered a potential means of treating a number of diseases affecting the immune, cardiovascular, and nervous systems and, therefore, had significant commercial potential. It is alleged that Zhu and Kimbara each signed a Participation Agreement upon coming to Harvard in which they agreed that all rights to any invention or discovery conceived or first reduced to practice as part of, or related to, their university activities were assigned to Harvard, and that their obligations would continue after the termination of their Harvard employment. Researchers in the laboratory funded in part by the National Institutes of Health and the American Cancer Society, used information, technology, and chemical reagents previously developed by the Harvard professor to screen drugs, proteins, and genes in an effort to determine those drugs that might control organ rejection, and those genes that might control calcineurin. The lab was kept locked and considered secure.

According to the complaint, by January or February 1999, Zhu and Kimbara began working from approximately 11:00 P.M. to approximately 9:00 A.M., thus enabling them to work without direct supervision from the Harvard professor and to conceal their activities from him. It is alleged that over time, the Harvard professor was able to determine that Kimbara was doing work that she was not sharing with him. It is alleged that, although Zhu and Kimbara reported the discovery of four genes as a result of the genetic screenings performed by them in the Harvard professor's lab, that, between February 1999 and August 1999, at least seven additional genes had been derived from preliminary genetic screenings performed by Zhu and Kimbara. On October 22, 1999, Harvard filed a provisional patent on the two genes and their products. It is alleged that, despite their legal and contractual obligations, Zhu and Kimbara took and conspired to take proprietary and highly marketable scientific information, belonging to Harvard, with them to Texas, with the intention of profiting from such information by collaborating with a Japanese company in the creation and sale of related and derivative products or otherwise capitalizing on the information.

It is alleged that beginning no later than December 27, 1999 to on or about January 1, 2000, Zhu and Kimbara removed, without permission or authorization, at least twenty cartons, including some Styrofoam containers commonly used to ship perishable biological materials, from the Harvard professor's laboratory in the very early morning hours or at night. It is alleged that between approximately December 22, 1999 and January 1, 2000, Zhu and Kimbara made arrangements to ship more than thirty boxes of biologicals, books, and documents to the University of Texas, unbeknownst to Harvard or the Harvard professor and without permission or authorization. It is alleged that beginning on approximately January 3, 2000, other Harvard laboratory personnel observed that significant amounts of biological material, equipment, and scientific documentation were missing from the lab.

It is alleged that on approximately January 11, 2000, Zhu and Kimbara met with officials from Harvard, including the Harvard professor. During that meeting, Zhu and Kimbara denied removing reagents, materials, and primary data from the lab and also denied hiding the results of work conducted while they worked in the lab. Zhu and Kimbara announced they were resigning their positions at Harvard and relocating to other research positions. They further stated that they had turned over all the primary data for the research they conducted, and they denied that they took anything from the laboratory other than personal belongings.

According to the complaint, in approximately June 2000, a significant percentage of the materials taken from Harvard by Zhu and Kimbara were recovered from their workspace at the University of Texas. However, many of the materials allegedly taken by Zhu and Kimbara from the Harvard professor's laboratory have not yet been recovered.

On December 13, 1999, Zhu received an offer of employment from the Institute of Biotechnology at the University of Texas, San Antonio (University of Texas). It is alleged that the day after receiving the offer, and while still employed at Harvard, Zhu sent an e-mail to a biochemical company in Japan in which he stated his intent to collaborate with another researcher after he left Boston to commercialize the antibodies suggested by the research done in the Harvard laboratory. It is alleged that Zhu sent three new genes to Japan for the purpose of the Japanese biochemical company making antibodies against them, without the knowledge or authorization of the Harvard professor and in direct violation of the Participation Agreement signed by both Zhu and Kimbara. It is alleged that the Japanese company did in fact produce antibodies against two of the genes and shipped these antibodies to Zhu at the University of Texas between February and May 2000.

Zhu accepted the position with the University of Texas, both to run his own lab and to teach. Kimbara was also hired to work in the University of Texas laboratory.

Tse Thow Sun

The U.S. Attorney's Office for the Northern District of California announced that Tse Thow Sun pled guilty on April 9, 2003 to theft of trade secrets. Mr. Sun, 32 at the time, a citizen of Singapore, was indicted by a federal grand jury on April 9, 2002. He was charged with theft of trade secrets, in violation of 18 U.S.C. Section 1832(a)(3); attempted theft of trade secrets, in violation of 18 U.S.C. Section 1832(a)(4); and interstate transportation of stolen goods, in violation of 18 U.S.C. Section 2314. Under the plea agreement, Mr. Sun pled guilty to theft of trade secrets.

In pleading guilty, Mr. Sun admitted that in early 2002, he was employed as an IT specialist with Online Interpreters in Chicago, Illinois. The company was in the business of providing real-time translation services over the phone for a variety of clients who had non-English-speaking customers. Mr. Sun admitted that in March 2002, he approached the president of a competing business located in Northern California with an offer to sell confidential information about Online Interpreters. Mr. Sun demanded $3 million for the information. At a meeting on March 29, 2002, Mr. Sun delivered a laptop computer and a hard drive that contained trade secrets and confidential propriety information about Online to the competitor. Mr. Sun admitted that he stole this information from his employer.

John Berenson Morris

Colm F. Connolly, U.S. Attorney for the District of Delaware, announced that John Berenson Morris of Mt. Kisco, New York, entered a guilty plea to one count of attempting to steal and transmit trade secret information belonging to Brookwood Companies, Inc., a textile company based in New York, New York. Morris was prosecuted under the EEA, which makes the theft of trade secrets a federal criminal offense. He faces up to 10 years' imprisonment and a fine of up to $250,000 on this charge.

During July and August 2002, Morris attempted to sell Brookwood's proprietary pricing information to one of its competitors, Newark-based W.L. Gore & Associates, Inc. This pricing information related to a then-outstanding multimillion-dollar U.S. DoD solicitation for bid for the production of certain military fabric products. From July 26, 2002 to August 5, 2002, Morris placed a series of phone calls to a man he believed to be a Gore employee, in which Morris offered to sell Brookwood's trade secrets for $100,000. What Morris did not know at the time, however, was that this man was actually an undercover DoD agent. The phone calls culminated in a meeting at a rest stop on the New Jersey Turnpike on August 5, 2002, where Morris was arrested.

W.L. Gore contacted federal law enforcement shortly after Morris placed his first phone call to Gore to propose the illegal sale of information. This action enabled law enforcement to arrange for the undercover special agent to receive and respond to Morris' subsequent overtures.

The case was investigated by agents with the DoD, Office of the Assistant Inspector General for Investigations, Defense Criminal Investigative Service. The case was prosecuted by Assistant U.S. Attorney Keith M. Rosen.

Mikahel K. Chang and Daniel Park

The U.S. Attorney's Office for the Northern District of California announced that Mikahel K. Chang pled guilty on December 4, 2001 to theft of a trade secret and criminal forfeitures. Also, Daniel Park pled guilty to aiding and abetting criminal copyright infringement.

Mr. Chang, 32 at the time, and Mr. Park, 33 at the time, both of San Jose, California, were indicted by a federal grand jury on June 14, 2000. Both defendants were charged with one count of theft of a trade secret in violation of Title 18, United States Code, Sections 1832(a)(1) and (a)(3). Mr. Chang was charged with two counts of criminal forfeiture pursuant to Title 18, United States Code, Sections 1834(a)(1) and (a)(2). Mr. Park was charged with one count of criminal forfeiture pursuant to Title 18, United States Code, Section 1834(a)(2).

Under the plea agreements, Mr. Chang pled guilty to all three counts and Mr. Park pled guilty to a superseding information charging the criminal copyright infringement violation. In pleading guilty, Mr. Chang admitted to having received, possessed, and without authorization appropriated stolen trade secret information belonging to Mr. Chang's former employer, Semi Supply, Inc., of Livermore, California, knowing such information to have been stolen, obtained, and converted without authorization. Specifically, Mr. Chang admitted to having received, possessed, and appropriated without authorization customer and order information in databases relating to Semi Supply's sales.

In pleading guilty, Mr. Park admitted to having aided and abetted the willful infringement of a copyright for purposes of commercial advantage and private financial gain. Mr. Park admitted to having aided and abetted the willful infringement of a copyright by accessing a FoxPro database program, which he knew had been copied without authorization and which had been infringed for the purposes of commercial advantage and private financial gain. Specifically, Mr. Park admitted that the FoxPro database program was used to access the stolen trade secret information belonging to Semi Supply.

The maximum statutory penalty for a violation of the theft of trade secrets statute is 10 years' imprisonment, and a fine of $250,000 or twice the gross gain or twice the gross loss (whichever is greatest), plus restitution if appropriate. However, the actual sentence will be dictated by the Federal Sentencing Guidelines, which take into account a number of factors, and will be imposed at the discretion of the court.

The prosecution was the result of an investigation by agents of the High Tech Squad of the FBI, which was overseen by the Computer Hacking and Intellectual Property (CHIP) Unit of the U.S. Attorney's Office.

Xingkun Wu

On July 31, 2001, Special Agent in Charge Peter J. Ahearn, Buffalo Division, FBI, announced the filing of a federal criminal complaint and the issuance of a federal arrest warrant against Mr. Xingkun Wu, age 40 at the time, of Los Angeles, California. The complaint and arrest warrant were the result of an investigation conducted by FBI Special Agents assigned to the Elmira, New York, Resident Agency, with the assistance of the New York State Police, the FBI's Los Angeles Division, and Corning Incorporated.

The Criminal Complaint, which was issued on July 30, 2001, charged Wu, a former employee of Corning Incorporated, with violations of Title 18, United States Code, Section 1832, which pertains to theft of trade secrets. The Criminal Complaint alleged that on or about March 10, 2000, and May 4, 2000, in the Western District of New York, Wu knowingly attempted to convert a trade secret to the economic benefit of someone other than its owner (Corning Incorporated), knowing that the offense would injure Corning Incorporated as the owner of the trade secret. Investigation by the Los Angeles Division of the FBI has developed information that Wu may have returned to his native country, China.

Junsheng Wang and Bell Imaging Technology Corporation

The U.S. Attorney's Office for the Northern District of California announced that Junsheng Wang and Bell Imaging Technology Corporation pled guilty on April 26, 2001 to theft and copying of the trade secrets of Acuson Corporation.

Mr. Wang, age 53 at the time, of Fremont, and Bell Imaging Technology Corporation, a California corporation based in Fremont, were charged in a criminal information filed in federal court on April 19, 2001. Mr. Wang was charged with theft of trade secrets in violation of Title 18, United States Code, Section 1832(a)(1), and Bell Imaging Technology Corporation was charged with copying of trade secrets in violation of Title 18, United States Code, Section 1832(a)(2). A related company, Belson Imaging Technology Company Limited, a joint venture based in the PRC, was also charged in the information with copying trade secrets, and that charge remains pending.

In pleading guilty, Mr. Wang and Bell Imaging Technology Corporation admitted that prior to August 24, 2000, Mr. Wang took without authorization and copied for Bell Imaging Technology Corporation a document providing the architecture for the Sequoia ultrasound machine that contained the trade secrets of Acuson Corporation. According to Mr. Wang's plea agreement, he had been able to obtain access to the Acuson trade secret materials because his wife was employed as an engineer at that company and because she had brought that document into their home. After Mr. Wang had copied the document, he took it with him in the year 2000 on business trips to the PRC for Bell Imaging Technology Corporation. According to Bell Imaging Technology Corporation's plea agreement, it is a California corporation involved in the manufacture and distribution of ultrasound transducers, and has been a partner with Henson Medical Imaging Company, a Chinese company, in Belson Imaging Technology Company Limited, the final defendant in this case. Mr. Wang was arrested carrying the Acuson trade secret documents at San Francisco International Airport as he was about to board a flight for Shanghai, PRC, in August 2000.

The prosecutions were the result of an investigation by agents of the FBI with cooperation from agents of the U.S. Customs Service.

Fausto Estrada

A five-count complaint unsealed on March 21, 2001 in Manhattan federal court charged Fausto Estrada with theft of trade secrets, mail fraud, and interstate transportation of stolen property. According to the complaint, Estrada was a contract food services employee working at MasterCard's headquarters in Purchase, New York. The complaint charged that in February 2001, Estrada, using the alias "Cagliostro," mailed a package of information he had stolen from MasterCard to Visa's offices located in California. Estrada allegedly offered to sell to Visa sensitive and proprietary information that he had stolen from MasterCard's headquarters and allegedly offered to record high-level meetings within MasterCard if Visa paid Estrada and provided him with recording equipment. According to the complaint, among the items Estrada offered to sell to Visa was a business alliance proposal valued in excess of $1 billion between MasterCard and a large U.S. entertainment corporation.

As part of a sting operation conducted by the FBI's Computer Intrusion and Intellectual Property Squad, an FBI agent posed as a Visa representative and negotiated for the purchase of the MasterCard documents in Estrada's possession. These negotiations culminated in a covert meeting at which an undercover FBI agent met with Estrada in a hotel room to exchange money for the stolen proprietary documents.

Peter Morch

The U.S. Attorney's Office for the Northern District of California announced that Peter Morch, a resident of San Francisco and a citizen of Canada and Denmark, was arrested on March 21, 2000 pursuant to a criminal complaint charging him with theft of trade secrets in violation of Title 18, United States Code, Section 1832.

According to an affidavit filed in support of the criminal complaint, Mr. Morch resigned from his position as a software engineer at Cisco Systems in Petaluma, California. While at Cisco, Mr. Morch was a team leader for a research and development project pertaining to voice-over and optical networking. The day before his final date of employment at Cisco, Mr. Morch was alleged to have burned onto CDs numerous proprietary documents, including but not limited to Cisco project ideas, general descriptions, requirements, specifications, limitations of design, and procedures to overcome the design difficulties for a voice-over and optical networking software product. Shortly after, Mr. Morch started working at Calix Networks, a potential competitor with Cisco.

Steven Craig Hallstead and Brian Russell Pringle

Two California men, Steven Craig Hallstead, 29 at the time, and Brian Russell Pringle, 34 at the time, were sentenced to prison terms on December 4, 1998 in federal court in Sherman, Texas, for attempting to sell trade secrets that belonged to the Intel Corporation. The two pled guilty to attempting to sell several prototype computer central processing units (CPUs) that belonged to the Intel Corporation, to the Cyrix Corporation, a competitor of Intel. The men were convicted under the EEA. According to prosecutors, approximately five of the prototype CPUs, known at Intel as "Slot II" CPUs, were stolen in a burglary in California in April 1998. The Slot II CPUs, which contained various trade secrets, were in the prototype stage and were not scheduled to be released on the public market until June of that year. In May 1998, Hallstead, identifying himself on the telephone only as "Steve," contacted a representative of the Cyrix Corporation in Richardson, Texas, offering to sell the Slot II CPUs to Cyrix. Hallstead told the officials at Cyrix that the CPUs were being developed by Intel and that they would be valuable to Cyrix. Cyrix immediately contacted law enforcement officials to report the incident. At the request of the FBI, Cyrix officials cooperated with the FBI in carrying out a sting operation to identify the individual who was attempting to sell the sell the Slot II CPUs to Cyrix. Cyrix officials permitted an FBI agent to pose as a Cyrix employee and, through a series of telephone conversations, Hallstead offered to sell five of the Slot II CPUs to Cyrix for a total of $75,000. FBI agents in Dallas, working with FBI agents in California, were able to identify and locate Hallstead and his business partner, Pringle, in California. Hallstead arranged for Pringle to travel from California to Richardson to deliver two of the Slot II CPUs to the Cyrix offices in Richardson on May 15, 1998. Pringle was arrested on that date when he arrived at the Cyrix offices and delivered the CPUs to FBI agents who were posing as Cyrix employees. Hallstead was arrested later that day in California.

Mayra Justine Trujillo-Cohen

On July 30, 1998, James H. DeAtley, the U.S. Attorney for the Southern District of Texas, announced that Mayra Justine Trujillo-Cohen, 46 at the time, pled guilty to superseding criminal information, charging her with theft of trade secrets, a violation of 18 United States Code, Section 1832, and one count of wire fraud, a violation of 18 United States Code, Section 1343. This case was the first economic espionage case to be brought in the Southern District of Texas.

Trujillo-Cohen pled guilty to taking a proprietary SAP Implementation Methodology, considered to be intellectual property, from her employer, ICS, Deloitte & Touche, and then attempting to convey that methodology as her own creation for personal financial gain, after she had been terminated from ICS, Deloitte & Touche.

Trujillo-Cohen also pled guilty to wire fraud. She admitted to developing a scheme wherein she was able to use an insurance company's bank account to pay her American Express credit card bill through wire transfers. Over a period of several months, Trujillo-Cohen transferred approximately $436,000 from the insurance company's bank account to her American Express account, which she used to purchase such big-ticket items as a Rover sports utility vehicle; furniture; and jewelry, including several Rolex watches.

Steven L. Davis

Steven L. Davis, 47 at the time, pled guilty on January 27, 1998 to federal charges that he stole and disclosed trade secrets of the Gillette Company.

At the plea hearing, a federal prosecutor told the court that in February and March 1997, Davis stole and disclosed trade secrets concerning the development of a new shaving system by the Gillette Company, which is headquartered in Boston, Massachusetts. Davis, was employed as a process controls engineer for Wright Industries, Inc., a Tennessee designer of fabrication equipment, which had been hired by Gillette to assist in the development of the new shaving system. The new shaving system project was extremely confidential and was treated so by both Gillette and Wright Industries. Davis told the court that in anger at a supervisor and, fearing that his job was in jeopardy, he decided to disclose trade secret information to Gillette's competitors. The disclosures were made to Warner-Lambert Company, Bic, and American Safety Razor Company.

This case was investigated by the Boston office of the FBI with assistance from the FBI's Nashville office. The case was being prosecuted in Tennessee by Assistant U.S. Attorney Jeanne M. Kempthorne, Deputy Chief of Stern's Economic Crimes Unit, with the assistance of Assistant U.S. Attorney Wendy Goggin, of the U.S. Attorney's Office in Nashville.

Jack Shearer and William Robert Humes

In December 1999, the Honorable U.S. District Judge Sidney A. Fitzwater sentenced Jack Shearer, age 54 at the time, of Montgomery, Texas, to 54 months' imprisonment and ordered him to pay $7,655,155 in restitution. William Robert Humes, age 60 at the time, of Arlington, Texas, was sentenced to 27 months' imprisonment and ordered to pay $3.8 million in restitution. Corporate defendants Tejas Procurement Services, Inc.; Tejas Compressor Systems, Inc.; and Procurement Solutions International, L.L.C. were each sentenced to 5 years' probation and ordered, jointly and severally, to pay $7,655,155 in restitution.

Jack Shearer pled guilty in December 1999 to two counts of an Information, which charged him with conspiracy to steal trade secrets, in violation of Title 18, United States Code, Section 1832(a)(5). William Robert Humes also pled guilty to one count of conspiracy to steal trade secrets, in violation of Title 18, United States Code, Section 1832(a)(5).

Three corporations founded by Jack Shearer – Tejas Procurement Services, Inc.; Tejas Compressor Systems, Inc.; and Procurement Solutions International, L.L.C. – pled guilty, by their duly appointed representatives, in December 1999 to federal charges of conspiracy to steal trade secrets. Tejas' revenues from the stolen trade secrets were in excess of $7 million.

Shearer admitted that he stole intellectual property, or proprietary trade secrets, from his former employer, Solar Turbines, Inc. (Solar), headquartered in San Diego, California. After receiving the proprietary information, Jack Shearer used this information for his own economic benefit as well as the benefit and private commercial advantage of his companies, Tejas and Procurement Solutions International, L.L.C. (PSI), an oil and gas parts company Shearer founded in the fall of 1998 to compete with Tejas. He advised his employees to "sanitize" the Solar plans, drawings, designs, and schematics by removing Solar's proprietary warnings and transferring the information to third-party machine shops. However, in some cases, Jack Shearer transferred the Solar plans, drawings, designs, and schematics to third-party machine shops with Solar's proprietary warnings still affixed and clearly visible. Solar parts have a specialized form, fit, and function, and plans depicting Solar parts are readily identifiable as Solar proprietary plans and specifications.

Over the years, Tejas developed a collection of Solar plans that numbered in the many hundreds, and Tejas provided various third parties with trade secret manufacturing information contained in these plans pertaining to hundreds of Solar parts. Various third-party machine shops received Solar's trade secrets and began to manufacture counterfeit Solar parts at Shearer's direction. Because the counterfeit parts produced by these machine shops were not manufactured to Solar's safety standards, their use raises serious safety concerns.

Once these third-party machine shops had manufactured the counterfeit Solar parts, the parts were either shipped directly from the machine shops or to Tejas for Shearer's customers. Jack Shearer acknowledges that he knew the sale of the counterfeit Solar parts would injure Solar, the true owner of the trade secrets. This trade secret information could only be obtained from Solar and was not available to be purchased by the general public. Jack Shearer and Tejas instructed its sales employees to falsely represent to customers that the counterfeit Solar parts made by the third-party machine shops were in fact genuine. Using the Solar drawings as a guide, Jack Shearer and Tejas instructed its employees to place identical Solar parts numbers on the counterfeit manufactured parts in order to deceive Tejas customers. Jack Shearer and Tejas also instructed its employees to create "Certificates of Compliance" for the counterfeit parts that were similar to genuine Solar certificates. These certificates were created specifically for Tejas customers that requested proof of genuine Solar parts.

Shearer would also, on behalf of PSI, purchase stolen Solar trade secret information, specifically information on Solar fuel control valves for its top-of-the-line turbine engine, from Jack Edward Nafus in return for cash payments. From January to May 1999, PSI paid Nafus at least $6,500 in cash for the stolen Solar trade secret information. Shearer and PSI passed the trade secret information to a machine shop in order to manufacture counterfeit Solar valves for Tejas' main customer, an Iranian national businessman who operated an oil and gas parts broker business in Uppsala, Sweden. This businessman placed millions of dollars of orders per year with Tejas, and orders he placed were designed for oil field applications and painted desert beige. Solar designs and manufactures industrial gas turbine engines and turbo machinery systems for the production and transmission of crude oil, petroleum products, and natural gas; generating electricity and thermal energy for a wide variety of industrial applications; and for the fast ferry marine market. Solar's equipment, distributed worldwide, was used to provide electrical power for industrial operations such as oil drilling operations. Solar, with approximately 5,100 employees worldwide, is a wholly owned subsidiary of Caterpillar, Inc., the world's leading manufacturer of construction and mining equipment, diesel and natural gas engines, and industrial gas turbines.

Shearer worked for Solar for 26 years until his employment was terminated in 1992. While he was employed at Solar, Shearer lived overseas and serviced a sales territory that included Libya, Jordan, Syria, Lebanon, Iraq, Iran, and Saudi Arabia. When Shearer was terminated from Solar, he started Tejas Compressor Systems, Inc., and Tejas Procurement Services, Inc., headquartered in Conroe, Texas, in order to compete with his former employer.

Shearer obtained Solar's trade secret information and used that information to manufacture counterfeit Solar parts through Tejas. Shearer obtained this confidential trade secret information through at least three individuals, defendant William Robert Humes and defendant Jack Edward Nafus, as well as a third named individual, now all former employees of Solar. Defendant Jack Edward Nafus, age 51, of River Ridge, Louisiana, also pled guilty in December 1999 to conspiracy to sell trade secrets. Tejas, at Shearer's direction, paid each of these Solar employees to provide Solar drawings, plans, and schematics that included confidential specifications describing the dimensions and manufacturing details of Solar parts. Shearer was aware that these payments constituted unlawful transactions and knew that stealing this proprietary trade secret information would injure Solar.

Tejas and a number of its employees became suspicious that the parts ordered by this Iranian national businessman were going to prohibited countries, such as Iran. One of Tejas' suppliers refused to manufacture parts for Tejas because it determined, based merely on the type of gear sought to be manufactured, that it was a proprietary Solar part of a Solar turbine engine located in Iran. Among other reasons, the manufacturer refused to manufacture the part for Tejas because it was in violation of the Presidential Order for selling such parts to prohibited countries such as Iran. In another instance, a Tejas employee called Jack Edward Nafus to inquire about a price quote for an order placed by this Iranian national businessman and learned from Nafus the type of shaft she was inquiring about and trying to procure belonged to a turbine unit located in Iraq. Nafus refused to provide the information to Tejas unless Tejas could provide verification that the shaft was not destined to a customer in an embargoed country.

The use of Solar's confidential information to manufacture counterfeit Solar parts was profitable for Tejas and, in fact, the substantial revenue generated from this activity became the predominant source of Tejas' income. By 1998, Tejas revenues were in the $8 million to $9 million range. Of that amount, the substantial majority was based on procurement activity including, in substantial part, the manufacture of counterfeit Solar parts using Solar's confidential and proprietary information.

What Do These Cases Tell Us So Far?

Criminal activity involving sophisticated technology or economic espionage have attracted attention in recent years. Eight years have passed and just forty cases have been prosecuted under the EEA. Is the EEA being effectively used? Given the reported severity of the foreign trade secret theft problem that drove the passage of the EEA, one might wonder why the number of prosecutions is not higher. One of the fears surrounding the passage of the EEA was that publicly traded companies might be hesitant to report the theft of their trade secrets for fear that doing so might adversely affect their stock prices.[164,165] Have the cases so far proven that to be true?

A number of important lessons can be learned from the cases to date. The cases confirm that the government will, in fact, devote significant resources to the investigation, prosecution, and enforcement of the EEA.[166] The amount of resources that the government has invested thus far illustrates that it takes the EEA seriously. Many of these cases arose out of FBI sting operations where extensive evidence was accumulated.[167] There was little dispute in any of the cases as to whether the defendant had the requisite criminal intent to satisfy the act.[168] No defendant could credibly argue that he or she had acted "inadvertently," "negligently," or "unintentionally" in disclosing trade secrets.[169]

In several cases, the indicted individuals and/or important players were outside agents, independent contractors, or temporary employees, not full-time regular employees.[170] This is consistant with an ASIS report that such individuals often pose the greatest threat to a company's trade secrets.

For those in the competitive intelligence industry, there was fear that the risk of prosecution under the EEA would have a large impact on how competitive intelligence professionals conduct their activities.[171] However, in light of the cases the government has filed thus far, this fear appears to have been misplaced.[172]

Most of the cases involved section 1832 (the domestic activity section), not section 1831 (the foreign activity section). Thus, we have yet to see more section 1831 cases brought by the government, even though that was the single most important reason behind the passage of the EEA.[173]

A New Solution for Guarding Secrets

The EEA is a comprehensive device to combat trade secret misappropriation. It has significantly raised the stakes with respect to protecting trade secrets. In light of its penalties, businesses must take careful notice of its provisions. Under the act, businesses have three major responsibilities: (1) establish reasonable safeguards to protect company trade secrets, (2) prevent the contamination of the firm through the inadvertent misappropriation of the trade secrets of others, and (3) institute measures to prevent employees from intentionally stealing the trade secrets of others.

Businesses must take a close look at their procedures involving confidential information. Rules for entering into nondisclosure agreements should be implemented to control the process of assuming, tracking, and enforcing confidentiality obligations to third parties. Hiring practices should be reviewed to avoid improper hiring of trained employees and consultants and to emphasize respect for IPRs as part of a company's training program. Perhaps most importantly, a company must examine its business relationships to determine the procedures and behaviors of those who may create vicarious liability under the EEA.

Overall, the EEA should prove to be a substantial improvement in the battle against industrial espionage. It has created a national standard governing trade secret misappropriation, supplementing the multitude of federal and state laws that were previously used to prosecute trade secret misappropriators with only mild results. In so doing, the EEA has filled a significant gap in the protection of trade secrets in the global information age.

Multinational Conspiracy or Natural Evolution of Market Economy

MODERN TECHNOLOGY has facilitated a dramatic rise in economic espionage committed by private companies, criminal organizations, and national governments.[1] Enterprises are faced with unprecedented risks associated with the pervasive infusion of technologies into virtually every corner of their operations. Today's managers are faced with a daunting array of technology-driven risks to navigate. Economic espionage, privacy, employee productivity, regulatory compliance, and systems integrity are but a few of these issues that cut across all areas of operation. These issues, if not properly handled, can have devastating consequences to an enterprise's viability. Unfortunately, far too many enterprises have failed to grasp the severity of these risks and take the necessary measures to mitigate them.

The focus on economic espionage ultimately reflects an underlying belief in the need for industrial policy on a worldwide basis. Information is a vital asset of the global economy and is vulnerable to economic espionage if not adequately protected by national laws and international agreements. Trade secret protection is becoming a common form of IPR and must receive heightened and explicit recognition in bilateral and multilateral agreements.

Despite the increasing importance of trade secrets to world economies, there is no global law on trade secrets or even a universal definition of a trade secret. Patents, copyrights, and trademarks are addressed in comprehensive international legal treaties, but trade secrets are not fully included. What can be protected as a trade secret differs from country to country, and, in some nations, trade secrets have no legal standing at all. International intellectual property law does not help because it is quite weak in this area. At the present time, it does not provide much protection to countries that are regular victims of economic espionage.[2]

In response to these trends, the United States enhanced its civil and criminal trade secret protection in federal laws.[3] An increase in intellectual property crimes, combined with the lack of deterrence associated with civil remedies, led the federal government and most states to enact statutes with criminal provisions designed to prevent the theft of intellectual property rights. Was this a good idea, and should other nations follow this lead?

U.S. Emphasis on Protection of Intellectual Property

In more recent years, the U.S. Congress has taken an especially strong interest in intellectual property crimes as well as intellectual property law generally. The protection of intellectual property is firmly rooted in American jurisprudence.[4] The federal interest in intellectual property is no recent or transitory development.[5] Rather, the protection of U.S. intellectual property both domestically and internationally has been a major policy objective of the U.S. government for years.

Intellectual property crimes were formally designated a "priority" by Deputy Attorney General Eric Holder on July 23, 1999.[6] In announcing an Intellectual Property Rights Initiative, Deputy Attorney General Holder stated that the Department of Justice, the FBI, and the U.S. Customs Service had concluded that they must make investigating and prosecuting intellectual property crime "a major law enforcement priority." In making the announcement, he noted that:

> [a]s the world moves from the industrial age to the information age, the United States' economy is increasingly dependent on the production and distribution of intellectual property. Currently, the U.S. leads the world in the creation and export of intellectual property and IP-related products.[7]

Deputy Attorney General Holder also observed that "[a]t the same time that our information economy is soaring, so is intellectual property theft." Because intellectual property theft undermines the federally established legal systems, it is especially appropriate that investigation and prosecution of these crimes are a federal law enforcement priority.

The United States has consistently pushed for international agreements to protect intellectual property, as well as the extension of state and federal remedies for the theft of trade secrets.[8] Global "harmonization" of intellectual property laws has been a top American policy priority in more recent years, but trade secrets are still at a disadvantage. Germany and Japan require public trials for lawsuits, for example, and anyone seeking redress must first reveal his or her trade secret. In other countries, confidential data are revealed when submitted for government review. In the international arena, the United States has regularly pressed for stringent protection and enforcement of intellectual property rights in the world.[9] The United States hopes to compel other nations to provide stronger protection for U.S. innovations.[10]

International Espionage for Commercial Advantage

Economic espionage will continue to rise unless nations make joint efforts to deal with the problem. As foreign corporate ownership becomes widespread, as multinationals expand, as nation-states dissolve into regions and coalesce into supranational states, traditional concepts of ownership are fading. However, the notice of "proprietary information" is here to stay, and theft will never cease as long as there is profit to be made.[11]

Because of the dramatic changes to the world's military and economic divisions caused by the end of the Cold War, the probability is great that nations will continue to commit economic espionage against one another. Illicit gathering of competitor nations' economic information is what allows many nations to compete effectively in the world market. Those who take part in economic espionage will not be readily willing to stop, especially if it means losing any clout they have as members of the global economy. World leaders recognize that economic power is fundamental to national power. If nations persist in placing their domestic priorities above international norms, the international economy will suffer. For the world to achieve stable economic conditions, individual governments must be willing to put aside their short-term parochial interests and begin harmonizing business practices, along with their legislative initiatives, with one another. It is vital that global leaders form an agreement on economic espionage. The world's economic future depends on it.

Cyberterrorism – An Emerging Threat

Terrorist groups are increasingly computer-savvy, and some are probably acquiring the ability to use cyberattacks to inflict isolated and brief disruptions. Due to the prevalence of publicly available hacker tools, many of these groups already have the capability to launch denial-of-service and other nuisance attacks against Internet-connected systems. As terrorists become more computer-savvy, their attack options will only increase.[12]

Terrorists worldwide have ready access to information on chemical, biological, radiologic, and nuclear weapons via the Internet. Attacks against high-tech businesses would cripple IT and jeopardize thousands of jobs. The financial sector now depends on telecommunications for most of its transactions. Disruption of critical telecommunications nodes can create severe hardships until services are restored. The results of sabotage could persist for longer durations, creating difficult repairs and recovery and intensifying uncertainty and economic losses.[13]

Adapting to a Changing Culture

In 1908 in the United States, to answer the need for a federal investigative body, Attorney General Charles Bonaparte established a group of special agents within the DOJ now known as the FBI.[14] During the organization's early days, its agents delved into violations involving fraud, bankruptcy, and antitrust crime. When the Mann Act was passed in 1910, the bureau's sleuthing expanded into investigating criminals who evaded state laws, but had no other federal violations. World War I brought more responsibility with draft violations, espionage, sabotage, and sedition. The National Motor Vehicle Theft Act, passed in 1919, gave the bureau even more to do.[15]

During Prohibition and the gangster era, the United States witnessed the passage of federal criminal and kidnapping statutes, and special agents were given authority to carry firearms and make arrests. World War II brought increased growth to the bureau's size and jurisdiction, and, with the emergence of the atomic age, background checks into security matters for the executive branch of the government became its responsibility.[16] Jurisdiction over civil rights violations and organized crime followed in the 1960s; white-collar crime, drugs, violent crimes, and counterterrorism in the 1970s and 1980s; and computer crimes, health care fraud, economic espionage, and threats from weapons of mass destruction in the 1990s.[17]

Today we recognize that punishment of financial and economic crimes is vital, both to the prosperity of a nation's economy and to people's faith in the criminal justice system. Although crimes of violence and routine property crimes will always be with us, the criminal justice system is poorly equipped to address the dramatic increases in crimes perpetrated with a computer or the Internet. Too few law enforcement departments in the United States even know of the legal requirements for obtaining a search warrant for a computer, and even fewer have personnel with expertise to capture the data sought. Most prosecutors lack the training and experience to provide guidance. The debate over the proper venue for a computer-based crime poses other problems. The ease with which computers cross jurisdictional boundaries means law enforcement agencies, often proud of their independence, must learn better cooperation. When more than 100 bank account records are finally obtained, who has the time and expertise to find the "smoking gun" buried within them? When a dispatcher receives a call about identity theft, does he or she even recognize the nature of the call and know how to aid the victim and properly route the problem? These issues must be addressed as the criminal justice system ventures into the new millennium.

Criminalization of Trade Secret Misappropriation in the United States

Criminalizing misappropriation of trade secrets implicitly treats the interest at issue as property. When the focus of a criminal law is to punish certain conduct, the property approach is implicated; condemning conduct that involves some interest inevitably sweeps that interest into a protected category. In the case of the EEA, however, U.S. Congress's adoption of the property basis was more explicit.

History demonstrates that many infringers will not be deterred by civil liability, which can be treated as a cost of doing business. For example, even when a permanent injunction or consent decree is in force, they do not necessarily deter some defendants. Some defendants may respond to such civil remedies by changing the item upon which they are infringing, such as counterfeiting shirts bearing marks of Major League Baseball teams after being the subject of an injunction obtained by the National Football League. Others close shop only to quickly reopen under a different corporate identity. Criminal prosecution can better deter a violator from repeating the crime.

Criminal prosecution of intellectual property crimes also is important for general deterrence. Many individuals may commit intellectual property crimes not only because they can be relatively easy to commit (e.g., copying music), but also because they believe they will not be prosecuted. Criminal prosecution plays an important role in establishing public expectations of right and wrong. Even relatively small-scale violations, if permitted to take place openly and notoriously, can lead other people to believe that such conduct is acceptable. Although some cases of counterfeiting or piracy may not result in provable direct loss to the holder of the IPR, the widespread commission of intellectual property crimes with impunity can be devastating to the value of such rights. Industry groups representing victims of intellectual property crimes are acutely aware of their need for law enforcement protection for intellectual property. These victims widely publicize successful prosecutions to send a message. The resulting public awareness of effective prosecutions can have a substantial deterrence effect.

Although the EEA prohibits a broad range of behavior, the United States does not appear to have been motivated by a desire to maintain commercial morality or to prevent unfair competition. Rather, in the view of the United States, trade secrets are much like any other property.[18] The United States effectively gave owners the right to control any use of the information.[19] The person or entity holding a trade secret can authorize certain uses, and an unauthorized use undertaken with the requisite mental state is a crime.[20]

Value of Lost Information

The United States' stated goal in passing the EEA was to promote the general economic well-being of the nation. The United States was undoubtedly influenced by the value of secret information and its importance to the economy, and may have equated value with property. The concern over value, however, is problematic for two reasons. In this specific case, the estimated financial value of lost information cannot be considered as entirely reliable, in part because the estimates vary so wildly. The estimates of lost value are often based on an assumption that infringers would have purchased the object if it was not otherwise available, and there after is no evidence of that.[21] Moreover, self-interested parties provide the estimates of losses, and their conclusions should be viewed skeptically.

Another more general problem is that relying on value to determine whether an object is property is circular: An object has market value in large part because legislators or courts have given some individual or entity the right to exclude others from using it.[22] Even if value were a valid standard for deeming an object worth protecting, criminal law does not guard every valuable interest.[23]

Some have argued that criminalizing trade secret takings is a double-edged sword because, although the EEA may deter such takings, unintended consequences of enforcement may very well undermine the goal of economic growth. In other words, protecting trade secrets in order to encourage innovation is not costless. One cost of enhanced rights in trade secrets is that exercising those rights impedes the ability of employees to take jobs in other firms or to start new businesses. Loss of employee mobility leads to another cost, or inefficiency, by affecting regional economic performance. However, there is no evidence in any of the cases that would support predictions that the EEA was "designed to employ foreign spies"[24] or that it would "destroy employee mobility."[25]

The passage of the EEA marks a significant milestone in the prosecution of global economic crime. The United States and foreign citizens, as well as foreign governments, who attempt to steal their way into unearned profits now face substantial monetary penalties and jail time. The use of the EEA also greatly increases the likelihood that victims will obtain just compensation for their injuries and will further allow courts to ensure the confidentiality of U.S. companies' most valuable economic assets. Finally, the international cybercriminal who specializes in surreptitious computer theft can no longer feel secure that his or her conduct will go undetected or that he or she can escape liability because he or she is not a U.S. citizen or not physically located in the United States. These new laws, and increased emphasis on federal enforcement and prosecution, certainly will help the owners of valuable intellectual property protect their assets.

Challenges to Overcome for Public–Private Partnership

Marketing the concept to corporations that the federal government can and will play an active role in assisting with the protection of proprietary trade secrets hinges on convincing corporate executives that the economic espionage threat is real and is growing steadily. Historically, many barriers have impeded the public–private partner relationship. Many of these barriers are attitudes from a bygone era of mistrust and bad interactions between the government and businesses. Today's fluid marketplace and vulnerability to terrorism in a post-9/11 world demand a new, more cooperative set of attitudes and relationships.

There remain many challenges to overcome in ensuring cooperation, but it is important to recognize that these challenges and roles are often different for industry and the government. Because most of America's critical infrastructure is owned or operated by the private sector, these businesses and companies face a greater degree of threat than the government, and should therefore feel a greater incentive to engage in increased protection and security. However, this is not the same for the rest of the industrialized world.

The private sector is driven by profits, consumer and shareholder confidence, and market forces, which are strong incentives for increased security. However, a change in focus is necessary for this process to succeed. The threat cannot be countered with the prevailing reliance on the research and development of new product lines as the main defense against corporate espionage. Such an approach will eventually drain corporate assets to unacceptable levels because inefficient economies of scale will be realized from each generation of products. In addition, very few corporate executives have any type of experience in security measures or with intelligence services. This creates an environment in which the corporation has a natural tendency to distance itself from the federal government rather than seeking assistance.

Yet, civil remedies may be futile under various circumstances. For example, intellectual property crimes are unusual because they generally are committed without the victim's knowledge, even after the fact. The victim usually has no direct relationship with the infringer – before, during, or after the commission of the crime. If a victim is unaware of a violation by a particular defendant, civil remedies will generally be unavailing. Furthermore, without criminal sanction, infringers or counterfeiters might treat the rare case of the victim's civil enforcement of its rights as a cost of doing business.

Finally, more laws on the books do not necessarily increase the level of protection. The real key is investigation, enforcement, and prosecution of the laws. There are at least two problems with the increased criminalization of intellectual property violations. First, it makes the threat of criminal sanctions an attractive litigation tool. A plaintiff could easily refer, or threaten to refer, a case of willful counterfeiting, infringement, or trade secret misappropriation to government prosecutors. Although there are many reasons not do this, the mere threat of a criminal investigation could provide additional leverage in a civil case. This may create a second problem by turning borderline behavior into criminal behavior. In most cases, these criminal statutes criminalize the same basic behavior that is also punishable civilly. This means that virtually any infringement could be criminalized, and a vindictive litigant could refer a case to prosecutors as a competitive tool or litigation strategy.

The Need for International Cooperation

There is presently much debate, both within nations and internationally, about the ways in which economic espionage should be controlled. Internationally, there is a push to harmonize criminal laws in the new economy area. There are three international organizations looking at some of these issues: the G-8 subgroup on high-tech crime, the UN, and the COE.[26] The debate revolves around unilateral and multilateral action.[27] Industrialized countries are the leaders in implementing this action. They are attempting to reach agreements that would prohibit bribes and other corrupt practices in doing business abroad.[28] Corrupt business practices are illegal in all industrialized countries. Hence, the proposed agreement will simply extend that prohibition to activities abroad, potentially leading to higher ethical standards in developing countries where corruption runs rampant.

States must come to terms with what specifically constitutes the key elements of unjustifiable, unreasonable, or discriminatory conduct with respect to economic espionage, thereby defining the problem in explicit detail.[29] States must recognize what is and what is not economic espionage if they are to combat it. The first step is to identify laws that address the problem of economic espionage. Unfortunately, international laws and courts are still too weak in enforcement to provide much help. It may be possible to construe economic espionage as a violation of customary law or of Article 2 of the UN Charter, as a "threat or use of force against the territorial integrity . . . of any state, or in any manner inconsistent with the purposes of the United Nations" if the spying moves from passive observation to proactive influencing of economic events within the nation.[30] Again, however, enforcement would probably reduce to general political pressure from the victim's government, which is quite unpredictable. International agreements may actually point a plaintiff back to individual countries for recourse, though. Under NAFTA, "member countries must protect trade secrets from unauthorized acquisition, disclosure or use."[31] GATT/TRIPS provides that same misappropriation remedies requirement for member countries.

States also must incorporate existing law, both national and international, that may apply to economic espionage, and propose new law where existing law fails to control economic espionage.[32] On the "supply side" of the economic espionage problem, states must make efforts to control their own exports and heighten individual corporate security.[33] On the "government side" of the economic espionage problem, states need to take advantage of existing governments and intelligence agencies of individual nations to curb economic espionage through law enforcement mechanisms. States need to specify the roles that individual nations will play in identifying and countering the threats that economic espionage imposes on the industry of all nations, paying special attention to the manner in which such functions and roles are coordinated.[34] States must identify what constitutes the industrial threat, by discussing the threat to the nations' industry of economic espionage and any trends in that threat, including the number and identity of the governments conducting economic espionage, the industrial sectors and types of information and technology targeted by such espionage, and the methods used to conduct such espionage. Finally, states need to work together toward an international criminal law solution, discussing the possibility of creating a coherent, modem body of international criminal law that deters and/or penalizes economic espionage.[35]

The Japanese authorities have long been irritated by accusations of economic espionage leveled against Japanese corporations. Several scandals in the new technology field and mainly in the United States, where Japanese engineers found themselves charged under the EEA, have convinced Japan to take some action in this regard. The economic and industrial ministry has submitted a bill to the parliament making it a crime to steal industrial secrets. The bill, which will bring Japan's laws into line with those practiced in the United States, France, Germany, and other industrialized countries, is being debated in the Diet. But some have criticized the bill because it allows only civil legal action against violators.[36] The bill, which would revise the Unfair Competition Prevention Law, is aimed at protecting corporate secrecy to strengthen the international competitiveness of Japanese companies. Japan wants to keep pace with other nations in protecting its companies' proprietary industrial information. France, Germany, and other industrialized nations consider industrial espionage a matter of criminal law. Unfair Competition Prevention Law prohibits the theft, leakage, or misuse of such corporate secrets by labeling these acts as "unfair competition." With the rapid growth of IT and biotechnology, the Japanese ministry believed it was necessary to draft a criminal law to cover cases of misuse of confidential business information. The ministry also plans to revise the Unfair Competition Prevention Law to relax its stricter provisions under which companies whose information was stolen should verify specific damages so victims can properly be compensated for the damage caused.[37]

What Have We Accomplished?

In passing the EEA, the U.S. Congress tightened a seam in the existing patchwork of federal criminal laws that helps safeguard intellectual property. Although there certainly will be many important cases prosecuted under the new act, and although great care must be taken in the defense and prosecution of these cases, the government likely will be very selective in undertaking prosecutions and usually will handle only the most egregious cases that send an appropriate message to private industry and would-be trade secret thieves.

Ultimately, the EEA's greatest importance will probably be the role it plays in heightening the awareness of the seriousness of trade secret theft. The potential punitive stakes now include civil and criminal remedies, and a new code of commercial conduct in the area of intellectual property is emerging as a result. As long as corporations and other owners of trade secrets adhere to that code and appropriately weave the provisions of the act into their compliance programs, business dealings, and employment practices, greater trade secret protection in the private sector undoubtedly will result, often with no direct involvement by the government whatsoever.

Nations whose profits depend on trade secrets typically consider their workers a potential threat to the nation's interests. Indeed, one would not be wrong in concluding that the historical impetus for trade secret law was to restrain employees from competing with their employers. Although the incongruent interests of employees and employers are well understood,[38] the trade secret issue raises a special application that involves a societal interest. Nations have an interest in maintaining their competitive advantage by keeping trade secrets and business information from their competitors abroad. Employees, however, want the freedom to work for whichever business values them most highly.[39] Not so obviously, the community has an independent interest in a sound and growing economy that may be aligned with either interest.

Overall, the importance of states working together to combat economic espionage cannot be stressed enough. This already occurs between some states, and others must follow such a lead. For example, some FBI agents in the United States regularly make contact with Scotland Yard or with the French police and work collectively in attempting to stop international criminals who are being investigated by both countries.[40] This kind of activity may open doors for creating relationships at a higher level, such as mutual legal assistance treaties for dealing with economic espionage crimes. The U.S. DOJ already has such treaties, which provide procedures to share evidence and facilitate cooperative law enforcement with many countries throughout the world. However, it does not presently have such treaties with any of the countries of Eastern Europe or the former Soviet Union,

which began increasing their economic espionage activity with the end of the
Cold War.

Setting the Stage for a New Code of Commercial Conduct in the Global Marketplace

Some critics, such as Vandana Shiva,[41] argue that imperial power has always
been based on a convergence of military power used in the defense of trade.
She argues that this convergence was at the heart of the gunboat diplomacy
during colonialism. A similar convergence is now taking shape around the
defense of trading interests in a period of globalization and free trade. This,
she argues, can be seen in the EEA legislation passed by the U.S. Congress
in 1996, which views IPRs as vital to national security. It can be interpreted
as criminalizing the natural development and exchange of knowledge as it
empowers U.S. intelligence agencies to investigate the activities of ordinary
persons worldwide in an effort to protect the intellectual property rights of
U.S. corporations.

There are deep differences in the positions and attitudes of developed
and developing countries to the protection of intellectual property by legislation. Developed countries and particularly the most industrialized among
them see intellectual property as the fruit of the creative capacity and intellectual effort of their individual citizens and companies and as the legitimate
basis for these individuals and companies to earn trading advantage. Such
advantage cannot be exercised unless the intellectual property concerned is
given protection against use by others. They believe, in the absence of such
protection and the promise of later reward, research and development that
leads to inventions and new products of value to all would simply not take
place.

Developing countries have a different perspective. They do not in general
dispute the case for patent and copyright protection. However, their individual citizens and companies have little intellectual property of their own to
protect, and they do not see reason to give support to international standards
of protection that would require them to pay large sums to use technology.
These matters, which are of domestic interest to developing countries in
terms of right to health and right to development, are perceived as issues of
trade by northern corporations that are seeking new global markets.

The lack of international legislation addressing intellectual property
crimes is understandable in the context of yesterday's technology. However, as society becomes ever more dependent on new technology, individual countries and the international community must address intellectual
property crimes. Individual countries must enact laws to address both the
national and international aspects of these types of crimes and likewise,
the international community must form an international agreement that
enables the successful enforcement of such laws.

The central question is whether the taking of information or knowledge ought to be criminalized. In analyzing this problem, it is useful to remind ourselves of some basic truths. First, few would dispute the notion that the advancement of scientific knowledge is by far the most important source of increasing wealth and prosperity in human history. If you just look at the evolution of technology over the past two centuries alone, no one can doubt that the standard of living of most people on earth has improved in terms of quality of medicine, health, food, comfort – all the positive values that Jeremy Bentham's utilitarian view of law and society say should be maximized for the good of the whole.

Second, it is hard to dispute that, in a free market economy, intangible assets such as knowledge and technological advancements must be accorded some form of property right; otherwise, there will be insufficient individual incentive to develop those advancements. The failure of communism and other economic systems to provide individual property rights should be proof enough that there is good justification for recognizing property interest in knowledge.

A property right also finds support in the philosophical theories developed by John Locke. Under his labor theory of property, there is an inherent justification to recognizing property rights in knowledge and information due to the fact that it was brought about through human effort and investment. So the question is not whether there should be a property interest or some form of ownership in the fruits of one's intellectual labor, but rather the question is how powerful should that property interest be since there is a countervailing societal interest in the dissemination of knowledge for the benefit of all.

In an ideal world, every increment of greater knowledge would be measured separately and accorded sufficient property rights to compensate its creator for the labor and investment that was needed to bring it into existence. That would be the ideal measure of the property interests needed to preserve the incentive to create and expand knowledge, while imposing the least societal cost. That, however, is impossible to accomplish. Thus, the legal regimes surrounding intellectual property must use other yardsticks to protect new knowledge.

In the case of patents, for example, the lifetime of that property interest has been set, somewhat arbitrarily, at 20 years. In some cases, that may result in a pharmaceutical company, for example, reaping vastly excessive economic rewards from a new drug far beyond its research investment and, at the same time, deprive sick people in less developed countries of access to that medical discovery. Conversely, the scope of the protection of a patent might be insufficient to prevent very close imitation and thereby fail to provide adequate return on investment. Both of these outcomes are the consequence of uniform laws. On balance, we need to strike the right trade-off between adequate property protection and the interest of the world community in reaping the benefits of technological advancement at a reasonable cost.

One of the factors that has changed in more recent history that influences this balance is the widespread growth of IT. As we have seen in the discussion in this book, the rapid proliferation of IT worldwide has made it easier for the institutions that generate knowledge and technological advancements to have the benefits of that work taken away. This is due to the increased portability of information, the rapid development of information networks spanning vast geographic regions, and the increased mobility of the means of production. In other words, the developer of a new technology can no longer rely on difficulties of travel or access as a barrier to imitation. This increased portability means that the potential for information theft is riskier today than ever before. In addition, the procedural and geographic difficulties presented to an intellectual property owner whose valuable information has been misappropriated thousands of miles from his or her home make traditional civil remedies all the less effective.

One way to counteract these effects is to increase the deterrence effect from the laws surrounding intellectual property. The most effective way to do that, given the nature of these crimes and the actors who engage in them, is through criminal sanctions. This raises the liability stakes and the accountably. As Jeremy Bentham recognized with his utilitarian "spirit of calculation" theory of criminal justice, the nature of the actors are such that they will rationally choose not to engage in prohibited behaviors if the potential sanction is high enough to outweigh the potential gain of the misconduct. In another words, there must be some higher price to pay than simply restitution to the knowledge creator; there must be serious consequences to deter misappropriation. This would seem to be especially true where the scheme is promoted or fostered by competing governments. Otherwise, all nations run the risk of an escalating race toward technological espionage.

Theft of trade secrets through corruption and bribery has serious economic consequences. Corruption makes economies less competitive because it undermines investment and leads to capital outflows.[42] Furthermore, the more resources the U.S. government and U.S. companies spend on measures to perpetuate or defend against foreign espionage, the less money is available for public projects or tax incentives that might enhance private research and development.[43] Therefore, greater protection of trade secret rights through international and bilateral agreements and decreased offensive economic espionage would protect citizens and private companies and foster economic growth throughout the world.

Judge Posner contended that "the distinctive doctrines of the criminal law can be explained as if the objective of that law were to promote economic efficiency," and has argued specifically that "[t]the major function of criminal law in a capitalist society is to prevent people from bypassing the system of voluntary, compensated exchange – the 'market,' explicit or implicit – in situations where, because transaction costs are low, the market is a more efficient method of allocating resources than forced exchange."[44] Judge Posner specifically noted that "the market-bypassing approach provides a straightforward economic rationale for forbidding theft and other acquisitive crime...."[45]

Some sociologists have expressed the view that the existing legal regime already tilts too heavily in favor of protection of IPRs, including the well-known sociologist John Braithwaite in his book *Information Feudalism,* co-authored with Peter Drahos.[46] In their view, new intellectual property regimes are entrenching new inequalities. Although access to information is fundamental to so much of modern life, Braithwaite and Drahos argue that IPRs have been used to lock up vital information. The result, they argue, will be a global property order dominated by a multinational elite, an elite that expropriates anything from AIDS drugs for Africa, to seeds for developing world farmers, to information on the human genome.

The concerns of Vandana Shiva, Peter Drahos, and John Braithwaite do not so much apply to the issue here, however, because their concerns are primarily addressing patents, which by definition involve public dissemination of knowledge in the body of the patent document. In contrast, economic espionage involves nonpublic, secret knowledge. This is a different category of information.

No one disagrees, however, that some form of protection is needed to foster the development of advancement of technology. It seems unlikely that there is some vast conspiracy at work between the industrial sectors and Western governments to bring about a new kind of feudalism. Experience shows, in fact, that mistrust between the private sector and government is rampant and, consequently, there is insufficient cooperation between law enforcement, legislators, and the private sector to rein in the increasing level of information theft. Such conspiracy theories seem highly unlikely with all these disparate forces working in the marketplace.

As Peter Grabosky has noted, the burden of enforcement is too great to be carried by law enforcement alone. A mixture of law as well as technological and market-base solutions will emerge. Nonetheless, the better course of action would be for governments in developed nations worldwide to adopt a uniform policy toward criminalizing misappropriation of knowledge. Only then can there be effective deterrence and can we avoid a decline into open intelligence warfare among nations.

UNITED STATES CODE
TITLE 18 – CRIMES AND CRIMINAL PROCEDURE
PART II – CRIMINAL PROCEDURE
CHAPTER 90 – PROTECTION OF TRADE SECRETS

Cite as the "Economic Espionage Act of 1996"

§ 1831. Economic espionage

(a) In General – Whoever, intending or knowing that the offense will benefit any foreign government, foreign instrumentality, or foreign agent, knowingly –

(1) steals, or without authorization appropriates, takes, carries away, or conceals, or by fraud, artifice, or deception obtains a trade secret:

(2) without authorization copies, duplicates, sketches, draws, photographs, downloads, uploads, alters, destroys, photocopies, replicates, transmits, delivers, sends, mails, communicates, or conveys a trade secret:

(3) receives, buys, or possesses a trade secret, knowing the same to have been stolen or appropriated, obtained, or converted without authorization:

(4) attempts to commit any offense described in any of paragraphs (1) through (3); or

(5) conspires with one or more other persons to commit any offense described in any of paragraphs (1) through (4), and one or more of such persons do any act to effect the object of conspiracy.

shall, except as provided in subsection (b), be fined not more than $500,000 or imprisoned not more than 15 years, or both.

(b) ORGANIZATIONS – Any organization that commits any offense described in subsection (a) shall be fined not more than $10,000,000.

§ 1832. Theft of trade secrets

(a) Whoever, with intent to convert a trade secret, that is related to or included in a product that is produced for or placed in interstate or foreign commerce, to the economic benefit of anyone other than the owner thereof, and intending or knowing that the offense will, injure any owner of that trade secret, knowingly –

(1) steals, or without authorization appropriates, takes, carries away, or conceals, or by fraud, artifice, or deception obtains such information;

(2) without authorization copies, duplicates, sketches, draws, photographs, downloads, uploads, alters, destroys, photocopies, replicates, transmits, delivers, sends, mails, communicates, or conveys such information;

(3) receives, buys, or possesses such information, knowing the same to have been stolen or appropriated, obtained, or converted without authorization;

(4) attempts to commit any offense described in paragraphs (1) through (3); or

(5) conspires with one or more other persons to commit any offense described in paragraphs (1) through (3), and one or more of such persons do any act to effect the object of the conspiracy, shall, except as provided in subsection (b), be fined under this title or imprisoned not more than 10 years, or both.

(b) Any organization that commits any offense described in subsection (a) shall be fined not more than $5,000,000.

§ 1833. Exceptions to prohibitions

This chapter does not prohibit –

(1) any otherwise lawful activity conducted by a governmental entity of the United States, a State, or a political subdivision of a State; or

(2) the reporting of a suspected violation of law to any governmental entity of the United States, a State, or a political subdivision of a State, if such entity has lawful authority with respect to that violation.

§ 1834. Criminal forfeiture

(a) The court, in imposing sentence on a person for a violation of this chapter, shall order, in addition to any other sentence imposed, that the person forfeit to the United States –

(1) any property constituting, or derived from, any proceeds the person obtained, directly or indirectly, as the result of such violation; and
(2) any of the person's property used, or intended to be used, in any manner or part, to commit or facilitate the commission of such violation, if the court in its discretion so determines, taking into consideration the nature, scope, and proportionality of the use of the property in the offense.

(b) Property subject to forfeiture under this section, any seizure and disposition thereof, and any administrative or judicial proceeding in relation thereto, shall be governed by section 413 of the Comprehensive Drug Abuse Prevention and Control Act of 1970 (21 U.S.C. 853), except for subsections (d) and (j) of such section, which shall not apply to forfeitures under this section.

§ 1835. Orders to preserve confidentiality

In any prosecution or other proceeding under this chapter, the court shall enter such orders and take such other action as may be necessary and appropriate to preserve the confidentiality of trade secrets, consistent with the requirements of the Federal Rules of Criminal and Civil Procedure, the Federal Rules of Evidence, and all other applicable laws. An interlocutory appeal by the United States shall lie from a decision or order of a district court authorizing or directing the disclosure of any trade secret.

§ 1836. Civil proceedings to enjoin violations

(a) The Attorney General may, in a civil action, obtain appropriate injunctive relief against any violation of this section.

(b) The district courts of the United States shall have exclusive original jurisdiction of civil actions under this subsection.

§ 1837. Applicability to conduct outside the United States

This chapter also applies to conduct occurring outside the United States if –

(1) the offender is a natural person who is a citizen or permanent resident alien of the United States, or an organization organized under the laws of the United States or a State or political subdivision thereof; or
(2) an act in furtherance of the offense was committed in the United States.

§ 1838. Construction with other laws

This chapter shall not be construed to preempt or displace any other remedies, whether civil or criminal, provided by United States Federal, State, commonwealth, possession, or territory law for the misappropriation of a trade secret, or to affect the otherwise lawful disclosure of information by any Government employee under section 552 of title 5 (commonly known as the Freedom of Information Act).

§ 1839. Definitions

As used in this chapter

(1) the term 'foreign instrumentality' means any agency, bureau, ministry, component, institution, association, or any legal, commercial, or business organization, corporation, firm, or entity that is substantially owned; controlled, sponsored, commanded, managed, or dominated by a foreign government;
(2) the term 'foreign agent' means any officer, employee, proxy, servant, delegate, or representative of a foreign government;
(3) the term 'trade secret' means all forms and types of financial, business, scientific, technical, economic, or engineering information, including patterns, plans, compilations, program devices, formulas, designs, prototypes, methods, techniques, processes, procedures, programs, or codes, whether tangible or intangible, and whether or how stored, compiled, or memorialized physically, electronically, graphically, photographically, or in writing if –
    (A) the owner thereof has taken reasonable measures to keep such information secret; and
    (B) the information derives independent economic value, actual or potential, from not being generally known to, and not being readily ascertainable through proper means by, the public; and
(4) the term 'owner', with respect to a trade secret, means the person or entity in whom or in which rightful legal or equitable title to, or license in, the trade secret is reposed.

FEDERAL GOVERNMENT GETS 'D' ON SECURITY

GRADES		
Agency	2003	2002
Nuclear Regulatory Commission	A	C
National Science Foundation	A−	D−
Social Security Administration	B+	B−
Labor Department	B	C+
Education Department	C+	D
Veterans Affairs Department[a]	C	F
Environmental Protection Agency	C	D−
Commerce Department	C−	D+
Small Business Administration	C−	F
Agency for International Development	C−	F
Transportation Department	D+	F
Defense Department[a]	D	F
General Services Administration	D	D
Treasury Department[a]	D	F
Office of Personnel Management	D−	F
NASA	D−	D+
Energy Department	F	F
Health and Human Services Department	F	D−
Interior Department	F	F
Agriculture Department	F	F
Housing and Urban Development Department	F	F
State Department	F	F
Homeland Security Department	F	−
Governmentwide average	D	F

[a] No independent evaluation from the inspector general.

Source: House Government Reform Committee's Subcommittee On Technology, Information Policy, Intergovernmental Relations, and the Census.

ECONOMIC ESPIONAGE ACT CASE CHART

Following is a summary chart of cases prosecuted under the Economic Espionage Act (EEA), 18 U.S.C. §§ 1831–9. This chart does not reflect ongoing investigations into the theft of trade secrets. This appendix also provides information about significant cases that involve allegations of trade secret theft, but did not include or have not as of December 2003 resulted in a formal charge under the EEA. The table contains only those cases in which charges have been publicly filed as of 2003.

Economic Espionage Act Cases Colloquial Case Name (District) Press Release Date or Date of Most Recent Court Activity	Violations EEA Comp. Intrusion ITSP Copyright Mail Fraud Wire Fraud	Defendants Ind.	Corp.	Method of Theft Insider Ex-Employee Competitor Outsider	Trade Secret Type of Information Stolen	Punishment Incarceration or Probation in Months	Fine Forfeiture Restitution	Other
U.S. v. Serebryany (C.D. Cal.) September 8, 2003	**EEA**	1	–	Insider	Access card control information	60	146K	
U.S. v. Branch (*Erskine*) (C.D. Cal.) June 25, 2003	**EEA** **Conspiracy**	2	–	Ex-employee, competitor	Competitor proprietary documents	–	–	
U.S. v. Garrison (N.D. Cal.) May 23, 2003	**Comp.** **Intrusion**	1	–	Insider	Engineering drawings and data	–	–	
U.S. v. Woodard (N.D. Cal.) May 14, 2003	**EEA**	1	–	Ex-employee	Proprietary databases	–	–	
U.S. v. Sun (N.D. Cal.) April 11, 2002	**EEA**	1	–	Insider	Customer and business information	–	–	FBI sting

(continued)

(continued)

Economic Espionage Act Cases — Colloquial Case Name (District) — Press Release Date or Date of Most Recent Court Activity	Violations	Defendants Ind.	Defendants Corp.	Method of Theft (Insider / Ex-Employee / Competitor / Outsider)	Trade Secret Type of Information Stolen	Punishment Incarceration or Probation in Months	Punishment Fine Forfeiture Restitution	Other
	EEA Comp. Intrusion ITSP Copyright Mail Fraud Wire Fraud							
U.S. v. Murphy (N.D. Cal.) April 2, 2003	**EEA, Comp. Intrusion**	1	–	Ex-employee	Computer source code	–	–	
U.S. v. Ye (N.D. Cal.) December 4, 2002	EEA **Conspiracy**	2	–	Ex-employee	Project information	–	–	
U.S. v. Morris (D. Del.) October 17, 2002	EEA	1	–	Ex-employee	Proprietary pricing information	–	–	
U.S. v. Kissane (S.D.N.Y.) October 15, 2002	EEA	1	–	Ex-employee	Computer source code	24	–	
U.S. v. Keppel (W.D. Wash.) August 23, 2002	EEA Copyright	1	–	Outsider	Test material	–	–	

192

Case	Charges			Defendant	Trade secret	Sentence	Fine/Restitution	Notes
U.S. v. Zhu (D. Mass.) June 19, 2002	EEA ITSP	2	–	Insider	Genetic screening discoveries	–	–	–
U.S. v. Dorn (D. Kan.) June 3, 2002	EEA	1	–	Insider, outsider	Customer information	–	–	–
U.S. v. Okamoto (N.D. Ohio) May 1, 2002	EEA ITSP	2	–	Insider	DNA cell line	–	–	First indictment under 18 *U.S.C.* § *1831*
U.S. v. ComTriad (D.N.J.) April 11, 2002	EEA Conspiracy	3	1	Insider, outsider	Computer source code	–	–	–
U.S. v. Daddona (D. Conn.) March 12, 2002	EEA Comp. Intrusion	1	–	Insider	Engineering plans	5 home detention 36 prob.	Fine: 4K Rest: 10K	Pled guilty to § 1832 violation
U.S. v. Rector (M.D. Fla.) January 28, 2002	**EEA Comp. Intrusion**	2	–	Insider, ex-employee	Drug delivery system formulas	14	–	FBI sting
U.S. v. Say Lye Ow (N.D. Cal.) December 11, 2001	EEA	1	–	Ex-employee	Microprocess or research	24	–	–
U.S. v. Chang (N.D. Cal.) December 4, 2001	**EEA**	2	–	Insider	Customer information	12	60K	–

(*continued*)

193

(continued)

Economic Espionage Act Cases	Violations	Defendants		Method of Theft	Trade Secret	Punishment		Other
Colloquial Case Name (District) Press Release Date or Date of Most Recent Court Activity	EEA Comp. Intrusion ITSP Copyright Mail Fraud Wire Fraud	Ind.	Corp.	Insider Ex-Employee Competitor Outsider	Type of Information Stolen	Incarceration or Probation in Months	Fine Forfeiture Restitution	
U.S. v. Petrolino (S.D. Fla.) November 29, 2001	EEA EEA Conspiracy	2	–	Outsider	Securities broker customer and account information	–	–	
U.S. v. Wu (W.D.N.Y.) July 31, 2001	EEA	1	–	Ex-employee	Network switch plans	–	–	
U.S. v. Wang (N.D. Cal.) April 26, 2001	EEA	1	1	Insider	Ultrasound machine blueprints	–	–	
U.S. v. Estrada (S.D.N.Y.) March 21, 2001	EEA Comp. Intrusion ITSP	1	–	Outsider	Confidential documents	–	–	FBI sting

Case								
U.S. v. Dai (W.D.N.Y.) August 23, 2001 (sentencing)	**Other**	1	–	Ex-employee	Computer source code	24 prob.	50K	Pled guilty to § 2701 violation
U.S. v. Morch (N.D. Cal.) March 21, 2001	**EEA Comp. Intrusion**	1	–	Ex-employee	Software design documents	36 prob.	–	Charged under EEA; pled to *§ 1030* violation
U.S. v. Corgnati (S.D. Fla.) June 12, 2000 (sentencing)	**EEA**	1	–	Outsider	Software	60 prob.	120K	
U.S. v. Everhart (W.D. Pa.) March 30, 2000 (sentencing)	**EEA**	1	–	Ex-employee	–	–	–	

Glossary

For the purposes of the EEA Case Chart, the following words or phrases are defined:

Violation – This category lists the U.S. Code provisions of the charging document or offenses that were the basis of conviction.

  EEA – The Economic Espionage Act prohibits foreign economic espionage and the theft of trade secrets, 18 U.S.C. §§ 1831–1839.

  Comp. Intrusion – The Computer Fraud and Abuse Act protects the confidentiality, integrity, and availability of electronically stored data, 18 U.S.C. § 1030.

  ITSP – Interstate Transportation of Stolen Property, 18 U.S.C. § 2314.

  Copyright – Criminal copyright infringement, 18 U.S.C. §§ 2318–2319.

  Mail fraud – Prohibits use of the mails in furtherance of a scheme to defraud, 18 U.S.C. § 1341.

  Wire fraud – Prohibits the use of interstate wires in furtherance of a scheme to defraud, 18 U.S.C. § 1343.

Defendants – This category lists the number and type of defendants (individual and/or corporate).

Method of theft – This category indicates the status of the defendant relative to the victim.

  Insider – Crime and arrest occurred while defendant was employed by the victim.

  Ex-employee – Crime may have occurred in part while the defendant was employed by the victim, but arrest occurred after defendant left victim's employ.

  Competitor – Includes individuals or corporations that are in a competitive relationship with the victim.

  Outsider – Includes individuals or corporations that steal trade secrets for their own use or to sell to a third party.

  Trade secret – This category provides a brief description of the stolen trade secret.

Punishment

  Incarceration or probation (months) – Refers to number of months of incarceration (prison, home confinement) imposed on the lead defendant or, if no incarceration was imposed, the number of months of probation.

  Fine, forfeiture, restitution – The combined amount that the lead defendant must pay in fines, restitution, and forfeiture.

Other – This column to note unusual aspects of the case.

Notes

Chapter One

1. Loeb et al. (2001), sec. A, p. 1.
2. Martin (1995), 10.
3. Locke (1884), Chapter V, Book II.
4. See Ewing (1929); Walker (1980).
5. Kant (1887), 195–6.
6. Bentham (1843), 396, 402.
7. The EEA was heavily supported by the U.S. Department of Justice and the FBI, which jointly drafted the first version of the EEA for Congress's consideration. Counterintelligence Executive Notes 13–96 (accessed 2004); National Counterintelligence Executive. "Annual Report to Congress on Foreign Economic Collection ad Industrial Espionage 2001." Accessed June 2004. Available at: <http://www.ncix.gov/docs/fecie_fy01.pdf>. see House Report No. 104-788 (1996), 6 (inapplicability of federal criminal laws). U.S. Congress. House of Representatives. Committee on the Judiciary. House Report no. 104-788 (to accompany H.R. 3723). Washington: GPO, 1996, reprinted in 1996 U.S.C.C.A.N. 402.
8. Murray (accessed 2003).
9. King & Bravin, Call it Mission Impossible, Inc. – Corporate Spying Firms Thrive, *Wall St. J.*, July 3, 2000, at B1. "Revictimization . . . " (2001).
10. Fialka (1997), 18.
11. King & Bravin (2000).
12. Ibid.
13. Ibid.
14. Ibid.; see also Robbins, In the New World of Espionage the Targets are Economic, *N.Y. Daily News*, September 5, 1994 ("American business executives were stunned in 1991 when the former chief of the French intelligence service revealed that his agency had routinely spied on U.S. executives traveling abroad [and] that his agency had regularly bugged first-class seats on Air France so as to pick up conversations by traveling execs, [and] then [entering] their hotel rooms to rummage through attaché cases.").

15. King & Bravin (2000).
16. Ibid.
17. See Gomes (1999), sec. B, p. 1, noting how Microsoft has formed a shadow team around Linux to better understand and anticipate the software and firms offering it.
18. See Wingfield (2000), sec. B, p. 1; see also Lisser (1999), sec. A, p. 1.
19. McCarthy (2000), sec. A, p. 1.
20. Bennett & Mantz (2000), sec. A, p. 34.
21. See Bridis et al. (2000), sec. A, p. 1, noting Oracle sifting through Microsoft's trash.
22. "Revictimization..." (2001).
23. See Nelson and Anders (1999), sec. A, p. 2.
24. See McCartney (2000), sec. B, p. 1.
25. See Bridis et al. (2000), sec. A, p. 1; Stone, B. (2000), 49.
26. "Annual Report to Congress on Foreign..." (1995).
27. See Senate, S12201 S12207, 104th Cong., 2d sess., *Cong. Rec.* (2 October 1996), 142. Congressional Record. "Economic Espionage Act of 1996." Accessed October 2003. Available at: <http://thomas.loc.gov/cgi-bin/query/R?r104:FLD001:S62208-S62210>.
28. See Senate Report No. 104-359 (1996), 8.
29. Freeh statement (1996).
30. Schweizer (1996), 11.
31. Ibid.
32. See "CIA Fingers France..." (1996), sec. A, p. 12; see also Jackamo (1992), 944, citing Gertz (1992), sec. A, p. 1; Behar (1997), 64.
33. See Berthelsen (1994), 28.
34. Foley, T. D. (1994), 143; Dreyfuss, R. (1996), 39; Berthelsen (1994), 28; Alster (1992), 200. "Revictimization..." (2001).
35. See Lowry, T. (1998), sec B, p. 1.
36. Silicon Valley is probably the most targeted area due to the concentration of electronics, aerospace, and biotechnological industries; its ties to Asia; and the mobility and sophistication of its workforce. See Foley, T. D. (1994), 143. See Alster (1992), 200, 204.
37. Freeh statement (1996), 12; see Senate, S12208 S12211, 104th Cong., 2d sess., *Cong. Rec.* (2 October 1996), Freeh, Louis. Statement. Economics Espionage: Joint Hearing Before the Select Comm. on Intelligence of the U.S. Senate and the Subcomm. on Terrorism, Tech., and Gov't Info. of the Comm. on the Judiciary of the U.S. Senate. 104th Cong., 2d Sess., (4 December 1996). Accessed June 2004. Available at: <http://thomas.loc.gov/cgi-bin/query/R?r104:FLD001:S62208-S62210>. 142; Burchette (1994), sec. F, p. 1; "Economic Espionage – Spies Come..." (1991), sec. A, p. 3.
38. Farnham (1997), 114.
39. Yates (1993a), sec. C, p. 1; Freeh statement (1996), 14; Higgins statement (1996).
40. Foley, T. D. (1994), 141–2.
41. King and Bravin (2000), sec. B, p. 1.
42. Ibid.

43. A 3.5-in. computer disk can store approximately 720 pages of double-spaced type. Toren (1996). As one commentator summarized the problem: "An employee can download trade secret information from a company's computer to a diskette, transfer the information to the hard drive of a home computer and then upload it to the Internet, where it can be transmitted worldwide within minutes.... Within days, a U.S. company can lose complete control over its trade secrets forever" Halligan (1996). See also Senate Report No. 104-359 (1996), 18.
44. Davis (1996), 42, 44.
45. Foley, T. D. (1994), 143; Dreyfuss, R. (1996), 39; Berthelsen (1994), 28; Alster (1992), 200.
46. "Russians Arrest..." (1995), sec. D, p. 5.
47. Swartz (1997), sec. A, p. 1 (Statement of Daniel Greer, Director of Engineering for Open Market). "Revictimization..." (2001).
48. Approximately 70% of the market value of a typical U.S. company is in IP assets. See American Society of Industrial Security (1999) (accessed 2003).
49. World Intellectual Property Organization (2003).
50. Ibid.
51. Ibid.
52. Carey (1995), sec. A, p. 8; according to 2000 data, Intel Corp. spends approximately $3.9 billion on research and development annually. Intel Corp. (2000), "2000 Annual Report."
53. Cole (1997), sec. B, p. 10.
54. "Worming Out the Truth," (2000), 89.
55. Industrial espionage is a corporation's use of illegal techniques to collect information, such as trade secrets, not voluntarily provided by the source. See, generally Gilad et al. (1988).
56. Bergier (1969), 3.
57. Jackamo (1992), 945.
58. Ryan (1998).
59. Fraumann (1997).
60. See Specter statement (1996).
61. *USC*, title 18, sec. 1831 (2000).
62. Moyer (1994), 182.
63. Kober (1998), 10.
64. Moyer (1994), 182.
65. Quoted in Schweizer (1993), 9.
66. Bluestein (1996), sec. A, p. 28.
67. "CIA: Israel Among Most 'Extensive' Economic Espionage" (1996), 16.
68. Capaccio (1996), 1.
69. U.S. General Accounting Office (1996), 1.
70. Capaccio (1996), 1
71. Hirst and Breslan (1995), 34.
72. Kaslow (1995), 1.
73. "Shift in Espionage Trends" (2001).
74. See Foley, T. D. (1994); Clark (1997).
75. Schweizer (1996).

76. Gallagher (1998).
77. Canadian Security Intelligence Service, "1996 Public Report, Economic Security" (accessed 2003).
78. *Economic Espionage Act of 1996* (U.S. Statutes at Large, 1996) *USC,* title 18, secs. 1831–1839 (1997).
79. Keithly and Ferris (2002).
80. Jackamo (1992), 945.
81. Boadle (1994).
82. Bergier (1969), 3.
83. Ibid.
84. Fialka (1997).
85. See Schweizer (1993), 5.
86. Burchette (1994), sec. F, p. 1.
87. See Schweizer (1993), 5.
88. Intelligence is categorized as strategic or tactical. See Watson (1990), xi. Strategic intelligence is "information on events, threats, and individuals that create major problems for the federal government." Id. Tactical intelligence is (1) information used to assess military threats against the U.S. armed forces and (2) covert and clandestine operations used to collect information or to influence events.
89. Counterintelligence "may include tracking suspected foreign intelligence operatives, passing on deceptive information to foreign spies, and working with indigenous industries to prevent infiltration by foreign intelligence services" Foley, T. D. (1994), 141–2.
90. See Freeh statement (1996); Fraumann (1997).
91. See Jackamo (1992), 942.
92. Vaknin (2002b).
93. President Clinton stated: "Economic security is vital to U.S. interests. The collection and analysis of intelligence related to economic development will play an increasingly important role in helping policymakers understand economic trends." University of Lethbridge ... *Management Matters* (1997).
94. Carr et al. (2000), 164; House Report No. 104-788 (1996), 5; Senate Report No. 104-359 (1996), 7.
95. *United States v. Hsu,* 155 F.3d 189 (3d Cir. 1998).
96. Carr et al. (2000). "Revictimization ... " (2001).
97. Keithly and Ferris (2002).
98. See *Congressional Record,* 142d Cong., S12208, daily ed. 2 October 1996 (Statement of Sen. Specter).
99. Fialka (1997).
100. Glickman (1994), 144. "With the end of the Cold War, Americans accept today more than ever the premise that economic strength defines national security."
101. See Schweizer (1996), 13.
102. See Cooper statement (1996).
103. See Sherr (1994/1995), 59.
104. See Schweizer (1993), 5.
105. Ibid.

106. Boren (1992), 854.
107. Fialka (1997).
108. See Desmet (1999), 98.
109. Richelson (2000), 41–4.
110. Waller (1995), 50.
111. Richelson (2000), 41–4.
112. Pincus (1996), sec. A, p. 18.
113. Waller (1995), 50.
114. "French Won't Expel U.S. Diplomats" (1995), sec. A, p. 10.
115. Sanger and Weiner (1995), sec. F, p. 1.
116. Landers (1996), sec. D, p. 1.
117. Kelsey and Leppard (1996).
118. Morris et al. (1996), 26.
119. Kelsey and Leppard (1996).
120. Richelson (2000), 41–4.
121. Ibid.
122. Ibid.
123. See *Echelon*, "Answers to Frequently Asked Questions About Echelon," nn. 14, 16, 18, 25, & 28, and accompanying text (accessed 2003). Note that the NSA is actually the American intelligence agency behind Echelon, but the CIA is being implicated for use of the information derived from Echelon.
124. Matthews (2000).
125. Drozdiak (2000), 4.
126. Paine (1991), 250.
127. Landes et al. (1991).
128. *Restatement (Third) of Unfair Competition*, sec. 39, comment a (1995).
129. Deutch (1997), listing English cases.
130. *Vickery v. Welch*, 36 Mass. (1 Pick.) 523, 526 (1837).
131. See *Kewanee Oil Co. v. Bicron Corp.*, 416 U.S. 470, 481–82 (1974), discussing the broad policies supporting trade secret law.
132. See Jager (1996), 1.03, 1–4; 1–8.
133. Ibid.
134. See *Restatements of Torts*, sec. 757 (1939): One who discloses or uses another's trade secret, without a privilege to do so, is liable to the other if (a) he discovered the secret by improper means, or (b) his disclosure or use constitutes a breach of confidence reposed in him by the other in disclosing the secret to him, or (c) he learned the secret from a third person with notice of the facts that it was a secret and that the third person discovered it by improper means or that the third person's disclosure of it was otherwise a breach of his duty to the other, or (d) he learned the secret with notice of the facts that it was a secret and that its disclosure was made to him by mistake.
135. *Restatement (First) of Torts*, sec. 757 (1939).
136. Band et al. (1997).
137. Steiker (1997).
138. Mann, K. (1992), 1807.
139. Fisse (1983), 1147.

140. Steiker (1997).

141. Mossinghoff et al. (1997).

142. See generally, Collins (1997).

143. See Epstein (1995), 1–28.

144. *Economic Espionage Act of 1996* (U.S. Statutes at Large, 1996), 3488; see Mossinghoff et al. (1997), 191–5, discussing reasons for enactment of EEA.

145. *Economic Espionage Act of 1996 section 1831.* Penalties for those convicted of this activity include fines up to $500,000 or imprisonment for up to 15 years, or both.

146. Damadian testimony (1996).

147. Yates (1996), sec. C, p. 1.

148. Damadian testimony (1996).

149. Fialka (1996).

150. The United States is a member of the World Intellectual Property Organization (WIPO) and the World Trade Organization (WTO), both of which administer agreements that have established international IP standards. The WTO's Agreement on Trade Related Aspects of Intellectual Property Rights (TRIPS), Sept. 27, 1994, is the most comprehensive agreement to date, and the first to include enforcement provisions.

151. See *United States Code* (USC), title 18, sec. 2710 (2000) (wrongful disclosure of videotape rental or sales records).

152. See Senate, testimony of Arlen Specter, S12207–08, 104th Cong., 2d sess., *Cong. Rec.* (2 October 1996), 142.

153. See Carr et al. (2000), 168–70. "Revictimization . . . " (2001).

154. "World Forum Designed . . . " (2000), 35.

Chapter Two

1. See Gorelick testimony (1996), 150, 155, describing how technology generally, and information networks specifically, play critical roles in the functioning and development of these important areas.

2. Science and Technology in U.S. International Affairs (1992), 6.

3. See Toffler and Toffler (1993), 19, discussing what they view as the "Third Wave" of civilization.

4. See Arquilla and Ronfeldt (1996), 33–5, explaining that the "network form" involves large-scale use of interconnected groups of information storage and retrieval technologies such as computers.

5. Ramo (1997), 54.

6. Carey (1995), sec. A, p. 8.

7. Cole (1997), sec. B, p. 10.

8. Carey (1995), sec. A, p. 8.

9. See Winton (1995), sec. A, p. 1; "Man Charged . . . " (1995), 8.

10. Simmonsen (2002), sec. A, p. 1.

11. Rosecrance (2000), "News-Early" section, p. 20.

12. Rodger (2000), sec. A, p. 1.

13. The National Fraud Center, Inc. (2000).

14. Young (1996), 70.
15. See Bick (1998).
16. The National Fraud Center, Inc. (2000).
17. O'Reilly (accessed 2003).
18. Lynch (accessed 2003).
19. Approximately 70% of market value of atypical U.S. company is in IP assets. American Society for Industrial Security (1999) (accessed 2003).
20. Department of Justice Website (accessed 1999).
21. Sciglimpaglia (1991), 245.
22. See generally, Stoll (1989).
23. "Cyber-Attacks, Information Theft..." (2001).
24. Ibid.
25. Clark (1997).
26. See Schwartau (1994), 308–10, describing how a concerted attack against critical financial and communication networks could result in widespread panic and lead to a situation resembling anarchy.
27. Ibid.
28. See Schleslinger testimony (1996), arguing that the break-up of the Soviet Union and the Warsaw Pact caused the dissolution of the only military force capable of challenging the advanced "Western" countries on a global scale. The Gulf War indicated the superiority of U.S. and European military forces over regional powers such as Iraq.
29. See Knowles (1997), describing how the U.S. Air Force is now conducting intensive studies of both offensive and defensive information warfare.
30. Toffler (1990).
31. See, e.g., Seper (1993), sec. A, p. 5.
32. See, e.g., Starkman (1998), sec. A, p. 6.
33. See, e.g., Seper (1993), sec. A, p. 5.
34. See, e.g., "911 Lines..." (1997), sec. D, p. 4.
35. See, e.g., McAllester (1997), sec. A, p. 41.
36. See, e.g., "Israeli Teenager Questioned..." (1998), sec. A, p. 4.
37. See, e.g., "Israel Indicts Hackers" (1999), sec. A, p. 4.
38. Wray (1999).
39. Harmon (1998), sec. A, p. 1.
40. See "Cybercrimes," (1998) reporting that Britain, France Germany, Italy, Japan, Russia, and the United States have agreed to work together to ensure sufficient numbers of trained personnel are properly equipped to fight high-tech crime, ensure criminals may be prosecuted where they have fled in the absence of an extradition treaty, ensure important information on computer networks is preserved and tampering is prevented, ensure each country's legal system will support investigation and prosecution of computer crime, promote efforts within the computer industry to detect and prevent computer crime, and permit witnesses to testify through the use of new technologies.
41. See Geist (1998), 551–4, summarizing various countries' policy papers on regulating Internet. Although the EC's 1991 Software Directive is aimed at harmonizing European copyright laws rather than computer security per se,

it does mandate that member states adopt prescribed penalties for software piracy and procedures for seizing illegally copied software, which is a first step toward addressing broader issues raised by computer crimes. See Council Directive 91/250/EEC. *The Legal Protection of Computer Programs.* O.J. (L122) (14 May 1991), 42; 44–6.

42. See Basiouni (1990), 20.
43. See Soma et al. (1997), 343–5.
44. See Charney and Alexander (1996), 949.
45. See Perritt (1996), 51–4.
46. For example, the United Kingdom's computer misuse act provides for broad jurisdiction over crimes that take place on computer networks in the United Kingdom. *Computer Misuse Act,* (1990), ch. 18, secs. 4–9 (England).
47. See, e.g., Ferdinand (1998), sec. A, p. 23; "Argentine Hacker..." (1997), sec. B, p. 10.
48. Ibid.
49. See Beatty (1998), 375.
50. See *USC,* title 18, sec. 2703 (1994 & Supp. 1997).
51. See, e.g., *USC,* title 18, sec. 3123 (1994).
52. See Part III. A. The G-8 is made up of Canada, France, Germany, Italy, Japan, Russia, the United Kingdom, and the United States.
53. See Soma et al. (1997), 343–5.
54. See Heymann (1997), 390.
55. For example, at the FBI, data forensics (i.e., extracting information from computers) is coordinated by the Computer Analysis and Response Team (CART), which is headquartered in Washington, DC, with trained agents in offices nationwide. Similarly, for computer intrusion cases, FBI efforts are coordinated by the National Infrastructure Protection Center (NIPC). See National Infrastructure Protection Center web site (accessed 2003). On the prosecution side, these efforts are coordinated in Washington, DC, by the Department of Justice's Computer Crime and Intellectual Property Section (CCIPS) and throughout the country by Assistant U.S. Attorneys designated as Computer-Telecommunications Coordinators (CTC). See U.S. Department of Justice, CCIPS Introduction (accessed 2003).
56. See Goodman (1997), 489.
57. See Shackelford (1992), 503.
58. See Aldrich (2000).

Chapter Three

1. Yellen and Kalamajka (2002), 1.
2. See U.S. Department of Justice, CCIPS Introduction (accessed 2003), mentioning increasing concern over intellectual property crime as societal reliance on intellectual property grows.
3. See Welsh et al. (2001); "Corporate Raiding: Handling, Preventing and Litigating..."(2001); Reno (accessed 2001).
4. "India: Netspionage Coming of Age..." (2001).

5. Hulme (2002), 36.
6. Ibid.
7. See U.S. International Trade Commission (1988), 1-1, 4-2.
8. Gilpin (1987), 112.
9. The Clinton Administration established the National Economic Council to give economic issues the same importance the National Security Council gives national security. See Kober (1998).
10. Nelan (1993), 29.
11. See Freeh statement (1996).
12. See Schweizer (1996), 13.
13. Intangible property "has no intrinsic and marketable value, but is merely the representative or evidence of value, such as certificates of stock, bonds, promissory notes, copyrights, and franchises." Garner (1999).
14. See Heffernan testimony (1996), noting a survey that found that intangible assets of U.S. manufacturing companies rose from 38% to 52% of market value from 1982 to 1992.
15. See Toren (1994), 60–1.
16. Fraumann (1997).
17. See Freeh statement (1996).
18. Sennott (1997b), sec. F, p. 2.
19. Barth (1998), 34, quoting John Schiman, special agent of the FBI in Los Angeles.
20. Ibid.
21. Ibid.
22. Sepura (1998).
23. Ibid.
24. Ibid.
25. McGugan (1995), 99.
26. Fialka (1997), 18.
27. Schweizer (1996).
28. "Trade in Secrets" (1994).
29. Schweizer (1996).
30. Ibid.
31. Moyer (1994), 182.
32. Jackamo (1992), 945.
33. Fialka (1997), 18.
34. See Clarke (1998), 21. Clark relates Israel's motivations for engaging in economic espionage. However, these motivations are equally applicable to all nations, whether emerging or already successful.
35. Crock (1997), 17.
36. See *G.S. Rasmussen & Assoc., Inc. v. Kalitta Flying Serv., Inc.*, 958 F.2d 896, 900 (9th Cir. 1992).
37. U.S. Congress, Senate Report No. 105-190 (1998), 10.
38. Sepura (1998), 131.
39. Jackamo (1992), 945.
40. "Trade in Secrets" (1994).

41. See *Intermedics, Inc. v. Ventritex, Inc.*, 822 F. Supp. 634, 642–643 (N.D. Cal. 1993), discussing, in part, the "continuing tort theory" and whether the various jurisdictions view "the principal interest protected by... trade secret law as 'property' or as 'confidential relationships.'"

42. See Winkler (1997), xvi.

43. See Pace (1995), 436.

44. *Kewanee Oil Co. v. Bicron Corp.*, 416 U.S. 470, 487 (1974), holding that state protection of trade secrets does not operate to frustrate the achievement of the congressional objectives served by the patent laws.

45. American Society of Industrial Security (2000) (accessed 2003), 28.

46. "Revictimization..." (2001).

47. U.S. Congress, Senate Report No. 104-359 (1996), 11.

48. See Veltrop (1997), 6 ("The new 'Cold War' revolves around the battle for technology."), noting the burgeoning use of computers and the Internet to facilitate the theft and transmission of confidential databases and technology.

49. OECD, *Computer Related Crime...* (1986), 25.

50. Yushkiavitshus (1996), 51.

51. See Moyer (1994).

52. Boadle (1994).

53. Canadian Security Intelligence Service, "1996 Public Report, Economic Security" (accessed 2003).

54. Heffernan and Swartwood (1996), 4.

55. Senate, S12213, 104th Cong., 2d sess., *Cong. Rec.* (2 October 1996), 142.

56. See U.S. Congress, Senate Report No. 104-359 (1996), 8.

57. Nelson, J. (1998), sec. A, p. 1.

58. See U.S. Congress, House Report No. 104-788 (1996), 5–6.

59. See Dreyfuss, R. (1996), 37, 39 (statement of Frank Dudley Berry, Deputy District Attorney in the High Technology Unit of the Santa Clara District Attorney's Office) ("It's nonsense.... There isn't any [economic espionage]. It doesn't exist.").

60. See, e.g., Toren (1994), 62.

61. "House Judiciary Panel Backs..." (1996) ($24 billion); "Economic Espionage: The Corporate Threat" (accessed 1996) ($260 billion).

62. See "U.S. Losing High-Tech Secrets..." (1997).

63. Cillufo (2001).

64. See U.S. Department of Justice, CCIPS Introduction (accessed 2003).

65. Keithly and Ferris (2002).

66. "The Enemy Within" (2002), 9.

67. Ibid.

68. Parra (2002), Business Monday, sec. F, p. 6.

69. Hulme (2002), 36.

70. Iwata (2003), Money section B, p. 1.

71. Parra (2002), Business Monday, sec. F, p. 6.

72. "Proprietary Information Theft..." (2002).

73. Schneier testimony (2003).

74. Computer Security Institute. *Issues and Trends: 1998 CSI-FBI Computer Crime and Security Survey* (1998).

75. Honeynet Project (accessed 2004).

76. "Annual Report to Congress on Foreign..." (2001).

77. See Schweizer (1993), 5.

78. Yates (1993a), sec. C, p. 1.

79. See Senate, testimony of Arlen Specter, S12201–03, 104th Cong., 2d sess., *Cong. Rec.* (2 October 1996), 142.

80. Norton-Taylor (1997).

81. Fialka (1997), 18.

82. See *G.S. Rasmussen & Assoc., Inc. v. Kalitta Flying Ser., Inc.*, 958 F.2d 896, 900 (9th Cir. 1992).

83. See *Intermedics, Inc., v. Ventritex, Inc.*, 822 F. Supp. 634, 642–643 (N.D. Cal. 1993), discussing, in part, the "continuing tort theory" and whether the various jurisdictions view "the principal interest protected by... trade secret law as 'property' or as 'confidential relationships.'" For example, if company Z develops a cure for AIDS at a high cost, it must be allowed to profit significantly from that innovation to recoup its investment and encourage other firms to invest in finding cures for illnesses in the hope of achieving similar profits. However, if company A, a competitor of company Z, finds a comparatively inexpensive way to steal the formula for the AIDS cure from company Z, and subsequently manufactures its own AIDS cure for a fraction of the cost company Z incurred while sharing the humanitarian credit and financial windfall, it is likely that company Z will no longer invest in research and development because its return on investment will be quite low.

84. See Winkler (1997). However, see Senate, statement of Arlen Specter, S12207–08, 104th Cong., 2d sess., *Cong. Rec.* (2 October 1996), 142, positing that the absence of development costs can lead to reduced prices; Petersen (1998), sec. C, p. 1, reporting that competitor lured customers away by using lower prices.

85. *Kewanee Oil Co. v. Bicron Corp.*, 416 U.S. 470, 487 (1974), holding that state protection of trade secrets does not operate to frustrate the achievement of the congressional objectives served by the patent laws.

86. Shoichet (2002), 32.

87. Ibid.

88. For additional background on the motivation and legislative history of the act, see Pooley et al. (1997).

89. Heffernan and Swartwood (1996), 4, 15.

90. Howard (2002).

91. A sensitive technology is an unclassified subject/topic identified by the DOE that involves information, activities, and/or technologies that are relevant to national security. Disclosure of sensitive subjects has the potential for enhancing foreign nuclear weapons capabilities, divulging military critical technologies, or revealing other advanced technologies.

92. See Senate, statement of Senator Specter, S12201, S12210, 104th Cong., 2d sess., *Cong. Rec.* (2 October 1996), 142, incorporating Schweizer (1996).

93. Ibid.

94. Brockett (2002), 17.

95. Ibid.

96. Ibid.
97. "Pair from Cupertino..." Department of Justice press release (Dec. 4, 2002).
98. Ibid.
99. Ibid.
100. See Mathiason and Juarez (1995), 188, 189; see *California v. Eubanks*, 927 P.2d 310 (Cal. 1996), as modified and rehearing denied, 1997 Cal. Lexis 1016 (software company paid for services of two computer experts to assist prosecutor).
101. *Fraser v. Nationwide Mut. Ins. Co.*,135 F.Supp.2d 623 (E.D. Pa. 2001).
102. Ibid.
103. Ibid.
104. Carr et al. (2000), 172.
105. See Morse (1997), 8.
106. Carr et al. (2000), 172.
107. Toren (1994), 62.
108. See also Foley and Dash (1999), 9, discussing the high degree of employee mobility in today's society; Tyler (1997), FT Weekend, 1 ("The problem is the loyalty – or lack of it – of employees in a world of short contracts, rapid turnover and big inducements.").
109. "Revictimization..." (2001).
110. See Morse (1997), 8.
111. *Uniform Trade Secrets Act* sec. 2(a) (amended 1985), *ULA*, Title 14, Secs. 433–467 (Supp. 1998). The Uniform Trade Secrets Act has been passed by forty states and the District of Columbia.
112. "Cyber-Attacks, Information Theft..." (2001).
113. Carr et al. (2000), 173.
114. Senate, S12213, 104th Cong., 2d sess., *Cong. Rec.* (2 October 1996), 142.
115. Band et al. (1997), 1.
116. "Revictimization..." (2001).
117. *Rockwell Graphics Sys., Inc. v. Dev Indus., Inc.*, 91 F3d 914, 917 n.3 (7th Cir. 1996) (citation omitted).
118. Pooley et al. (1997), 195.
119. "Revictimization..." (2001).
120. See Milgrim (1999), 1.05[5], summarizing the legality of such study with respect to patents, copyrights, and trade secrets.
121. See *Kewanee Oil Co. v. Bicron Corp.*, 416 U.S. 470, 476 (1974), defining reverse engineering as "starting with the known product and working backward to divine the process which aided in its development or manufacture."
122. See *Brooktree Corp. v. Advanced Micro Devices, Inc.*, 977 F.2d 1555, 1570 (Fed. Cir. 1992), finding the accused infringer to have copied, rather than reverse engineered, the maskwork.
123. See, e.g., *USC*, title 17, sec. 906(a) (Supp. 1998), providing a defense to infringement of a protected maskwork where the reproduction was "solely for the purpose of teaching, analyzing, or evaluating the concepts or techniques embodied"; see also *Atari Games Corp. v. Nintendo of America Inc.*, 975 F. 2d 832, 845 Fed. Cir. 1992, finding that the replication of unnecessary instructions in

the resulting computer code was evidence of copying, not independent creation resulting from reverse engineering.

124. See *Brooktree Corp. v. Advanced Micro Devices, Inc.*, 977 F.2d 1555, 1567 (Fed. Cir. 1992), reviewing the requirements for a reverse engineering defense.
125. Pooley et al. (1997), 179–87.
126. Nelson, J. (1998), sec. A, p. 1.
127. See U.S. Constitution, article I, sec. 8, cl. 8.
128. Weisner and Cava (1988).
129. See Seidel (1984), 2.03.
130. See Marriot (1997), sec. B, p. 6.
131. See Heed (1996), 210–11, stating that, between 1985 and 1994, reported incidents of misappropriated trade secrets rose 260% and tripled from 1993 to 1995.
132. See Lowry, S. (1988), noting that "trade secret litigation is burgeoning."
133. See Toren (1994), 60–1.
134. See Bradsher (2000), sec. C, p. 1.
135. See Harmon (2001a), sec. C, p. 2.
136. See Harmon (2001b), sec. C, p. 4. Senate Report No. 105-190 (1998), 10.
137. Brockett (2002), 17.
138. Dilworth (accessed 2003).
139. Yates (1993a), sec. C, p. 1.
140. See Powell (1994).
141. Winter (2002), sec. D, p. 1.
142. Ibid.
143. Ibid.
144. Brockett (2002), 17.

Chapter Four

1. Porter (1980).
2. Meyerowitz and Fryer (2002), p. 5, col. 4.
3. "Shedding the Trench Coat" (2001), Features, p. 70.
4. "Annual Report to Congress on Foreign..." (1995). The 1996 report "noted little new in the origin of the threat, collection targets, or methods used in effecting economic collection and industrial espionage." "Annual Report to Congress on Foreign..." (1996).
5. Keithly and Ferris (2002).
6. O'Hearn and Sozio (2001).
7. Brockett (2002), 17.
8. Meyerowitz and Fryer (2002), p. 5, col. 4.
9. See Schweizer (1997b), sec. G, p. 5. The critical question is whether economic espionage is within the definition of economic intelligence, and hence within the act.
10. Pasternak and Witkin (1996), 45.
11. Meyerowitz and Fryer (2002), p. 5, col. 4.
12. Ibid.

13. Elliott (2002).

14. See Toren (1994). Rather than copying documents manually, a thief can down-load information onto a computer disk, which is then easily removed from an office. In his comments to the Senate Select Committee on Intelligence, FBI Di-rector Louis Freeh stated: "Where hackers formerly may have been motivated by the technical challenge of breaking into a computer system, the motivation may be shifting more toward hacking for profit. As more and more money is trans-ferred through computer systems, as more fee-based computer services are in-troduced, as more sensitive proprietary economic and commercial information is exchanged electronically, and as the nation's defense and intelligence commu-nities increasingly rely on commercially available information technology, the tendency toward information threats emerging as national security threats will increase." *Current and Projected Nat'l Sec. Threats to the U.S.: Hearings...* (1998), 35.

15. U.S. General Accounting Office (1996).

16. "Annual Report to Congress on Foreign..." (1995).

17. See Mills (1997), sec. C, p. 1.

18. Ryberg (1997), 44.

19. Stone, B. (1997), 53.

20. Ibid.

21. Ibid.

22. Barth (2001).

23. Ibid.

24. U.S. General Accounting Office (1996).

25. Iwata (2003), Money section B, p. 1.

26. Fialka (1997), 18.

27. See Schweizer (1993), 5.

28. "Annual Report to Congress on Foreign..." (1995).

29. Fialka (1997), 149–60, explaining how Chinese and Japanese students flood American schools and corporations.

30. "Annual Report to Congress on Foreign..." (1995).

31. Ibid.

32. Barth (1998), 34, quoting John Schiman, special agent of the FBI in Los Angeles.

33. See Schweizer (1993), 5.

34. Yates (1993a), sec. C, p. 1.

35. Canadian Security Intelligence Service, "1996 Public Report, Economic Security" (accessed 2003).

36. See "Annual Report to Congress on Foreign..." (1995); "Annual Report to Congress on Foreign..." (1996).

37. Yates (1993a), sec. C, p. 1.

38. Barth (1998), 34, quoting John Schiman, special agent of the FBI in Los Angeles.

39. "Annual Report to Congress on Foreign..." (1995).

40. See Robbins (1994), sec. C, p. 10.

41. Murray (accessed 2003).

42. See Murray (1998).

43. See DeYoung (1996), 12.

44. See Coile (1994), sec. D, p. 1.

45. See *Novell, Inc. v. Weird Stuff, Inc.*, No. C92-20467 JW/EAI, 1993 U.S. Dist. Lexis 6674, at 5 (N.D. Cal. May 14, 1993).
46. Fialka (1997), 18.
47. Boadle (1994).
48. "Annual Report to Congress on Foreign..." (2001).
49. Ibid.
50. Ibid.
51. See Schweizer (1993), 5.
52. "Annual Report to Congress on Foreign..." (2001).
53. Wheeler (2002), 26.
54. Ibid.
55. Ibid.
56. Ibid.
57. Ibid.
58. "Annual Report to Congress on Foreign..." (2001).
59. See Lowry, T. (1998), sec. B, p. 1.
60. Ibid.
61. "Annual Report to Congress on Foreign..." (2001).
62. Ibid.
63. Ibid.
64. See Schweizer (1993), 5.
65. See U.S. Congress, House Report No. 104-788 (1996), 4. "The United States produces the vast majority of the intellectual property in the world."
66. See Schweizer (1993), 5.
67. "Annual Report to Congress on Foreign..." (2001).
68. Ibid.
69. Ibid.
70. Katsh and Dierks (1995). For example, Canada, China, Germany, Italy, Japan, Korea, Mexico, the United Kingdom, and the United States have adopted express statutory protection for trade secrets.
71. Seita (1997), 486.
72. See Schweizer (1996), 13.
73. Yates (1993a), sec. C, p. 1.
74. "CIA: Israel Among..." (1996).
75. See Schweizer (1993), 5.
76. McGugan (1995), 99.
77. Ibid.
78. Hobson (accessed 1998). The Futures Group is a competitive intelligence consultant in the United States.
79. "Annual Report to Congress on Foreign..." (1995).
80. Canadian Security Intelligence Service, "1996 Public Report, Economic Security" (accessed 2003).
81. Kober (1998), 10.
82. Moyer (1994), 182.
83. Moyer (1994), 182; Jackamo (1992), 945.
84. Murray (accessed 2003).

85. See Jopeck and Sawka (accessed 1996).
86. See Freeh statement (1996); Fraumann (1997).
87. Yates (1993a), sec. C, p. 1.
88. See Freeh statement (1996); Fraumann (1997).
89. Wheeler (2002), 26.
90. Ibid.
91. Ibid.
92. Shoichet (2002), 32.

Chapter Five

1. Molander et al. (1998), 34.
2. Clinton (1998).
3. Toffler and Toffler (1980).
4. Pethia testimony (2003).
5. Ibid.
6. Ibid.
7. Ibid.
8. Ibid.
9. Ibid.
10. Ibid.
11. Ibid.
12. Reno keynote address (accessed 2003).
13. Pethia testimony (2003).
14. Ibid.
15. See Olivenbaum (1997), 574–5, arguing that "the protean difficulty of defining computer crime," victims' reluctance to report it, and dual system of prosecution have made statistical figures suspect.
16. See Charney and Alexander (1996), 934, stating that term "computer crime" eludes precise definition.
17. See Friedman and Bissinger (1996).
18. A joint study of the Business Software Alliance (BSA) and the Software & Information Industry Association (SIIA) estimated that the global software industry lost $11 billion to software piracy in 1998; the loss for 1997 was estimated to be $11.4 billion. See 1998 Global Software Piracy Report (1999). A WarRoom Research study showed that of 236 corporations studied, 58% reported suffering computer break-ins in the previous year. See Friedman and Bissinger (1996). Of those 58%, 66% incurred damages exceeding $50,000 and 18% suffered losses in excess of $1 million.
19. Sen (2000).
20. "Air Force Websites . . . " (1996), 32.
21. Most computer hacking that causes injury is penalized under one or more federal or state statues. See, e.g., *USC*, title 18, sec. 1030 (2000).
22. See Dillon et al. (1998), 543.
23. Swartz (1997), sec. A, p. 1 (statement of Daniel Geer, director of engineering for Open Market in Cambridge, Massachussets).

24. "Russians Arrest..." (1995), sec. D, p. 5.

25. Bowman (1996), 1943.

26. Sen (2000).

27. See Branscomb (1990), 24–6.

28. Sen (2000).

29. *United States v. Morris*, 928 F.2d 504 (2d Cir. 1991), cert. denied, 502 U.S. 817 (1991).

30. Ibid.

31. "Computer Whiz Guilty of Planting Rogue Virus," *Chicago Sun-Times*, Jan. 23, 1990, at 3, available in 1990 WL 4381438.

32. *United States v. Morris*, 928 F.2d 504 (2d Cir. 1991), cert. denied, 502 U.S. 817 (1991).

33. Ibid.

34. See, e.g., *United States v. Morris*, 928 F.2d 504 (2d Cir. 1991), cert. denied, 502 U.S. 817 (1991). Robert Morris was convicted under the CFAA, *USC*, title 18, sec. 1030(a)(5)(A) (2000), for releasing a worm that eventually caused 6,000 computers to crash. However, Morris did not have a criminal mens rea when he released the program. He merely wanted to prove his ability to write a program capable of accessing as many computer systems as possible without destroying, damaging, or copying any data contained therein. He actually attempted to warn potential victims about his program when he realized it was out of control.

35. See Costantini (1996).

36. See Zuckerman (1996), sec. B, p. 4.

37. See Sieber (1993), 69–70.

38. Taiwan and South Korea have indicted companies for illegally copying software for internal use. See Business Software Alliance (1991), *BSA World-wide Report 1990–1991*. In Great Britain, software piracy carries prison terms up to 2 years. See Business Software Alliance, *United Kingdom: Software Piracy and the Law*. Similar French laws also provide for restitution, doubled penalties for repeat offenders, and court-ordered business closings. See Business Software Alliance, *France: Software Piracy and the Law*. Singapore provides for up to five years' imprisonment for illegally copying software. See Business Software Alliance, *Singapore: Software Piracy and the Law*. See generally, the Intellectual Property Crimes section in this Report.

39. See Park (1990), 433–4.

40. Charney and Alexander (1996), 934.

41. Sieber (1986).

42. "United Nations Manual on Prevention..." (accessed 2003), citing Carroll (1996).

43. Barton (1995), 469–76, citing definitional problems arising from application of old statutes criminalizing communications to computer transmissions.

44. Adams, J. (1996), 408, cited in Parker, D.B. (1989), 2.

45. See Dillon et al (1998), 543.

46. Goodman (2001).

47. See, e.g., Knoll (1996).

48. The OECD is comprised of twenty-nine countries: Australia, Austria, Belgium, Canada, the Czech Republic, Denmark, Finland, France, Germany, Greece, Hungary, Iceland, Ireland, Italy, Japan, Luxembourg, Mexico, The Netherlands, New Zealand, Norway, Poland, Portugal, South Korea, Spain, Sweden, Switzerland, Turkey, the United Kingdom, and the United States. Although the OECD does not have legal powers, its guidelines, reports, and publications can have a major policy impact on policy making for both member and non member countries. The OECD's Internet address is http://www.oecd.org.
49. "United Nations Manual on Prevention..." (accessed 2003), citing Carroll (1996).
50. The British Misuse Act takes an approach simpler than either of those proposed by the international bodies, choosing to group all computer crimes under three broad offenses: unauthorized access, unauthorized access with further criminal intent, and intentional unauthorized modification. Computer Misuse Act (1990).
51. See Soma et al. (1997), 359–60, listing actions called for by United Nation's resolution on computer-related crimes.
52. "Proprietary Information Theft..." (2002).
53. U.S. Department of Justice, CCIPS Introduction (accessed 2003).
54. The Computer Emergency and Response Team Coordination Center (CERT/CC) was formed by the Defense Advanced Research Projects Agency (DARPA), part of the U.S. Department of Defense, in November 1988 to work with the Internet community in detecting and resolving computer security incidents as well as taking steps to prevent future incidents. CERT/CC is now part of the Survivable Systems Initiative at the Software Engineering Institute, a federally funded research and development center at Carnegie Mellon University. See Carnegie Mellon Software Engineering Institute, CERT Coordination Center.
55. CERT Coordination Center 1998 Annual Report.
56. Ibid.
57. See Vistica (2000), 48, noting that attacks on computer systems has concerned federal officials who fear penetration of U.S. computers by foreign countries.
58. See Persico (1999), 155–6.
59. See Shackelford (1992), 494, describing globalization of access to computer systems.
60. See Lange (1996), estimating that $800 million was lost by banks and other corporations because of attacks on their computer systems, such as one perpetrated by Russian programmer Vladimir Levin, who tampered with Citibank's computer system by transferring $10,000,000 to various bank accounts around the world.
61. See, generally, Solomon (1995), 645, reporting on use of new computer technology as effective and dangerous mechanism exploited by international criminals.
62. See Nobel (1999), 48–52.
63. Ibid.
64. See Reno statement (accessed 2003).
65. "Cyber-Attacks, Information Theft..."(2001).
66. Computer Security Institute. *CSI-FBI Computer Crime Security Survey* (2003).

67. Sen (2000).
68. For a description of various Denial of Service (DoS) attacks, see http://searchsecurity.techtarget.com/sDefinition/O,,sid14_gci557336,00.html.
69. See CERT Coordination Center, "Trends in Denial..." (2001).
70. Hulme (2002), 36.
71. See Denial of Service (DoS) attack, PC Webopedia Definition and Links.
72. See Dungan (accessed 2003).
73. See Husman (accessed 2003).
74. See CERT Coordination Center Research, "Denial-of-Service Incidents" (accessed 2003).
75. Center for Strategic and International Studies (1998) (accessed 2003).
76. Goodman (2001).
77. Ibid.
78. Ibid.
79. Ibid.
80. Ibid.
81. Ibid.
82. Ibid.
83. Welch (2002), sec. C, p. 3.
84. See Reno statement (accessed 2003).
85. See FBI Press Room – "Congressional Statement for the Record of Charles L. Owens..." (accessed 1997).
86. See Reno statement (accessed 2003).
87. Ibid.
88. Ibid.
89. See Hatcher et al. (1999), 420–1.
90. See Tillett (accessed 2003).
91. See Piller (2000), sec. A, p. 1, providing an overview of the state of cybercrime and associated concerns.
92. See Rovella (2000), sec. A, p. 1, noting that one such position exists in each of the nation's ninety-three U.S. Attorney's Offices.
93. See Markey and Boyle (1999), 23, stating that the CFAA was enacted to help stop computer abuse and has had many revisions in order to achieve semifunctioning.
94. See Vistica (2000), 48, noting that attacks on computer systems has concerned federal officials who fear penetration of U.S. computers by foreign countries.
95. See, generally, Cilluffo et al. (1999), 130, 140, providing illustrative examples of how vulnerable computer systems can become.
96. Welch (2002), sec. C, p. 3.
97. See Barbaro (2002), sec. E, p. 5.
98. To learn more about the CSI (a San Francisco-based international association of computer security professionals) or its survey, visit the CSI web site.
99. See CSI, "Cybercrime..." (accessed 2002).
100. Ibid. The respondents who were capable of quantifying their losses said they lost close to $115.8 million due to financial fraud and $170.8 million from the theft of proprietary information.

101. Simmonsen (2002), sec. A, p. 1.
102. Hulme (2002), 36.
103. Nadlemann (1993), 1.
104. Harris memorandum (1998).
105. See Ford (2000), 1.
106. See Behar (1997), 56, 66.
107. See Nash (1993), 2, noting that the case actually involved prosecution against two individuals, former Borland International Vice President Eugene Wang and Symantec CEO Gordon Eubanks.
108. See Behar (1997), 56, 66.
109. See "Reno Opposes..." (1999), noting, alternatively, the FBI proposes that companies provide the FBI with a "key" to unlock the code.
110. See O'Harrow (2000), sec. E, p. 1, recognizing former computer hacker Kevin Poulsen as editorial director of a web site called SecurityFocus.com.
111. See Olivenbaum (1997), 577–8, discussing federal legislation and the need to consider new alternatives.
112. Ibid.
113. See James (2001), sec. C, p. 1, reporting consumer class action brought against online companies for failing to secure consumers' credit card data adequately; "Nike Sued..." (2001), reporting threatened suit against Nike for loss of business resulting from Nike's alleged failure to secure computers.
114. Latham (1979).
115. Commons (1924); Friedman (1978), 300–6.
116. Barnouw (1966).
117. Edelman (1979).
118. "Cyber-Attacks, Information Theft... "(2001).
119. See, e.g., Soma et al (1996), 226–30, positing that twenty-three different U.S. Code sections criminalize certain conduct involving computers and information networks.
120. *USC*, title 18, sec. 1030 (2000).
121. See Markey and Boyle (1999), 23, stating that the CFAA was enacted to help stop computer abuse and has had many revisions in order to achieve semifunctioning.
122. *USC*, title 18, sec. 1030(a) (2000).
123. *USC*, title 18, sec. 1030(a)(5)(A) (2000).
124. *USC*, title 18, sec. 1030(g) (2000).
125. *USC*, title 17, sec. 506 (1994).
126. See Schwartau (1994), 308–10, describing how a concerted attack against critical financial and communication networks could result in widespread panic and lead to a situation resembling anarchy.

Chapter Six

1. *Peabody v. Norfolk*, 98 Mass. 452, 457 (Mass. 1868).
2. See *Act of 4 March 1909, U.S. Statutes at Large* 35 (1909), 1082.
3. See Public Law No. 97-180, *U.S. Statutes at Large* 96 (1982), 92.

4. See Public Law No. 102-561, *U.S. Statutes at Large* 105 (1992), 4233.
5. See Public Law No. 103-325, *U.S. Statutes at Large* 108 (1994), 2111.
6. See Public Law No. 104-253, *U.S. Statutes at Large* 110 (1996), 1386.
7. See Net Act (16 December 1997).
8. See *USCA*, title 18, sec. 2319(b)(1) (West Supp. 1998).
9. See *Economic Espionage Act of 1996* (codified at USC, title 18, secs. 1831–1839 [Supp. II 1996]).
10. Senate, statement of Senator Specter, S12207–08, 104th Cong., 2d sess., *Cong. Rec.* (2 October 1996), 142.
11. Paris Convention (1883).
12. Paris Convention (1883), reprinted in Leaffer (1997), 20–43.
13. Dreyfuss, R. C. (2001), 423.
14. Paris Convention (1883).
15. *International Treaties on Intellectual Property* 561 (Marshall A. Leaffer ed., BNA Inc. 2d ed. 1997).
16. Convention Establishing the World Intellectual Property Organization, July 14, 1967, 21 U.S.T. 1749, 829 U.N.T.S. 3 [hereinafter WIPO Convention], Available at: http://www/wipo.org/members/convention/conl.html (last visited Oct. 14, 2001).
17. Agreement on Trade-Related Aspects of Intellectual Property Rights (1994), 81.
18. Katsh and Dierks (1995). For example, Canada, China, Germany, Italy, Japan, Korea, Mexico, the United Kingdom, and the United States have adopted express statutory protection for trade secrets.
19. GATT (1993).
20. Combeau (1996), 58.
21. GATT (1993).
22. "North American Free Trade Agreement (NAFTA)," (1992), 612, approved by Congress on 3 December 1993, *USC*, title 19, sec. 3311(a) (2000).
23. *Restatement of Torts*, sec. 757 cmt. b (1939).
24. General Assembly Resolution 1236 (1957).
25. General Assembly Resolution 2131 (1965).
26. Palmer (1999), Business section, 16.
27. Convention on Combating Bribery of Foreign Public Officials in International Business Transactions (accessed 2003).
28. The OECD is a Paris-based multilateral organization founded in 1960 with an annual budget of approximately $200 million. It consists of thirty member countries that together produce two-thirds of the world's goods and services and includes the home countries of almost all large multinational enterprises. OECD, "About OECD" (accessed 2003).
29. "1998 OECD Convention . . . " (2000).
30. Hansen (1998), 1–1.
31. "Treaty Establishing the European Economic Community" (1957).
32. Waterschoot (1998), 2-1.
33. "Treaty Establishing the European Economic Community" (1957).
34. See Simensky et al. (1999), 25.10.
35. The Treaty provisions have been renumbered. Article 81(3) was formerly 85(3).

36. "Commission Regulation No. 2658/2000..." (accessed 2003).
37. "Commission Regulation No. 566/89..." (1989), 1.
38. "Commission Regulation No. 240/96..." (1996), 2.
39. Aoki (1998), 22–23.
40. Blair (2000), sec. B, p. 7.
41. See, e.g., American Bar Association, "Section of Intellectual Property Law" (accessed 2003), listing upcoming intellectual property protection seminars.
42. The "rust belt" is the "economic region in the NE quadrant of the United States, focused on the Midwestern ... states of Illinois, Indiana, Michigan, and Ohio, as well as Pennsylvania." Encyclopedia.com (accessed 2003) (on file with the *Connecticut Law Review*).
43. *Economic Espionage Act of 1996, USC*, title 18, secs. 1831, 1832 (1997).
44. Howard (2002).
45. U.S. Congress, House Report No. 104-788 (1996), 5, reprinted in 1996 U.S.C.C.A.N. 4021, 4024.
46. See Simon (1998).
47. Tucker D. S. (1997), 1110. This intrusion can be attributed to intelligence resources that were once used to secure military technologies now becoming available.
48. Pooley et al. (1997), 179.
49. *USC*, title title 18, sec. 1905 (1994 & Supp. IV 1998).
50. See Mossinghoff et al. (1997), 196.
51. See U.S. Congress, House Report No. 104-788 (1996), 12–13.
52. See U.S. Congress, Senate Report No. 104-359 (1996), 6.
53. See generally, Kerr (1997), 27–8, discussing lengthy discovery processes and low-priority docket scheduling for noncriminal cases.
54. Freeh statement (1996); see also Loeb (1998), sec. A, p. 1, reporting that the CIA is recruiting candidates with technical skills to strengthen its espionage.
55. See Cundiff (1997), 9, 22.
56. See *Economic Espionage Act of 1996*.
57. *United States v. Hancock*, Crim. No. CR88–319A (N.D. Ga. 1988) (prosecuted by Kent Alexander).
58. *United States v. Huang Dao-Pei*, Crim No. 2:98m04090 (D.N.J. 1998).
59. *National Stolen Property Act* (1940).
60. Howard (2002).
61. See U.S. Congress, House Report No. 104-788 (1996), 7, reprinted in 1996 U.S.C.C.A.N. 4021, 4025–26.
62. Ibid.
63. Howard (2002).
64. Ibid.
65. See generally, Kerr (1997), 27–8, discussing lengthy discovery processes and low-priority docket scheduling for noncriminal cases.
66. *Kewanee Oil Co. v. Bicron Corp.*, 416 U.S. 470, 489–490 (1974).
67. Available at: <http:www.nsi.org/Library/Espionage/usta.html>.
68. Slind-Flor (1997), sec. A, p. 11.
69. "Reviewing..." (2002), 1.

70. Rush et al. (2000), 21.
71. Chatterjee (1996), 856.
72. See *Restatement of Torts*, sec. 757 (1939).
73. "What Purchasing Managers..." (2001).
74. Ibid.
75. Ibid.
76. *Restatement (Third) of Unfair Competition* sec. 39 (1995).
77. Ibid.
78. "What Purchasing Managers..." (2001).
79. Ibid.
80. Ibid.
81. Ibid.
82. Carr et al. (2000), 172.
83. *USC*, title 18, sec. 1839(3)(B) (Supp. V 1999).
84. See Fraumann and Koletar (1999), 64.
85. "Revictimization..." (2001).
86. Toren (1994).
87. Arkin (1996), 3.
88. See USC, title 35, secs. 100–105 (Supp. 1998), outlining the requirements for patenting an "invention."
89. USC, title 35, sec. 102 (1994), detailing the "novelty" requirement for patentability.
90. See USC, title 35, sec. 103 (Supp. 1998), detailing the "non-obvious subject matter" requirement for patentability.
91. See USC, title 35, sec. 115 (Supp. 1998), requiring the inventor to submit an oath stating that he believes himself to be the first inventor.
92. USC, title 35, sec. 102(b) (1994), denying patentability if an invention is patented, described in a printed publication, publicly use, or placed on sale more than 1 year prior to the date of the application.
93. Chisum (2000), OV[1].
94. USC, title 35, sec. 284 (1998), providing for damages not less than a reasonable royalty, including interest and costs.
95. *Amstar Corp. v. Envirotech Corp.*, 730 F 2d 1476, 1481–82 (Fed. Cir. 1984), explaining that patent infringement is determined by comparing the accused product and the patent claims, not by comparing the accused and patented products.
96. Chisum (2000), OV[1].
97. See Epstein (1995), 1.03, 1–28.
98. See Pace (1995), 436.
99. See U.S. Congress, Senate Report No. 104-359 (1996), 11.
100. See Pace (1995), 446–447; Lao (1998), 1671–4.
101. See Waller and Byrne (1993), 7–8, noting that the United States has made the enforcement a top priority, often conditioning trade concessions on the enforcement of IPRs by recipient nations.
102. See Samuels and Johnson (1990), 49–51.
103. *Uniform Trade Secrets Act*, sec. 1, *ULA*, title 14, sec. 438 (1990). The UTSA defines misappropriation as: (i) acquisition by improper means; or (ii) disclosure or

use of a trade secret of another without express or implied consent by a person who (A) used improper means to acquire knowledge of the trade secret; or (B) at the time of disclosure or use, knew or had reasons to know that his knowledge of the trade secret was (I) derived from or through a person who had utilized improper means to acquire it; (II) acquired under circumstances giving rise to a duty to maintain its secrecy or limits its use; or (III) derived from or through a person who owed a duty to the person seeking relief to maintain its secrecy or limits it use; or (C) before a material change of his [or her] position, knew or had reason to know that it was a trade secret and that knowledge of it had been acquired by accident or mistake.

104. See Augustini (1994), 475.
105. See Freeh statement (1996); Loeb (1998), sec. A, p. 1, reporting that the CIA is recruiting candidates with technical skills to strength its espionage.
106. "What Purchasing Managers..." (2001).
107. Ibid.
108. Ibid.
109. See Pooley et al. (1997), 200.
110. "Revictimization..." (2001).
111. Howard (2002).
112. See *USCA*, title 18, sec. 1832(a) (2000).
113. See Pooley et al. (1997), 200.
114. Carr et al. (2000).
115. See U.S. Congress, House Report No. 107-788 (1996), 7.
116. For more detailed discussion of how a company might satisfy this "reasonable measures" hurdle, see Carr et al. (2000).
117. See Senate, S12213, 104th Cong., 2d sess., *Cong. Rec.* (2 October 1996), 142.
118. Ibid.
119. Ibid.
120. "Revictimization..." (2001).
121. Carr et al. (2000).
122. 18 U.S.C. §1837(2).
123. Carr et al. (2000).
124. *USC*, title 18, sec. 1837(1) (2000).
125. Pooley et al. (1997), 204.
126. "Revictimization..." (2001).
127. Toren (1996), 648. As one commentator summarized the problem: An employee can download trade secret information from a company's computer to a diskette, transfer the information to the hard drive of a home computer, and then upload it to the Internet, where it can be transmitted worldwide within minutes.... Within days, a U.S. company can lose complete control over its trade secrets forever. Halligan (1996), sec. B, p. 6; see also U.S. Congress, Senate Report No. 104-359 (1996), 20, available in 1996 WL 497065.
128. *USC*, title 18, sec. 1837 (1998).
129. See Hodkowski (1997), 222.
130. See U.S. Congress, House Report No. 104-788 (1996), 5–7, reprinted in 1996 U.S.C.C.A.N. 4021, 4023–26.
131. See Crock and Moore (1997), 76, 77–8.

132. Case No. 97-CR-288 (N.D. Ohio); see *United States V. Yang*, No. 1:97 CR 288, 1999 WL 1051714 (N.D. Ohio, Nov. 17, 1999), denying the defendants' motion for a new trial or reconsideration of their motion for a mistrial.
133. *United States v. Pin Yen Yang*, Criminal No. 1:97MG0109 (N.D. Ohio 1997).
134. See Starkman (1997), sec. B, p. 1, 4.
135. See Arevalo et al. (1999).
136. See FBI Press Release (accessed 1999).
137. See "Business Watch Legal" (1997), sec. D, p. 3.
138. See "Spies Step Up Attacks..." (1998), 60.
139. See "Ex-Kodak Employee Sentenced" (1997), sec B, p. 2, pt. A.
140. U.S. Department of Justice Press Release (1997a, 1997b).
141. Nelson, E., et al. (1996), sec. A, p. 1.
142. Ibid.
143. McMorris (1998), sec. B, p. 5.
144. Halligan (accessed 2003), citing *United States v. Kai-L Hsu*, Criminal No. 97–323 (E.D. Pa. 1997).
145. Rovella (1999), sec. B, p. 1.
146. See *United States v. Hsu*, 982 F. Supp. 1022, 1022–23 (E.D. Pa. 1997).
147. "EDPA Sentences..." (1991), 7.
148. Ibid.
149. See also *United States v. Kai-Lo Hsu, et al.*, 155 F.3d 189, 193 n.2 (1997).
150. Halligan (accessed 2003), citing *United States v. Worthington*, Criminal No. 97–9 (W.D. Pa. 1996).
151. See Schweizer (1997b), sec. A, p. 15.
152. See Crock and Moore (1997), 76, 77–8.
153. See *United States v. Worthing*, Crim. No. 97–9 (W.D. Pa., Crim. Complaint filed Dec. 9, 1996).
154. "Superseding Indictment..." (2002).
155. Ibid.
156. Gertz (2002), sec. A, p. 1.
157. Ibid.
158. Ibid.
159. "Veridian Targeted by Spy?" (2002).
160. No. 02–20145-JW, indictment issued (N.D. Cal. Dec. 4, 2002).
161. "Feds Charge Two..." (2003), 5.
162. Vrana (2003), 15.
163. Ibid.
164. See Carr et al. (2000).
165. "Revictimization..." (2001).
166. See Sennott (1997b).
167. See also Hosteny (1998).
168. The Four Pilliars, Indexx Labs, and RAPCO cases.
169. Seltzer and Burns (1999).
170. E.g., the Worthing, Gillette, Deloite & Touche, and Vactec cases.
171. See, e.g., Schweizer (1997), sec. A, p. 15.
172. See Horowitz (1998).
173. See Senate, S12207–08, 104th Cong., 2d sess., *Cong. Rec.* (2 October 1996), 142.

Chapter Seven

1. Gallagher statement (accessed 2003).
2. See Perry (1995).
3. Brandes et al. (2000), 659.
4. The U.S. Constitution grants Congress the power to "promote the Progress of Science and Useful Arts, by securing for limited times to Authors and Inventors the exclusive right to their respective writings and discoveries." U.S. Const. art. I, sec. 8, cl. 8.
5. See U.S. Const. art. I, sec. 8, cl. 8.
6. Holder (accessed 1999).
7. Ibid.
8. See Augustini (1995), 476–81, discussing Allied espionage against American business.
9. Schmetzer (1995), 3.
10. See Augustini (1995), 476–81, discussing Allied espionage against American business.
11. Vaknin (2002a).
12. Mueller statement (1996).
13. Ibid.
14. Edsall (2002), sec. E, p. 10.
15. Ibid.
16. Ibid.
17. Ibid.
18. Pooley et al. (1997), 196–7.
19. *USC*, title 8, sec. 1839(3)(A) (2000).
20. See *USC*, title 18, sec. 1832 (a)(1)–(3) (1998), specifying acts taken "without authorization."
21. Flaming (1993), 287.
22. Hohfeld (1913), 21–3.
23. See Feinberg (1984), 218–21.
24. See Dreyfuss, R. C. (1998).
25. See Goodin (1996).
26. Ros-Lehtinen hearing (2000).
27. Moyer (1994), 182.
28. Seita (1997), 486.
29. Moyer (1994), 182.
30. See Kanuck (1996), 276, quoting UN Charter, art. II, para. 4.
31. Halligan (accessed 2003), not citing the specific NAFTA provisions.
32. "Annual Report to Congress on Foreign . . . " (1995).
33. Moyer (1994), 182.
34. "Annual Report to Congress on Foreign . . . " (1995).
35. Fialka (1997), 18.
36. "Japan Changes . . . " (2002).
37. "Govt Aims to Fight Industrial Espionage" (2002), 22.
38. Rothstein et al. (1999), 642–70.
39. Coffee (1988), 139.

40. Shapiro (1995), 224.
41. Shiva (2001).
42. Sohmen (1999), 870.
43. Clark (1997).
44. Posner (1985).
45. Ibid.
46. Drahos and Braithwaite (2002).

References

"Across the Nation." *Seattle Times*, 21 August 2002.

Adams, James. *The Next World War: Computers Are the Weapons and the Front Line is Everywhere*. New York: Simon and Schuster, 1998.

Adams, Jo-Ann M. "Comment, Controlling Cyberspace: Applying the Computer Fraud and Abuse Act to the Internet." *Santa Clara Computer and High Technology Law Journal*, vol. 12 (1996). Cited in National Institute of Justice, U.S. Department of Justice, *Computer Crime: Criminal Justice Resource Manual*. Washington, DC: GPO, 1989.

Agre, Philip E. "Your Face Is Not a Bar Code: Arguments Against Automatic Face Recognition in Public Places." 9 September 2001. Accessed 9 September 2003. Available at: <http://dlis.gseis.ucla.edu/people/pagre/bar-code.html>.

Agreement on Trade-Related Aspects of Intellectual Property Rights, 15 April, 1994. "Marrakesh Agreement Establishing the World Trade Organization." Annex 1C, *Legal Instruments – Results of the Uruguay Round*, vol. 31, *International Legal Materials*, vol. 33 (1994) [TRIPS Agreement]. Reprinted in *International Treaties on Intellectual Property*, edited by Marshall Leaffer. Washington, DC: BNA Books, 1997.

"Air Force Websites Shut as Hackers Gain Access, Change Files." *Wall Street Journal*, 31 December 1996.

Akdeniz, Yaman, Clive Walker, and David Wall. *The Internet, Law and Society*. Harlow: Longman, 2000.

Aldrich, Richard W. "Cyberterrorism and Computer Crimes: Issues Surrounding the Establishment of an International Legal Regime." *INSS Occasional Paper* 32, Information Operation Series (April 2000). USAF Institute for National Security Studies, USAF Academy, Colorado Springs, Colorado.

"How Do You Know You Are at War in the Information Age?" *Houston Journal of International Law*, vol. 22 (fall 1999).

Allen, Mary. "Secret Trader Gets Weekends in Jail." *News Journal* (Delaware), 5 February 2003.

Alster, Norm. "The Valley of the Spies." *Forbes*, 26 October 1992.

American Bar Association. Section of Intellectual Property Law. *American Bar Association Homepage*. Accessed 4 July 2003. Available at: <http://www.abanet.org/intelprop/home.html>.

"American Chemistry Council Statement on EPA Computer Security." *U.S. Newswire*, 11 August 2000.

American Society of Industrial Security & Pricewaterhouse Coopers. "Trends in Proprietary Information Loss Survey Report 1999." Accessed 4 July 2003. Available at: <http://www.pwcglobal.com/extweb/ncsurvres.nsf/(ViewA-gentBy KeyDisplay)/all_all_us_eng>.

   "Trends in Proprietary Information Loss Survey Report 2000." Accessed 4 July 2003. Available at: <http://www.pwcglobal.com/extweb/ncsurvres.nsf/(ViewAgentByKey Display)/all_all_us_eng>.

Amstar Corp. v. Envirotech Corp., 730 F 2d 1476, 1481-82 (Fed. Cir. 1984).

"Annual Report to Congress on Foreign Economic Collection and Industrial Espionage." 1995. Accessed 3 July 2003. Available at: <http://www. fas. org/sgp/othergov/indust.html>.

   1996. Accessed 3 July 2003. Available at: <http://www.apg.army. mil/tenants/902dmi/ARTICLES/Fy96rpt.htm>.

   1998. Pacific Northwest National Laboratory.

   2001. Office of the National Counterintelligence. Accessed 20 July 2003. Available at: <http://www.ncix.gov/pubs/reports/fy01.htm>.

Anthes, Gary H. "Target: Electronic Spies Beefing Up Corporate Computer Security Alert Program." *Computer World*, 28 October 1996.

Aoki, Keith. "Neocolonialism, Anticommons, Property and BioPiracy in the (Not-so-Brave) New World Order of International Intellectual Property Protection." *Indiana Journal of Global Legal Studies*, vol. 6 (1998).

Arevalo, Penny, Steve Andersen, and Bruce Rubenstein. "Circuit by Circuit." *Corporate Legal Times*, July 1999. Available in Lexis-Nexis (Legal News).

"Argentine Hacker Who Invaded Pentagon Enters Guilty Plea." *Wall St. J.*, 8 December 1997.

Arkin, Stanley S. "When Theft of an Idea Can Be a Crime." *New York Law Journal*, 11 April 1996.

Arquilla, John, and David Ronfeldt. *The Advent of Net War*. Santa Monica, CA: RAND, 1996.

Asbrand, Deborah. "Who's Holding the Bag for the Hackers?" *The Standard: Intelligence for the Internet Economy*. Accessed 4 July 2003. Available at: <http://www.thestandard.com/article/0,1902,10840,00.html>.

Association for Computing Machinery. "Denial of Service." *University of Illinois, Urbana-Champaign*. Accessed 5 July 2003. Available at: <http://www.acm.uiuc.edu/workshops/security/deny.html>.

Atari Games Corp. v. Nintendo of America Inc., 975 F. 2d 832, 845(Fed. Cir. 1992).

Augustini, Jeff. "Note, From Goldfinger to Butterfinger: The Legal and Policy Issues Surrounding Proposals to Use the CIA for Economic Espionage." *Law and Policy in International Business*, vol. 26 (winter 1995).

Band, Jonathan, et al. "The Economic Espionage Act: Its Application in Year One." *Corporate Counsel*, November 1997.

Barbaro, Michael. "Internet Attacks on Companies up 28 Percent, Report Says." *Washington Post*, 8 July 2002.

Barkley, John. "Denial of Service." Accessed 5 July 2003. Available at: <http://csrc.nist.gov/publications/nistpubs/800-7/node117.html>.

Barnouw, Erik. *A History of Broadcasting in the United States, A Tower in Babel.* New York: Oxford University Press, 1966.

Barth, Steve. "Protecting the Knowledge Enterprise; Knowledge Management Techniques and Theory." *Knowledge Management* 4 (1 March 2001).

"Spy vs. Spy." *World Trade*, 1 August 1998.

Barton, Gene. "Taking a Byte out of Crime: E-Mail Harassment and the Inefficacy of Existing Law." *Washington Law Review*, vol. 70 (1995).

Basiouni, Mammoud Cherif. "Effective National and International Action Against Organized Crime and Terrorist Criminal Activities." *Emory International Law Review*, vol. 4 (1990).

Bass, Kenneth C., III. "Relevant Intelligence in the Post-Cold War World." Accessed 13 January 1997. Available at: <http://199.34.61.2/govern/fulltext.html>.

Beatty, Donna L. "Comment, Malaysia's 'Computer Crimes Act 1997' Gets Tough on Cybercrime but Fails to Advance the Development of Cyberlaws." *Pacific Rim Law and Policy Journal*, vol. 7 (1998).

Beck, Matthew E., and Matthew E. O'Brien. "Corporate Criminal Liability." *American Criminal Law Review*, vol. 36 (2000).

Behar, Richard. "Who's Reading Your E-mail?" *Fortune*, 3 February 1997.

Bennett, Johanna, and Beth Mantz. "Amgen's Patent Infringement Trail Draws Rivals' Lawyers in Search of Data." *Wall St. J.*, 26 June 2000.

Bentham, Jeremy. "Principles of Penal Law, Part II: Rationale of Punishment." In *The Works of Jeremy Bentham, vol. 1,* edited by John Bowring. Edinburgh: William Tait, 1843.

Bergier, Jacques. *Secret Armies: The Growth of Corporate and Industrial Espionage.* Translated by Harol J. Salemson. Indianapolis: Bobbs-Merrill Co., Inc., 1975.

Berthelsen, John. "Friendly Spies." *Far Eastern Economic Review*, 17 February 1994.

Bick, Jonathan D. "Why Should the Internet Be Any Different." *Pace Law Review*, vol. 19 (1998).

Blair, Margaret M. "New Ways Needed to Assess New Economy." *L.A. Times*, 13 November 2000. Lexis News Library, Lat File.

Blake, Harlan M. "Employee Agreements Not to Compete." *Harvard Law Review*, vol. 73 (1960).

Bluestein, Paul. "France, Israel Alleged to Spy on U.S Firms." *Washington Post*, 16 August 1996.

Boadle, Anthony. "Canada Spy-Catcher Says High-Tech Firms Targeted." *The Reuter European Business Report*, 13 April 1994.

Boren, David L. "The Winds of Change at the CIA." *Yale Law Journal*, vol. 101 (1992).

Borrus, Amy. "Why Pinstripes Don't Suit the Cloak-and-Dagger Crowd." *Business Week*, 17 May 1993.

Bowman, M.E. "International Security in the Post-Cold War Era: Can International Law Truly Effect Global Political and Economic Stability? Is International Law Ready for the Information Age?" *Fordham International Law Journal*, vol. 19 (1996).

Bradsher, Keith. "Former G.M. Executive Indicted on Charges of Taking Secrets." *N.Y. Times*, 23 May 2000.

Brandes, Ronnie Heather, et al. "Intellectual Property Crimes." *American Criminal Law Review*, vol. 37 (2000).

Branscomb, Anne W. "Rogue Computer Programs and Computer Rogues: Tailoring the Punishment to Fit the Crime." *Rutgers Computer and Technology Law Journal*, vol. 16 (1990).

Brendel, Neal, and Lucas Paglia. "The Economic Espionage Act." *Pennsylvania Law Weekly*, 7 July 1997.

Bridis, Ted, et al. "How Piles of Trash Became Latest Focus in Bitter Software Feud." *Wall St. J.*, 10 July 2000.

Brockett, Daniel L. "Companies Need to Keep Sharp Eye on Trade Secrets." *Crain's Cleveland Business*, 15 July 2002.

Brooktree Corp. v. Advanced Micro Devices, Inc., 977 F.2d 1555, 1570 (Fed. Cir. 1992).

Buckley, Neil, and Robert Graham. "Europe: MEP's to Vote on Probe of US-UK "Spying' Satellite." *Financial Times* (London), 5 July 2000.

Burchette, Lloyd M., Jr. "Economic Espionage is a Big Threat to National Security." *Greensboro News & Record* (North Carolina), 6 March 1994.

Burton, Mark. "Problems and Alternatives: Government Spying for Commercial Gain." Accessed 2002. Available at: <http://www.odci.gov/csi/studies/unclass1994.pdf>.

Business Software Alliance. "1998 Global Software Piracy Report." Accessed 4 July 2003. Available at: <http://global.bsa.org/usa/press/newsreleases//1999-05-25.239.phtml>.

Business Software Alliance. 1998 Global Software Piracy Report. Washington, D.C.: International Planning and Research Corporation for the Business Software Alliance, May 1999. Business Software Alliance. Software Piracy and the Law. Accessed July 2003. Available at: <http://global.bsa.org/usa/antipiracy/law/Piracy_Law03.pdf>.

Business Software Alliance. Eighth Annual BSA Global Software Piracy Study: Trends in Software Piracy, 1994–2002. June 2003. Accessed July 2003. Available at: http://www.bsa.org/globalstudy/loader.cfm?url=/commonspot/security/getfile.cfm &pageid=12927&hitboxdone=yes

BSA World-wide Report 1990–91. Washington, DC: BSA, United States, 1991.

"Business Trends; Management." *Electronic Business*, 1 January 2002.

"Business Watch Legal." *Sun-Sentinel* (Ft. Lauderdale), 14 November 1997.

Campbell, Duncan. "Inside Echelon." 25 July 2000. Accessed 2002. Available at: <http://www.heise.de/tp/english/inhalt/te/6929/1.html>.

Campbell, Duncan, and Paul Lashmar. "Revealed: 30 More Nations with Spying Stations." *Independent* (London), 9 July 2000.

Canadian Security Intelligence Service. "1996 Public Report, Economic Security." Accessed 7 July 2003. Available at: <http://www.csis-scrs.gc.ca/eng/publicrp/pub1996_e.html>.

Capaccio, Tony. "Report Highlights Espionage Threat from Israel, Allies." *Defense Week*, 26 February 1996.

Carey, Pete. "Software Engineer Charged in Theft of Pentium Plans from Intel." *Seattle Times*, 24 September 1995.

Carnegie Endowment for International Peace. Website. Accessed 15 September 2003. Available at: <http://www.ceip.org/>.

Carr, Chris, et al. "The Economic Espionage Act: Bear Trap or Mousetrap?" *Texas Intellectual Property Law Journal*, vol. 8 (winter 2000).

Carroll, John. *Computer Security. 3rd ed.* St. Louis, MO: Butterworth-Heinemann, 1996.

Carter, Jimmy. "Amendments to the Manual for Courts-Martial, United States, 1969 (Revised Edition)." Executive Order 12,238, 1 September 1980.

CCIPS, Introduction. Accessed 4 July 2003. Available at: <http://www.cybercrime.gov/ccips.html>.

CDT (Center for Democracy and Technology) "pages on wiretapping and surveillance." Accessed 15 September 2003. Available at: <http://www.cdt.org>. Policy Post 6.15.

Center for Strategic and International Studies (CSIS). Cybercrime...Cyberterrorism...Cyberwarefare...(1998). Accessed July 2003. Available at: <http://www.csis.org>.

Central Intelligence Agency. Accessed 1 July 2003. Available at: <http://www.cia.gov>.

CERT Coordination Center. "CERT/CC Statistics 1988–2000." Accessed 4 July 2003. Available at: <http://www.cert.org/stats/cert_stats.html>.

Computer Emergency Response Team 1995 Annual Report. Pittsburgh, PA: Carnegie Melon University, 1995.

CERT Coordination Center. *Computer Emergency Response Team 1998 Annual Report*. Pittsburgh, PA: Carnegie Melon University, 1998.

"Trends in Denial of Service Attack Activity" (October 2001). Accessed July 2003. Available at: <http://www.cert.org/archive/pdf/DoS_trends.pdf>.

CERT Coordination Center Research. "Denial-of-Service Incidents." Accessed 5 July 2003. Available at: <http://www.cert.org/research/JHThesis/Chapter11.html>.

CERT. "Home Network Security." Accessed 15 September 2003. Available at: <http://www.cert.org/tech_tips/home_networks.html>.

CERT Coordination Center. CERT Coordination Center 1998 Annual Report (Summary) (1999). Accessed July 2003. Available at: <http://www.cert.org/annual_rpts/cert_rpt_98.html>.

Cha, Ariana Eunjung. "Hackers Steal Subscriber Data from AOL Network." *Washington Post*, 17 June 2000.

Charney, Scott, and Kent Alexander. "Computer Crime." *Emory Law Journal*, vol. 45 (1996).

Chatterjee, Neel. "Should Trade Secret Appropriation be Criminalized." *Hastings Communications and Entertainment Law Journal*, vol. 19 (fall 1996).

Children's Online Privacy Protection Act. Public Law 277, 105th Con., 2d sess., (21 October 1998).

Chicago Lock Co. v. Fanberg, 676 F.2d 400, 404 (9th Cir. 1982).

Children's Online Privacy Protection Rule. 64 *Federal Register* 59888 (3 November 1999).

Childs, Kelvin. "Feds Arrest Two for Newspaper Espionage." *Editor and Publisher Magazine*, 21 February 1998.

Chisum, Donald S. *Chisum on Patents*. Albany, NY: Matthew Bender Publishing, 2000.

"CIA Fingers France, Israel for Economic Espionage." *Orlando Sentinel Tribune*, 15 August 1996.

"CIA: Israel Among Most 'Extensive' In Economic Espionage." *Defense Week*, 5 August 1996.

Cillufo, Frank J. "Security Threats to Americans Overseas, Congressional Testimony." Federal Document Clearing House (3 April 2001).

Cillufo, Frank J., et al. "Bad Guys and Good Stuff: When and Where Will the Cyber Threats Converge?" *DePaul Business Law Journal*, vol. 12, no. 30 (1999).

Clark, Michael T. "Economic Espionage: The Role of the United States Intelligence Community." *Journal of International Legal Studies*, vol. 3 (1997).

Clarke, Duncan L. "Israel's Economic Espionage in the United States." *Journal of Palestine Studies*, vol. 27 (1998).

Clinton, William J. Commencement Address to the U.S. Naval Academy. May 1998.

Coffee, John C. "Hush!: The Criminal Status of Confidential Information After McNally and Carpenter and the Enduring Problem of Overcriminalization." *American Criminal Law Review*, vol. 26 (1988).

Cohen, Jerry, and Alan S. Gutterman. *Trade Secrets Protection and Exploitation*. Washington, DC: BNA Books, 1998.

Coile, Zachary. "Better Shred Than Read." *San Francisco Examiner*, 29 August 1994.

Cole, Michelle. "Proliferation of High Tech Firms Fosters Espionage." *Idaho Statesman*, 27 April 1997.

Collins, Cindy. "Trade Secrets: The Economic Espionage Act, Friend or Foe?" *Inside Litigation*, September 1997.

Combeau, Jacques. "Protection of Undisclosed Information." In *Intellectual Property and International Trade: A Guide to the Uruguay Round TRIPS Agreement Paris, France*, edited by Tania Saulnier et al. New York: International Chamber of Commerce, 1996.

Commission Regulation No. 240/96 of 31 January 1996 on the application of Article 81(3) of the Rome Treaty to Certain Categories Technology Transfer Agreements. 1996 O.J. (L 31) 2.

Commission Regulation No. 566/89 of November 1988 on the application of Article 85(3) of the Rome Treaty to Certain Categories of Know-How Licensing Agreements. 1989 O.J. (L 61) 1.

"Commission Regulation No. 2658/2000 of 29 November 2000 on the application of Article 81(3) of the Treaty to Categories of Specialisation

Agreements." Accessed 3 July 2003. Available at: <http://europa.eu.int/smartapi/cgi/sga_doc?smartapi!celexapi!proc!CELEXnumdoc&lg=en&num doc=32000R2658&model=guichett>.

"Commission Regulation No. 2659/2000..." (accessed 2003). [Office for Official Publications of the European Communities, Commission Regulation (EC) No 2659/2000 of 29 November 2000, On the Application of Article 81(3) of the Treaty to Categories of Research and Development Agreements, at http://europa.eu.int/eur-lex/en/consleg/pdf/2000/en_2000R2659_do_001.pdf (last visited July 2003).

Commons, John R. *The Legal Foundations of Capitalism*. Madison: University of Wisconsin Press, 1924.

Computer Misuse Act. (1990), ch. 18, secs. 4–9 (England).

Computer Security Institute. "Cyber Attacks Rise From Outside and Inside Corporations: Dramatic Increase in Reports to Law Enforcement." Accessed 5 March 1999. Available at <http://www.gocsi.com/prelea990301.htm>.

CSI-FBI Computer Crime and Security Survey, vol. 8. San Francisco: CSI, 2003.

Issues and Trends: 1998 CSI-FBI Computer Crime and Security Survey. San Francisco: CSI, 1998.

Computer Security Institute web site. Accessed 4 July 2003. Available at: <http://www.gocsi.com>.

"Computer Whiz Guilty of Planting Rogue Virus." *Chicago Sun-Times*, 23 January 1990, 3. Available in 1990 WL 4381438.

Congressional Record. Washington, D.C.: GPO, 1996.

Convention Establishing the World Intellectual Property Organization. 14 July 1967. Accessed 3 July 2003. Available at <http://www.wipo.int/treaties/convention/index.html>.

Convention on Combating Bribery of Foreign Public Officials in International Business Transactions. 17 December 1997. Accessed 3 July 2003. Available at: <http://ue.eu.int/ejn/data/vol_c/9_autres_textes/20nov1en.html>.

Cooper, David E. Statement before U.S. Senate Committee on Intelligence of the U.S. Senate and the Subcomm. on Terrorism, Tech., and Gov't Info. of the Comm. on the Judiciary of the U.S. Senate. *Economic Espionage: Joint Hearing Before the Select Comm. on Intelligence of the U.S. Senate and the Subcomm. on Terrorism, Tech., and Gov't Info. of the Comm. on the Judiciary of the U.S. Senate*. 104th Cong., 2d Sess., (4 December 1996) [Cooper statement].

"Corporate Legal Times Roundtable: Protecting Trade Secrets Requires Multiple Approaches." *Corporate Legal Times*, October 1998.

Corporate Raiding: Handling, Preventing and Litigating the Theft of Corporate Employees and Information. New York: Practicing Law Institute, 2001.

Costantini, Peter. "Information Warriors Form New Army. *International Press Service*, 9 August 1996. Available in 1996 WL 10768646.

Council Directive 91/250/EEC. *The Legal Protection of Computer Programs*. May 14, 1991 O.J. (L122) 42; 44–46.

Council of Europe Criminal Law Convention. Accessed 3 July 2003. Available at: <http://conventions.coe.int/treaty/en/Treaties/Html/173.htm>.

Crock, Stan. "Business Spies: The New Enemy Within?" *Business Week*, 10 February 1997.

Crock, Stan, and Jonathan Moore. "Corporate Spies Feel a Sting." *Business Week*, 14 July 1997.

Cundiff, Victoria A. "The Economic Espionage Act and You." In *Third Annual Institute for Intellectual Property Law*, PLI Patents, Copyrights, Trademarks, and Literary Property Course Handbook Series, No. G-490, 1997.

Current and Projected Nat'l Sec. Threats to the U.S.: Hearings Before the Select Comm. on Intelligence of the U.S. Senate, 105th Cong., 2d Sess. 35 (1998).

"Cyber-Attacks, Information Theft, and the Online Shakedown: Preparing for and Responding to Intrusions of Computer Systems." *Electronic Banking Law and Commerce Reporter*, vol. 6 (October 2001).

"Cybercrime Bleeds U.S. Corporations, Survey Shows." Accessed 7 April 2002. Available at <http://www.gocsi.com/press/20020407.htm>.

"Cybercrimes." *Cyberspace Law*, vol. 3, no. 1 (1998).

Daly, James. "Netherlands, Mexico Chase After Hackers." *Computerworld*, 13 July 1992.

Damadian, Raymond. *Testimony before the House Comm. on the Judiciary Subcomm. on Crime*. Federal Document Clearing House, 9 May 1996. Available in 1996 WL 10163734 [Damadian testimony].

Davis, Susan E. "Gangster Tech." *California Lawyer*, June 1996.

"Defense Commissary Agency." Accessed 3 July 2003. Available at: <http://www.commissaries.com/>.

Denning, Dorothy E. "Cyberterrorism, Testimony before the Special Oversight Panel on Terrorism, Committee on Armed Services." U.S. House of Representatives. 23 May 2000. Accessed 2002. Available at: <http://www.cs.georgetown.edu/~denning/infosec/cyberterror.html>.

Desmet, Thierry Olivier. "The Economic Espionage Act of 1996: Are We Finally Taking Corporate Spies Seriously?" *Houston Journal of International Law*, vol. 22 (1999).

Deutch, Miguel. "The Property Concept of Trade Secrets in Anglo-American Law: An Ongoing Debate." *University of Richmond Law Review*, vol. 31 (1997).

Deutsch, Andrew L. "Practice Tip; Protecting the Co.'s Trade Secrets." *Start-Up & Emerging Companies Strategist*, vol. 3 (September 2002).

Devost, Matthew G., Brian K. Houghton and Neal A. Pollard. "Information Terrorism: Political Violence in the Information Age." Accessed 2002. Available at: <http://www.terrorism.com/Denning.html>.

DeYoung, H. G. "Thieves Among Us: If Knowledge Is Your Most Important Asset, Why Is It So Easily Stolen?" *Industry Week*, 17 June 1996.

Dickson, Paul, and Joseph Goulden. *Myth-Informed: Legends, Credos and Wrongheaded Facts We All Believe*. New York, NY: Perigree Books, 1993.

Dillon, Sheri A., Douglas E. Groene, and Todd Hayward. "Computer Crimes." *American Criminal Law Review*, vol. 35 (1998).

Dilworth, George "Toby." "The Economic Espionage Act of 1996: An Overview." Accessed 3 July 2003. Available at: <http://www.cybercrime. gov/usamay 2001_6.htm>.

Doane, Michael L. "The Uruguay Round Negotiations." In *International Intellectual Property Law*, edited by Anthony D'Amato and Doris Estelle Long. London; Boston: Kluwer Law International, 1997.

Dobbs, Dan B. *The Law of Torts*. St. Paul, MN: West Group, 2001.

Dolinar, Lou. "Spoofing Lets Hackers Hijack Computers, Officials Warn." *News Tribune* (Tacoma), 24 January 1995.

"DoS attack." PC Webopedia Definition and Links. Accessed 5 July 2003. Available at: <http://webopedia.internet.com/TERMS/D/DoS_attack.html>.

Drahos, Peter, and John Braitwaite. *Information Feudalism Who Owns the Knowledge Economy?* London: Earthscan Publications Ltd, 2002.

Dreyfuss, Robert. "Company Spies." *Mother Jones Mo Jo Wire.* Accessed 30 October 1997. Available at: <http://www.mojones.com/motherjones/MJ94/dreyfuss.html>.

"Tinker, Tailor Silicon Spy." *California Lawyer*, 15 May 1996.

Dreyfuss, Rochelle Cooper. "Intellectual Property Challenges in the Next Century." Article an Alert to the Intellectual Property Bar: The Hague Judgments Convention 2001. *University of Illinois Law Review*, no. 1 (2001).

"Trade Secrets: How Well Should We Be Allowed To Hide Them: The Economic Espionage Act of 1996." *Fordham Intellectual Property and Media Law Journal*, vol. 9 (1998).

Drozdiak, William. "U.S. Spy Agency Is Out in the Cold; Some Germans Question Presence of American Eavesdropping Site." *International Herald Tribune*, 25 July 2000.

Dungan, Sean. "Cybersabotage." *Infoworld.* Accessed 5 July 2003. Available at: <http://ask.elibrary.com/login.asp?c=&host=ask%2Eelibrary%2Ecom&script=%2Fgetdoc%2Easp&query=pubname%3DInfoWorld%26puburl%3Dhttp%7EC%7E%7ES%7E%7ES%7Ewww%2Einfoworld%2Ecom%26querydocid%3D29132249%40urn%3Abigchalk%3AUS%3BLib%26dtype%3D0%7E0%26dinst%3D0%26author%3DSean%2520Dugan%2520%2520%26title%3DENTERPRISE%2520COMPUTING%2520%253A%2520Cyber%2520sabotage%2520%2520%26date%3D02%2F10%2F1997%26refid%3Dency%5Fbotnm&title=ENTERPRISE+COMPUTING+%3A+Cyber+sabotage++&pubname=InfoWorld&author=Sean+Dugan++&date=02%2F10%2F1997>.

Echelon. "Answers to Frequently Asked Questions about Echelon." Accessed 1 July 2003. Available at: <http://www.aclu.org/echelonwatch/faq.html>.

"Economic Espionage." *Pittsburgh Post-Gazette*, 1 February 1997.

"Economic Espionage of U.S. Companies on the Rise: Report." *Agence France-Presse*, 24 February 1996. Available in NEXIS, News Library.

Economic Espionage Act of 1996. U.S. Code 18 (2000) § 1831.

"Economic Espionage – Spies Come in From the Cold Go After U.S. Business." *Seattle Times*, 6 November 1991.

"Economic Espionage: The Corporate Threat." Accessed 22 October 1996. Available at: <http://emporium.turnpike.net/IntlInt/econ.html>.

Edelman, Bernard. *Ownership of the Image: Elements for a Marxist Theory of Law.* Translated by E. Kingdom. London: Routledge and Kegan, Paul, 1979.

"EDPA Sentences Taiwanese Businessman to Probation in Taxol Theft Case." *Intellectual Property Litigation Reporter*, 21 July 1991.

Edsall, Margaret Horton. "Away We Go, Investigate FBI Headquarters in DC." *The Capital*, 11 August 2002.

Eells, Richard, and Peter Nehemkis. *Corporate Intelligence and Espionage.* New York, NY: Macillan, 1984.

"Electronic Intrusion Threats to National Security and Emergency Preparedness (NS/EP) Internet Communications." National Communications Systems. December 2000. Accessed 2002. Available at: <http://www.infowarrior. org/strategy/nsepcomms.pdf>.

Elliott, Marci. "MBA Students Learn the Art of Corporate Spying." *Scripps Howard News Service*, 6 August 2002.

Elron Software. "The Year 2001 Corporate Web and Email Study." Accessed 4 July 2003. Available at <http://www.elronsoftware.com/pdf/nforeport.pdf>.

Encyclopedia.com. Accessed 4 July 2003. Available at: <http://www.ency-clopedia.com/searchpool.asp?target=@DOCTITLE% 20Rust%20Belt>.

"Enemy Within, The." *Engineer*, 9 August 2002.

Epstein, Michael A. *Modern Intellectual Property.* Gaithersburg, MD: Aspen Law & Business, 1995.

Evans-Pritchard, Ambrose. "Bored CIA Spies Go Moonlighting." *Sunday Telegraph* (London), 24 November 1996.

Ewing, A.C. *The Morality of Punishment.* London: Kegan Paul, Trench, Trubner & Co., 1929.

"Exclusive Interview with Charles Neal, Supervisory Special Agent, FBI Computer Crime Squad." *E-Commerce Times.* Accessed 10 February 2000. Available at: <http://www.ecommercetimes.com/news/articles2000/000211-la.shtml>.

"Ex-Kodak Employee Sentenced." *Greensboro News and Record*, 15 November 1997.

Farnham, Alan. "How Safe Are Your Secrets?" *Fortune*, 8 September 1997.

"FBI: Ethnic Targeting Common Tactic in Economic Espionage." *Defense Week*, 25 March 1996.

FBI Press Release. 28 April 1999. Accessed 13 December 1999. Available at: <http:www.fbi.gov/pressrm/pressrel/avery.htm> (also on file with authors).

FBI Press Room – "Congressional Statement for the Record of Charles L. Owens, Chief Financial Crimes Section Federal Bureau of Investigation, Computer Crimes and Computer Related or Facilitated Crimes." Accessed 19 March 1997. Available at: <http://www.fbi.gov/congress/congress97/compcrm.htm>.

Federal Bureau of Investigation. Accessed 1 July 2003. Available at: <http://www.fbi.gov>.

"Feds Charge Two with Stealing Trade Secrets for China." *Intellectual Property Litigation Reporter*, vol. 9 (7 January 2003).

Fein, David B., and Mark W. Heaphy. "Companies Have Options When Systems Hacked Same Technologies That Empower Corporation Can Expose Vital Proprietary Information." *Connecticut Law Tribune*, vol. 27 (15 October 2001).

Feinberg, Joel. The Moral Limits of the Criminal Law: Harm to Others 218–21 (1984).

Ferdinand, Pamela. "Argentine Pleas Guilty to Hacking U.S. Networks: Wire Tap Led Authorities to Arrest." Washington Post, 20 May 1998.

Fialka, John J. "Stealing the Spark: Why Economic Espionage Works in America." Wasington Quarterly (autumn 1996).

 War by Other Means: Economic Espionage in America. New York: W.W. Norton & Co., Inc., 1997.

"Field Guide for Investigating Computer Crime." Accessed 2002. Available at: <http://www.securityfocus.com/cgi-bin/infocus.pl?head=Incidents: Forensics&id=1244>.

Fisse, Brent. "Reconstructing Corporate Criminal Law: Deterrence, Retribution, Fault and Sanctions." Southern California Law Review, vol. 56 (1983).

Flaming, Todd H. "Comment, The National Stolen Property Act and Computer Files: A New Form of Property, A New Form of Theft." University of Chicago Law School Roundtable (1993).

Florini, Ann M., and Yahya A. Dehqanzada. No More Secrets, Policy Implications of Commercial Remote Sensing Satellites. Washington, D.C.: Carnegie Endowment for International Peace, July 1999.

Foley, Mark J., and Michael E. Dash, Jr. "Inevitable Disclosure Cases in the Information Age." Legal Intelligencer (Philadelphia), 9 August 1999.

Foley, Timothy D. "The Role of the CIA in Economic and Technological Intelligence." Fletcher Forum of World Affairs, vol. 18 (winter/spring 1994).

Fonseca, Brian. "IT Security Under the Gun" Infoworld. Accessed 4 July 2003. Available at: <http://www.itworld.com/Sec/3832/itwnws010312 security/>.

Ford, Peter. "New Cooperation in Taming the Wild Web." Christian Science Monitor, 18 May 2000.

Fraser v. Nationwide Mut. Ins. Co.,135 F.Supp.2d 623 (E.D. Pa. 2001).

Fraumann, Edwin. "Economic Espionage: Security Missions Redefined." Public Administration Review, vol. 57 (1997).

Fraumann, Edwin, and Joseph Koletar. "Trade Secret Safeguards." Security Management, March 1999.

Freeh, Louis. Statement. See Cooper...Economic Espionage: Joint...(1996) [Freeh statement].

Freeh, Louis. Statement. Economic Espionage: Joint Hearing Before the Select Comm. on Intelligence of the U.S. Senate and the Subcomm. on Terrorism, Tech., and Gov't Info. of the Comm. on the Judiciary of the U.S. Senate. 104th Cong., 2d Sess., (4 December 1996). Accessed June 2004. Available at: <http://thomas.loc.gov/cgi-bin/query/R?r104:FLD001:S62208-S62210>................ Loeb, Vernon. "Wanted: A Few Good Spies; After Dry Spell, CIA Hiring Again." Washington Post, 27 November 1998, sec. A, p. 01. Accessed June 2004. Available at: <http://www.washingtonpost.com>.

"French Won't Expel U.S. Diplomats." Windsor Star, 28 February 1995.

Friedman, Lawrence. A History of American Law. New York: Simon and Schuster, 1978.

Friedman, Marc. S., and Kristin Bissinger. "'Infojacking': Crimes on the Information Superhighway." *Computer Law*, vol. 13 (1996).

Gallagher, Neil J. "Cybercrime, Transnational Crime, and Intellectual Property Theft: Hearing Before the J. Econ. Comm., 105th Cong. 2–4," 1998. Accessed 3 July 2003. Available at: <http://www.wiu.edu/library/govpubs/guides/intellect.htm> [Gallagher statement].

Gannon, John C. "Intelligence Challenges Through 2015." *National Intelligence Council*, 27 April 2000. See "Speeches and Testimony." Accessed 2002. Available at: <http://www.cia.gov/>.

Garner, Bryan A. *Black's Law Dictionary*. 7th ed. St. Paul, MN: West Group, 1999.

Geist, Michael A. "The Reality of Bytes: Regulating Economic Activity in the Age of the Internet." *Washington Law Review*, vol. 73 (1998).

Gelber, Daniel S. Testimony before Permanent Subcomm ... *Security in Cyberspace: Hearings Before the Permanent Subcomm. on Inv. of the Senate Comm. on Governmental Affairs*. 104th Cong., sess. 50 (1996) [Gelber testimony].

"General Agreement on Tariffs and Trade – Multilateral Trade Negotiations (The Uruguay Round): Agreement on Trade-Related Aspects of Intellectual Property Rights, Including Trade in Counterfeit Goods," 15 December 1993. *International Legal Materials*, vol. 33 [GATT].

Gertz, Bill. "SEC Aide Quits After Leak to Chinese; Threatened Firms, FBI Kept in Dark." *Washington Times*, 11 November 2002.

   "The New Spy: '90s Espionage Turns Economic." *Washington Times*, 9 February 1992.

   "U.S. Spy Center to Track Economic Espionage." *Washington Times*, 21 October 1994.

Gibson, Steve. "The Strange Tale of the Denial of Service Attacks Against GRC.COM." May 2001. Accessed 2002. Available at:<http://grc.com/dos/grcdos.htm>.

Gilad, Benjamin, and Tamar Gilad. *The Business Intelligence System: A New Tool for Competitive Advantage*. New York: American Management Association, 1988.

Gilpin, Robert. *The Political Economy of International Relations*. Princeton, NJ: Princeton University Press, 1987.

Glickman, Dan. "Intelligence After the Cold War." *Kansas Journal of Law and Public Policy*, vol. 3 (1994).

Goller, Mimi C. "Is A Padlock Better Than a Patent? Trade Secrets vs. Patents." *Wisconsin Lawyer*, May 1998.

Gomes, Lee. "Upstart Linux Draws a Microsoft Attack Team." *Wall St. J.*, 21 May 1999.

Goodin, Dan. "Busting Industrial Spies." *Recorder* 25 September 1996. Available in Lexis-Nexis (Legal News).

Goodman, Marc D. "Making Computer Crime Count." *The FBI Law Enforcement Bulletin*, vol. 70 (1 August 2001).

   "Why the Police Don't Care About Computer Crime." *Harvard Journal of Law and Technology*, vol. 10 (1997).

Gordon, Sarah. "The Generic Virus Writer II." Accessed 15 September 2003. Available at:<http://www.research.ibm.com/antivirus/SciPapers/Gordon/GVWII.html>.

Gore, Al. "Bringing Information to the World: The Global Information Infrastructure." *Harvard Journal of Law and Technology*, vol. 9 (1996).

Gorelick, Jamie S. Testimony . . . *See* Gelber . . . Security in Cyberspace: Hearings (1996) [Gorelick testimony].

"Govt Aims to Fight Industrial Espionage." *Daily Yomiuri* (Toyko), 13 February 2002.

Grabosky, Peter, and Russell G. Smith. *Crime in the Digital Age: Controlling Telecommunications and Cyberspace Illegalities.* Leichhardt, N.S.W.: The Federation Press, 1997.

Grabosky, Peter, Russell G. Smith, and Gillian Dempsey. *Electronic Theft: Unlawful Acquisition in Cyberspace.* Cambridge: Cambridge University Press, 2001.

Graham, Robert. "Carnivore FAQ." Accessed 2002. Available at: <http://www.robertgraham.com/pubs/carnivore-faq.html>.

G.S. Rasmussen & Assoc., Inc. v. Kalitta Flying Serv., Inc., 958 F.2d 896, 900 (9th Cir. 1992).

Gutowski, Robert J. "The Marriage of Intellectual Property and International Trade in the TRIPS Agreement: Strange Bedfellows or a Match Made in Heaven?" *Buffalo Law Review*, vol. 47 (1999).

Halligan, R. Mark. "Intellectual Property." *National Law Journal*, 9 December 1996.

"International Protection of Trade Secrets." Accessed 5 July 2003. Available at: <http://execpc.com/~mhallign>.

Hansen, Hugh C. "Introduction to Part I: Current Developments in European Union Intellectual Property Law." In *International Intellectual Property Law and Policy, vol. 3*, edited by Hugh C. Hansen. Yonkers, NY: Juris Publishing, 1998.

Harmon, Amy. "Group Says It Beat Music Security But Can't Reveal How." *N.Y. Times*, 15 January 2001 [2001a].

"'Hactivists' of All Persuasions Take Their Struggle to the Web." *N.Y. Times*, 31 October 1998.

"New Economy." *N.Y. Times*, 13 August 2001 [2001b].

Harris, John E. Director, OIA. Memorandum to Scott Charney, Chief, Computer Crime and Intellectual Property Section, 21 December 1998 [Harris memorandum].

Hartstein, Larry. "Man Sentenced for Conspiracy." *Atlanta Journal & Constitution*, 4 June 1998.

Hatcher, Michael, et al. "Computer Crimes." *American Criminal Law Review*, vol. 36 (1999).

Health Insurance Portability and Accountability Act of 1996. Office of the Federal Register. *Code of Federal Regulations*, vol. 45 (1996) sec. 164.530(c)(1).

Heed, Thomas P. "Comment, Misappropriation of Trade Secrets: The Last Civil RICO Cause of Action That Works." *John Marshall Law Review*, vol. 30 (1996).

Heffernan, Richard J. *Testimony with Regard to Economic Espionage Before the House Comm. on the Judiciary Subcomm. on Crime Subcomm. on Crime.* Committee on the Judiciary, U.S. House of Representatives. Washington, DC: GPO, 9 May 1996 [Heffernan testimony].

Heffernan, Richard J., and D.T. Swartwood. *Asis Special Report: Trends in Intellectual Property Loss.* Alexandria, VA: American Society for Industrial Security (ASIS), 15 March 1996.

Heller, Emily. "Stolen Plan No Big Secret, But Scheme Costs 90 Days." *Fulton County Daily Report,* 27 August 1998. Available in Lexis-Nexis (U.S. News, Southeast Regional Sources).

Heymann, Stephen P. "Legislating Computer Crime." *Harvard Journal on Legislation,* vol. 34 (1997).

Higgins, John J. Statement. *See* Cooper . . . Economic Espionage: Joint . . . (1996) [Higgins statement].

Hirst, Michael, and Karen Breslau. "Closing the Deal, Trade Is the Main Focus of Bill Clinton's Foreign Policy." *Newsweek,* 6 March 1995.

Hitchens, Ralph. "Computer Network Security and Risk Management." *MultiTech Communications.* Accessed 15 September 2003. Available at: <http://www.insurancetranslation.com/Language_Perils/01general. htm#12a>.

Hobson, Katherine. "Corporate Intelligence Seen as a Necessity." Accessed 30 September 1998. Available at: <http://www.abcnews.com/sections/ business/DailyNews/spy980924/index.html>.

Hodgson, Stephen S. "Trade Secrets, The U.S. Economic Espionage Act and You." *Chemical Engineering,* December 1998.

Hodkowski, William A. "Comment, The Future of Internet Security: How New Technologies Will Shape the Internet and Affect the Law." *Santa Clara Computer and High Technology Law Journal,* vol. 13 (1997).

Hohfeld, Wesley Newcomb. "Some Fundamental Legal Conceptions as Applied in Judicial Reasoning." *Yale Law Journal,* vol. 23 (1913).

Holder, Eric. Deputy Attorney General. Remarks at Press Conference Announcing the Intellectual Property Rights Initiative. Accessed 23 July 1999. Available at: <http://www.cybercrime.gov/dagipini.html>.

Honeynet Project. "Know Your Enemy: Statistics." 22 July 2001. Accessed 18 January 2004. Available at: <http://www.honeynet.org/papers/stats/>.

Horowitz, Richard. "The Economic Espionage Act: The Rules Have Not Changed." *Competitive Intelligence Review,* vol. 9 (1998).

Hosteny, Joseph N. "The Economic Espionage Act: A Very Mixed Blessing." *Intellectual Property Today,* February 1998. Available in Lexis-Nexis (Legal News).

"House Judiciary Panel Backs . . ." (1996) ($24 billion); "Economic Espionage: The Corporate Threat" (accessed 1996) ($260 billion). Perry, Sam. "Economic Espionage: The Corporate Threat." Accessed 22 October 1996. Available at: <http://emporium.turnpike.net/IntlInt/econ.html>.

Howard, Liz. "Criminal Penalties for Theft of Biological Materials." *BioPharm,* vol. 15 (1 June 2002).

Hudson, James E., III. "Trade Secret Theft Threatens Everyone with Corporate Economic Espionage Escapades." *Houston Bus. J. Tech. Q.* Accessed 1

October 1999. Available at:<http://www.bizjournals.com/houston/stories/1999/10/4/focus13.html>.

Hulme, George V. "Guarded Optimism – Even as Companies Plug More Holes, the Threats Grow More Sophisticated." *Information Week*, 8 July 2002.

Husman, Hans. "Introduction to Denial of Service." Accessed 5 July 2003. Available at: <http://secinf.net/misc/Introduction_to_Denial_of_Service_.html>.

Hyde, Alan. "The Wealth of Shared Information: Silicon Valley's High-Velocity Labor Market, Endogenous Economic Growth, and the Law of Trade Secrets." Accessed 4 July 2003. Available at <http://andromeda.rutgers.edu/~hyde/WEALTH.htm>.

"Independent Technical Review of the Carnivore System." 8 December 2000. Accessed 2002. Available at: <http://www.usdoj.gov/jmd/publications/carniv_final.pdf>.

"India: Netspionage Coming of Age – II: William Boni and Gerald L. Kovacich on Business, Crime and Security in the 21st Century Global Marketplace." *Global News Wire*, 3 September 2001.

Institute for Security Technology Studies, Dartmouth College. "Cyber Attacks During the War on Terrorism: A Predictive Analysis." September 22, 2001. Accessed 15 September 2003. Available at: <http://www.ists. dartmouth.edu/ISTS/counterterrorism/cyber_attacks. htm>.

Intel Corp. "2000 Annual Report." Accessed 3 July 2003. Available at: <http://www.intel.com/intel/annual00/>.

Inter-American Convention on Corruption. "Signatories." Accessed 3 July 2003. Available at: <http://www.oas.org/juridico/english/sigs/b-58. html>.

"Interception Capabilities 2000." European Parliament, Scientific and Technological Options Assessment (STOA). Accessed 15 September 2003. Available at: <http://www.cyber-rights.org/interception/stoa/interception_capabilities_2000.htm.>

Intermedics, Inc. v. Ventritex, Inc., 822 F. Supp. 634, 642-43 (N.D. Cal. 1993).

"Internet Insecurity." *Time*, 2 July 2001.

"Israel Indicts Hackers." *Pittsburgh Post-Gazette*, 10 February 1999.

"Israeli Teenager Questioned in Pentagon Hacking Case." *L.A. Times*, 19 March 1998.

Iwata, Edward. "More U.S. Trade Secrets Walk Out Door with Foreign Spies." *USA Today*, 13 February 2003.

Jackamo, Thomas J., III. "From the Cold War to the New Multilateral World Order: The Evolution of Covert Operations and the Customary International Law of Non-Intervention." *Virginia Journal of International Law*, vol. 32, no. 88 (1992). Citing Bill Gertz, "The New Spy: '90s Espionage Turns Economic," *Washington Times*, 9 February 1992.

Jager, Melvin F. *Trade Secrets* Law. New York: Clark Boardman Callaghan & Co, 1996.

James, Michael. "Small Thefts, Big Trouble." *Baltimore Sun*, 22 January 2001.

"Japan Changes Its Espionage Laws." *Intelligence Online*, no. 423, 14 February 2002.

Jauvert, Vincent. "Espionage – How France Listens to the Whole World." 5 April 2001. Accessed 2002. Available at:<http://all.net/iwar/archive/2001Q2/0098.html>.

Java Security. "Denial of Service." Accessed 5 July 2003. Available at: <http://java.sun.com/sfaq/denialOfService.html>.

Jopeck, Ed, and Ken Sawka. "Foreign Espionage: Is Your Business at Risk?" Accessed 25 September 1996. Available at: <http://www.scip.org/jan3.html>.

"Judge Convicts Man in Trade-Secret Case." *Milwaukee Journal Sentinel*, 10 December 1999.

Kalitka, Peter F. "Do They Know What You Know?" *Security Management*, vol. 44 (1 September 2000).

Kant, Immanuel. *The Philosophy of Law: An Exposition of the Fundamental Principles of Jurisprudence as the Science of Right.* Translated From German by W. Hastie, B.D. (Edinburgh: T. & T. Clark, 1887).

Kanuck, Sean P. "Information Warfare: New Challenges for Public International Law." *Harvard International Law Journal*, vol. 37 (1996).

Kaslow, Amy. "Behind White House Role as Pitchman for U.S. Firms." *Christian Science Monitor*, 28 March 1995.

Katsh, Salem M., and Michael P. Dierks. "Globally, Trade Secrets Are All Over the Map." *Journal of Property Rights*, vol. 7, no. 11 (1995).

Keithly, David M., and Stephen P. Ferris. "U.S. Companies Exposed to Industrial Espionage; Point of View." *National Defense*, vol. 87 (1 September 2002).

Kelsey, Tim, and David Leppard. "American Spies Hack into Euro Computers to Steal Trade Secrets." *Sunday Times* (London), 4 August 1996.

Kephart, Jeffrey, Gregory Sorkin, David Chess, and Steve White. "Fighting Computer Viruses. *Scientific American*, November 1997. Accessed 2002. Available at: <http://www.sciam.com/1197issue/1197kephart.html>.

Kerr, Orin. "Internet Surveillance Law After the USA Patriot Act." *Northwestern Law Review*, vol. 97 (2003).

Kerr, Thomas M. "'Trade Secrets,' i.e., Confidential Business Information or Business Intelligence." *Pittsburgh Legal Journal*, vol. 145 (December 1997).

Kewanee Oil Co. v. Bicron Corp., 416 U.S. 470, 481–82 (1974).

King, Neil, Jr., and Jess Bravin. "Call It Mission Impossible, Inc. – Corporate Spying Firms Thrive." *Wall St. J.*, 3 July 2000.
    "Corporate-Spying Firms Thrive: CIA Veterans, Dumpster-Divers Work in 'Competitive Intelligence': If the Trash is on the Curb, It's Fair Game." *Wall St. J.*, 4 July 2000, Europe edition.

Klevorick, Alvin K. "Legal Theory and the Economic Analysis of Torts and Crimes." *Columbia Law Review*, vol. 85 (1985).

Knoll, Amy. "Comment, Any Which Way But Loose: Nations Regulate the Internet." *Tulane Journal of International and Comparative Law*, vol. 4 (1996).

Knowles, J. "IW Battlelab to Go Operational This Month." *Journal of Electronic Defense*, 1 June 1997.

Kober, Stanley. "Why Spy? The Uses and Misuses of Intelligence." *USA Today Magazine*, 1 March 1998.

Korah, Valentine. *An Introductory Guide to EC Competition Law and Practice. 7th ed.* Oxford: Hart Publishing, 2000.

Lamb, Robert. "Economic and Financial Issues in Intellectual Property." In *International Intellectual Property Law and Policy, vol. 3,* edited by Hugh C. Hanson. Yonkers, NY: Juris Publishing, 1998.

Landers, Jim. "Foreign Spies Target Corporate Secrets." *Dallas Morning News*, 7 October 1996.

Landes, William, David Friedman, and Richard A. Posner. "Some Economics of Trade Secret Law." *Journal of Economic Perspectives,* vol. 5, no. 1 (1991).

Lange, Larry. "Trust a Hacker Under 30? You'd Better." *Elec. Engineering Times*, 19 August 1996.

Lao, Marina. "Federalizing Trade Secrets Law in an Information Economy." *Ohio State Law Journal*, vol. 59 (1998).

Latham, A. *Copyright Law.* New York: Rothman, 1979.

Leaffer, Marshall A. *International Treaties on Intellectual Property. 2nd ed.* Washington, DC: BNA Inc., 1997.

Leob, Vernon. "Wanted: A Few Good Spies." *Washington Post*, 27 November 1998.

Leob, Vernon, and Walter Pincus. "Invisible on the Inside; Knowing System Helped Suspect Go Undetected, FBI Says." *Washington Post*, 21 February 2001.

Lisser, Eleena de. "Hearing and Seeing Business Travel Blab and Laptop Lapses." *Wall St. J*, 8 November 1999.

"Local Man Pleads Guilty in Trade Theft Case." *Telegram & Gazette* (Massachusetts), 12 October 2002.

Locke, John. *Two Treatises on Civil Government.* Edited by H. Morley. London: George Routledge and Sons, 1884.

Lowry, Suellen. "Inevitable Disclosure Trade Secrets Disputes: Dissolutions of Concurrent Property Interests." *Stanford Law Review*, vol. 40 (1988).

Lowry, Tom. "Secrets at Stake, Fears of Chinese Spying Mount." *USA Today*, 29 January 1998.

Lynch, Ian. "EU Makes Blueprint for Echelon Inquiry." Accessed 9 September 2000. Available at: <http://www.vnunet.com/News/1110830>.

Overseas Offices Fall Prey to Crackers. Accessed 5 July 2003. Available at: <http://www.vnunet.com/News/1115279>.

MaCodrum, Donald, Hedieh Nasheri, and Timothy J. O'Hearn. "Spies in Suits: New Crimes of the Information Age from the United States and Canada Perspectives." *Information and Communications Technology Law*, vol. 10, no. 2 (June 2001).

"Man Charged in Theft of Trade Secrets." *Des Moines Register*, 26 September 1995.

"Man Offering to Sell Secrets to Rival Newspaper Sentenced." *Associated Press State & Local Wire*, 25 August 1998. Available in Lexis-Nexis (Wire Service Reports).

Mangel, John. "Economic Espionage Losses in the Billions Experts Say." *Plain Dealer* (Cleveland), 30 July 2001.

Mann, Charles C. "The Mole in the Machine." *The New York Times Magazine*, 25 July 1999. Accessed 15 September 2003. Available at:<http://www.nytimes.com/library/magazine/home/19990725mag-tech-secure-secrets.html>.

Mann, Kenneth. "Punitive Civil Sanctions: The Middleground Between Criminal and Civil Law." *Yale Law Journal*, vol. 101 (1992).

Marcus, Jon. "Scientist Arrested Over Trade Espionage." *N.Y. Times*, 30 August 2002, Higher Education Supplement, no. 1553.

Markey, John K., and James F. Boyle. "New Crimes of the Information Age." *Boston Bar Journal*, vol. 43 (May/June 1999).

Marriot, Anne. "Companies Gamble on Keeping Secrets." *Washington Times*, 20 March 1997.

Martin, Brian. "Against Intellectual Property." *Philosophy and Social Action*, vol. 21 (1995).

Mason, J. Derek, et al. "The Economic Espionage Act: Federal Protection for Corporate Trade Secrets." *Computer Law*, vol. 16 (1999).

Mathiason, Garry G., and Roland M. Juarez. "The Electronic Workplace: An Overview." *CEB's California Business Law Reporter*, 1995.

Matthews, Chris. "FBI Has Developed System for Monitoring the Internet." Hardball with Chris Matthews, *CNBC News Transcripts*, 18 July 2000.

McAllester, Matthew. "Feds Aid Miami Company in Global Hunt for Hacker." *Newsday*, 8 June 1997.

McCarthy, Michael. "The Pentagon Worries That Spies Can See Its Computer Screens." *Wall St. J.*, 7 August 2000.

McCartney, Scott. "System Breach Is Stirring Up Airline Rivalry." *Wall St. J.*, 27 June 2000.

McCurdy, Dave. "Glasnost for the CIA." *Foreign Affairs*, vol. 73 (January/February 1994).

McGugan, Ian. "The Spy Who Came in for the Gold." *Canadian Business*, 1 May 1995.

McMorris, Frances A. "Corporate-Spy Case Rebounds on Bristol." *Wall. St. J.*, 2 February 1998.

"Men Sentenced for Trying to Sell Prototype Computers." *Associated Press State and Local Wire*, 4 December 1998. Available in Lexis-Nexis (Wire Service Reports).

Meyerowitz, Steven A., and Donna Fryer. "Competitive Intelligence: A New Revenue Stream for Firms Looking to Gain an Edge." *New York Law Journal News*, vol. 228, 20 August 2002.

Milgrim, Roger M. *Milgrim on Trade Secrets*. New York: Matthew Bender, 1999.

Mills, Mike. "Testing the Limits on Trade Secrets; Kodak Lawsuit Is Likely to Have Broad Impact on Use of Confidential Data." *Washington Post*, 9 December 1997.

Mock, Lois F., and Dennis Rosenbaum. *A Study of Trade Secret Theft in High-Technology Industries*. Unpublished manuscript on file with the National Institute of Justice, May 1988.

Molander, Roger, Peter Wilson, David Mussington, and Richard Mesic. "Strategic Information Warfare Rising." Draft RAND Study. Santa Monica, CA: 1998.

Moore, David. "The Spread of the Code-Red Worm (CRv2)." Accessed 2002. Available at: <http://www.caida.org/analysis/security/code-red/>.

Moore, David, Geoffrey M. Voelker, and Stefan Savage. "Inferring Internet Denial-of-Service Activity." 2001. Accessed 2002. Available at: <http://www.caida.org/outreach/papers/backscatter/usenixsecurity01.pdf>.

Morris, Nomi, et al. "The New Spy Wars: Canada Is a Key Target in the Global Race for Economic Secrets." *Maclean's*, 2 September 1996.

Morse, Paige Marie. "Protecting Trade Secrets." *Chemical and Engineering News*, 1 December 1997.

Mossinghoff, Gerald J., et al. "The Economic Espionage Act: A New Federal Regime of Trade Secret Protection." *Journal of the Patent and Trademark Office Society*, vol. 79 (1997).

Moyer, Marc A. "Section 301 of the Omnibus Trade and Competitiveness Act of 1988: A Formidable Weapon in the War Against Economic Espionage." *Northwestern Journal of International Law and Business*, vol. 15 (1994).

Mueller, Robert S., III. Director, Federal Bureau of Investigation. Statement before the Senate Select Committee on Intelligence. *International Terrorism: Hearing Before the Senate Select Comm. on Intelligence.* 104th Cong., 2d sess. (1 August 1996) [Mueller statement].

Muller, Joann. "Raytheon Unit Is Accused of Industrial Espionage; Florida Firm Alleges Foul in $450 Million Aircraft Pact." *Boston Globe*, 22 January 1997.

Murray, Kevin D. "Ten Spy-Busting Secrets." Accessed 3 July 2003. Available at: <http://www.tscm.com/murray.html>.

Nadlemann, Ethan A. *Cops Across Borders: The International ization of U.S. Criminal Law Enforcement.* University Park: Pennsylvania State University Press, 1993.

Nash, Kim S. "Symantec Executives Charged with Stealing Borland Trade Secrets." *Computerworld*, 8 March 1993.

Nasheri, Hedieh. "Digital Crime." *Encyclopedia of Crime and Punishment*, vol. 2 (2002). Great Barrington, MA: Berkshire Publishing Group, 2002.

"The Intersection of Technology Crimes and Cyberspace in Europe: The Case of Hungary." *Information and Communications Technology Law*, vol. 12, no. 1 (2003).

Nasheri, Hedieh, and Timothy J. O'Hearn. "Crime and Technology: New Rules for a New World." *Information and Communications Technology Law*, vol. 7, no. 2 (June 1998).

"Hightech Crimes and the American Economic Machine." *International Review of Law, Computers and Technology*, vol 13, no. 2 (November 1999).

"The Worldwide Search for Techno-thieves: International Competition v. International Co-operation." *International Review of Law, Computers and Technology*, vol. 13, no. 3 (December 1999).

"The Worldwide Search for Techno-thieves: International Competition v. International Co-operation." In *Cyberspace Crime*, ed. D.S. Wall (London: Ashgate, 2002). First published in *International Review of Law, Computers and Technology*, vol. 13, no. 3 (December 1999).

National Counterintelligence Center. "Counterintelligence News & Developments," no. 1. Accessed 3 July 2003. Available at: <http://www.loyola.edu/dept/politics/hula/cind1.html>.

National Fraud Center, Inc., The, a LEXIS-NEXIS Company. "The Growing Global Threat of Economic and Cyber Crime." A white paper produced in conjunction with The Economic Crime Investigation Institute, Utica College, December 2000.

National Infrastructure Protection Center (NIPC). Accessed 3 July 2003. Available at: <http://www.nipc.gov>.

National Legal Center for the Public Interest. *Judicial Legislative Watch Report*, vol. 19, no. 6 (June 1998).

National Stolen Property Act. *United States Code*. Title 18, sec. 2314 (1940).

Nelan, Bruce. "A New World for Spies." *Time*, 5 July 1993.

Nelson, Carrington. "Ex-Engineer Jailed for Stealing Secrets." *Tennessean*, 29 April 1998.

Nelson, Emily, and George Anders. "Wal-Mart, Amazon.com Settle Fight Over Recruitment and Trade Secrets." *Wall St. J.*, 6 April 1999.

Nelson, Emily, George Anders, and Raju Narisetti. "How Kodak, Fearing Theft of Trade Secrets, Mounted Its Own Sting." *Wall St. J.*, 25 November 1996.

Nelson, Jack. "Spies took $300-Billion Toll on U.S. Firms in '97." *L.A. Times*, 12 January 1998.

"Network Security: The Business Value Proposition." *The Consultant Registry*. Accessed 15 September 2003. Available at: <http://www.consultant-registry.com/delivery/SWP2.pdf>.

"Nike Sued for Hacking Costs." *Newswire*, 28 March 2001.

Nimmer, Raymond T. *The Law of Computer Technology*. 3rd ed. St. Paul, MN: West Group, 1997.

"911 Lines Tied Up by Hacker – In Sweden." *Orlando Sentinel*, 8 March 1997.

1998 Global Software Piracy Report. International Planning and Research Corporation for the Business Software Alliance, May 1999.

"1998 OECD Convention: An Impetus for Worldwide Changes in Attitudes Toward Corruption in Business Transactions." *American Business Law Journal*, vol. 37 (2000).

No Electronic Theft (Net) Act, Pub. L. No. 105–147, 1997 U.S.C.C.A.N. (111 Stat. 2678). United States Code Congressional and Administrative News, 105th Congress, First Session, 1997, vol. 2. St. Paul: West Group, 1998.

No. 02-20145-JW, indictment issued (N.D. Cal. Dec. 4, 2002). [Indictment by Ross W. Nadel (Assistant U.S. Attorney) against Fei Ye and Ming Zhong in USA v. Ye(before Judge James Ware); USDOJ press release athttp://www.cybercrime.gov/yeIndict.htm]

Nobel, Johan J. Ingles-le. "Cyberterrorism Hype." *Jane's Intelligence Review*, 1 December 1999.

"North American Free Trade Agreement (NAFTA)." *International Legal Materials*, vol. 32 (17 December 1992).

Norton-Taylor, Richard. "Spooky Business." *Guardian* (Manchester, GB), 26 March 1997.

"Note, Trade Secrets in Discovery: From First Amendment Disclosure to Fifth Amendment Protection." *Harvard Law Review*, vol. 104 (1991).

Novell, Inc. v. Weird Stuff, Inc., No. C92-20467 JW/EAI, 1993 U.S. Dist. Lexis 6674, at 5 (N.D. Cal. May 14, 1993).

Nyberg, Alix. "The Spy Who Bugged Me." *CFO, The Magazine for Senior Financial Executives*, vol. 16 (1 September 2000).

Organization for Economic Co-operation and Development (OECD). "About OECD." Accessed 3 July 2003. Available at: <http://www.oecd.org/EN/home/0,,EN-home-0-nodirectorate-no-no-r_o-0,FF.html>.

Computer Related Crime: Analysis of Legal Policy. Washington, DC: OECD, 1986.

Office of the National Counterintelligence Executive. "Counterintelligence Executive Notes 13–96." Accessed 4 July 2003. Available at: <http://www.nacic.gov>.

O'Harrow, Robert, Jr. "Hacker Accesses Patient Records; Thousands of Files Easily Downloaded." *Washington Post*, 9 December 2000.

O'Hearn, Timothy, and Stephen Sozio. "Tech Secrets Can Be Troublesome, Economic Espionage Act of 1996." *Communications News*, vol. 38 (1 September 2001).

Olivenbaum, Joseph M. "Ctrl-Alt-Delete: Rethinking Federal Computer Crime Legislaton." *Seton Hall Law Review*, vol. 27, no. 4 (1997).

O'Reilly, John. "Online Propaganda the Corporate Way." Accessed 5 July 2003. Available at: <http://www.vnunet.com/analysis/1114674>.

O'Sullivan, Sean. "N.Y. Man Pleads Guilty To Stealing Trade Secrets." *News Journal*, 18 October 2002.

Pace, Christopher Rebel J. "The Case for a Federal Trade Secrets Act." *Harvard Journal of Law and Technology*, vol. 8 (1995).

Paine, Thomas. "The American Crisis." In *Heritage of American Literature Beginnings to the Civil War*, edited by James E. Miller, Jr. Fort Worth, TX: Harcourt Brace Jovanovich Collage Publisher, 1991.

"Pair from Cupertino and San José, California, Indicted for Economic Espionage and Theft of Trade Secrets from Silicon Valley Companies," U.S. Department of Justice press release December 4, 2002.

Palmer, Caroline. "How to Spot Your Office Spy." *Observer* (London), 17 October 1999.

Pappalardo, Denise. "Avoiding Future Denial-of-Service Attacks." *Network World Fusion*, 23 February 2000.

Paris Convention of Industrial Property. *United Nations Treaty Series*, vol. 828 (20 March 1883) [Paris convention].

Park, W. H. "The International Law of Intelligence Collection." In *National Security Law*, edited by John Norton Moore, et al. Durham, NC: Carolina Academic Press, 1990.

Parker, D. B. *Computer Crime: Criminal Justice Resource Manual*. Washington, DC: Department of Justice, National Institute of Justice, 1989.

Parra, Esteban. "The Enemy Is in the Internet." *The News Journal*, 16 December 2002.

Pasternak, Douglas, and Gordon Witkin. "The Lure of the Steal." *U.S. News and World Reports*, 4 March 1996.

Peabody v. Norfolk, 98 Mass. 452, 457 (Mass. 1868).

Perritt, Henry H. "Jurisdiction in Cyberspace." *Villanova Law Review*, vol. 41 (1996).

Perry, Sam. "Economic Espionage and Corporate Responsibility." *CJ International*, March/April 1995.

Persico, Brian A. "Under Siege: The Jurisdictional and Interagency Problems of Protecting the National Information Infrastructure." *CommLaw Conspectus*, vol. 7 (1999).

Petersen, Melody. "Lawsuits by Rivals Accuse Textile Maker of Corporate Espionage." *N.Y. Times*, 13 October 1998.

Pethia, Richard. "Cyber Security – Growing Risk from Growing Vulnerability." Testimony before the House Select Committee on Homeland Security Subcommittee on Cybersecurity, Science, and Research and Development. *Hearing on Overview of the Cyber Problem – A Nation Dependent and Dealing with Risk.* 25 June 2003 [Pethia testimony].

Piirto, Rebecca. "Health, Competitive Intelligence; What You Don't Know Will Hurt You." *Marketing Tools*, July/August 1996.

Piller, Charles. "Anti-Hacker Fights for Respect, Internet: Federal Agency Created to Combat the Rise in Cyber-crime Is Viewed with Distrust by Firms It Is Supposed to Protect." *L.A. Times*, 5 March 2000.

Pincus, Walter. "Agencies Debate Value of Being Out in the Cold: Spies Under "Nonofficial Cover" Are Among Most Sensitive Operations." *Washington Post*, 12 January 1996.

Pitz, Marylynne. "Brothers Charged in Scheme to Sell PPG Trade Secrets; Competitor Offered Documents, FBI Says." *Pittsburgh Post-Gazette*, 10 December 1996.

Pollit, Mark. "Cyberterrorism – Fact or Fancy?" Accessed 15 September 2003. Available at: <http://www.cs.georgetown.edu/~denning/infosec/pollitt.html>.

Pooley, James H. A., et al. "Understanding the Economic Espionage Act of 1996." *Texas Intellectual Property Law Journal*, vol. 5 (winter 1997).

Porter, Michael E. *Competitive Strategy: Techniques for Analyzing Industries and Competitors.* New York: Free Press, 1980.

"Portland Woman Faces Jail Term for E-mailing Company Secrets." *Associated Press State and Local Wire*, 23 July 1999. Available in Lexis-Nexis (Wire Service Reports).

Posner, Richard A. "An Economic Theory of the Criminal Law." *Columbia Law Review*, vol. 85 (1985).

Powell, Daniel P. "An Introduction to the Law of Trade Secrets." *Colorado Lawyer*, vol. 23 (1994).

Prentice, Robert A. "The Future of Corporate Disclosure: The Internet, Securities Fraud, and Rule 10b-5." *Emory Law Journal*, vol. 47 (1998).

Preston, Candace L. "Out-of-work Spies Find New Niche in Corporate Espionage." *Business First-Columbus*, 28 November 1997.

"Proprietary Information Theft #1 Threat to Information Systems; Vanguard Introduces ezRIGHTS, Ground Breaking Technology That Eliminates Risk." *Business Wire*, 21 October 2002.

Ramo, Joshua Cooper. "A Survivor's Tale." *Time*, 29 December 1997.

Rathmell, Andrew. "Assessing the IW Threat from Sub-state Groups." In *Cyberwar 2.0: Myths, Mysteries and Reality*, edited by Alan D. Campen and Douglas H. Dearth. Fairax, Virginia: AFCEA International Press, 1998.

"Relevant Intelligence in the Post-Cold War World." Accessed 10 September 1998, Available at: <http://www.venable.com/govern/fulltest.htm>.

Reno, Janet. Attorney General of the United States. Before the *United States Senate Committee on Appropriations Subcommittee on Departments of Commerce, Justice, State, the Judiciary, and Related Agencies, Cybercrime.* Accessed 4 July 2003. Available at <http://www.usdoj.gov/archive/ag/testimony/2000/reno21600.htm> [Reno statement].

Keynote address at the Meeting of the P8 Senior Experts' Group on Transnational Organized Crime (Chantilly, VA). 21 January 1997. Accessed 20 July 2003. Available at: <http://www.usdoj.gov/criminal/cybercrime/agfranc.htm> [Reno keynote address].

"The Threat of Digital Theft: Intellectual Property Theft Is Faster, Costlier, and More Dangerous Than Ever." Accessed 21 November 2001. Available at: <http://www.cybercrime.gov/Agdigitaltheft.htm>.

"Reno Opposes Eased Export Control." *Associated Press*, 13 July 1999. Available at 1999 WL 17823820.

Restatements of Torts, sec. 757 (1939): Chapter 36, § 757: "Liability for Disclosure or Use of Another's Trade Secret – General Principle." In Restatement of the Law of Torts: As Adopted and Promulgated by the American Law Institute at Washington, D.C., May 11, 1934. St. Paul: American Law Institute Publishers, 1934–1939.

Restatement (First) of Torts, sec. 757 (1939). Chapter 36, § 757: "Liability for Disclosure or Use of Another's Trade Secret – General Principle." In Restatement of the Law of Torts: As Adopted and Promulgated by the American Law Institute at Washington, D.C., May 11, 1934. St. Paul: American Law Institute Publishers, 1934–1939.

Restatement of Torts, sec. 757 cmt. b (1939). "Liability for Disclosure or Use of Another's Trade Secret – General Principle," in Chapter 36: Miscellaneous Trade Practices, Restatement of the Law of Torts As Adopted and Promulgated by the American Law Institute at Washington, D.C., May 11, 1934. St. Paul: American Law Institute Publishers, 1934–1939.

Restatement (Third) of Unfair Competition, sec. 39, comment a (1995). Section 39: "Definition of Trade Secret," comment a. In Restatement (Third) of the Law, Unfair Competition: As Adopted by the American Law Institute at Washington, D.C., May 11, 1993. St. Paul: American Law Institute Publishers, 1995.

Restatement (Third) of Unfair Competition sec. 39 (1995). "Definition of Trade Secret" Restatement (Third) of the Law, Unfair Competition: As Adopted by the American Law Institute at Washington, D.C., May 11, 1993. St. Paul: American Law Institute Publishers, 1995.

Restatement of Torts, sec. 757 (1939). "Liability for Disclosure or Use of Another's Trade Secret – General Principle," in Chapter 36: Miscellaneous Trade Practices, Restatement of the Law of Torts: As Adopted and

Promulgated by the American Law Institute at Washington, D.C., May 11, 1934. St. Paul: American Law Institute Publishers, 1934–1939.

"Revictimization of Companies by the Stock Market Who Report Trade Secret Theft Under the Economic Espionage Act, The." *Business Law*, vol. 57 (November 2001).

"Reviewing Current Issues on Trade Secrets." *New York Law Journal*, 1 April 2002.

Richelson, Jeffrey. "Examining US Intelligence Failures." *Jane's Intelligence Review*, vol. 12 (1 September 2000).

Robbins, Tom. "In the New World of Espionage, Targets Are Economic." *Houston Chronicle*, 11 September 1994.

Rockwell Graphics Sys., Inc. v. Dev Indus., Inc., 91 F3d 914, 917 n.3 (7th Cir. 1996).

Rodger, Will. "Warrants for Online Data Soar, Demands Served on Internet, E-mail Providers Up 800%, Study Finds." *USA Today*, 28 July 2000.

Ros-Lehtinen, Ileana. U.S. Representative. Holding Hearing on Corporate and Industrial Espionage and Its Effects. House International Relations Committee: Subcommittee on International Economic Policy and Trade Holds Hearing on Corporate and Industrial Espionage. *FDCH Political Transcripts*, Committee Hearing, 13 September 2000 [Ros-Lehtinen hearing].

Rosencrance, Linda. "Survey: Retail Fraud More Prevalent for Online Vendors." *ComputerWorld*, 24 July 2000.

Rovella, David E. "Preparing for a New Cyberwar: Justice Dept. Seeks Lawyers, Revised Laws to Fight Net Crimes." *National Law Journal*, 20 March 2000.

"Trail Nears for Untested Secrets Law." *National Law Journal*, 8 March 1999.

Rush, Mark A., Mark D. Feczko, and Thomas D. Manganello. "Protecting Trade Secrets from Dumpster Divers and Other Snoops: The Law Protects Those That Protect Themselves." *Mealey's Litigation Report: Trademarks*, vol. 8, no. 12 (7 August 2000).

"Russians Arrest 6 in Computer Thefts." *N.Y. Times*, 27 September 1995.

Ryan, Michael P. *Knowledge Diplomacy, Global Competition and the Politics of Intellectual Property*. Washington, DC: Brookings Institution Press, 1998.

Ryberg, William. "New Washers Put Town on Spy Alert." *Chicago Sun-Times*, 2 January 1997.

Samuels, Linda B., and Brian K. Johnson. "The Uniform Trade Secrets Act: The States' Response." *Creighton Law Review*, vol. 24 (1990).

Sanger, David E., and Tim Weiner. "CIA Targets Allies But Still Misses." *Sacramento Bee*, 22 October 1995.

Savage, Joseph R. Jr., and Lauren A. Stagnone. "Plot to Steal Trade Secrets Alleged." *Record* (Bergen County, NJ), 29 July 1998 [1998a].

"You Can't Hide Your Spying Eyes: EEA Issues Emerge." *Business Crimes Bulletin*, December 1998. Available in Lexis-Nexis (Legal News) [1998b].

Schleslinger, James. Testimony before the Senate Select Committee on Intelligence. *International Terrorism: Hearing Before the Senate Select Comm. on Intelligence*. 104th Cong., 2d sess. (1 August 1996) [Schleslinger testimony].

Schmetzer, Uli. "Optimism on Trade Accords; Agreements Could Open Market to U.S. Goods, Advance Human Rights." *Chicago Tribune*, 14 March 1995.

Schneier, Bruce. Testimony before the House Select Committee on Homeland Security Subcommittee on Cybersecurity, Science, and Research and Development. *Hearing on Overview of the Cyber Problem – A Nation Dependent and Dealing with Risk.* 25 June 2003 [Schneier testimony].

Schuldt, Gretchen. "Man Charged with Selling Trade Secrets." *Milwaukee Journal Sentinel,* 9 September 1999.

Schwartau, Winn. *Information Warfare: Chaos in the Electronic Superhighway.* New York: Thunder's Mouth Press, 1994.

Schweizer, Peter. *Friendly Spies: How American Allies Are using Economic Espionage to Steal Our Secrets.* New York: Atlantic Monthly Press, 1993.

"Hello, Cruel World: How to Succeed in Business." *News & Observer* (Raleigh), 9 March 1997 [1997a].

"New Spy Law Could Cramp Economy. *USA Today,* 20 November 1997 [1997b].

"The Growth of Economic Espionage: America Is Target Number One." *Foreign Affairs* (January/February 1996).

Science and Technology in U.S. International Affairs. *Report of the Carnegie Commission on Science, Technology, and Government,* January 1992.

Sciglimpaglia, Robert J., Jr. "Comment, Computer Hacking: A Global Offense." *Pace Yearbook of International Law,* vol. 3, no. 255 (1991).

SecureWorks website. Accessed July 2003. Available at: <www.secureworks. com>.

See USC, title 18, sec. 2703 (1994 & Supp. 1997). Section Name: "Requirements for governmental access" Title 18: "Crimes and Criminal Procedure," United States Code: Containing the General and Permanent Laws of the United States, in Force on January 4, 1995. 1994 ed., Washington: Government Printing Office, 1995–2000.

Seidel, Arthur H. *What The General Practitioner Should Know About Trade Secrets and Employment Agreements.* Philadelphia: ALI-ABA, 1984.

Seita, Alex Y. "Globalization and the Convergence of Values." *Cornell International Law Journal,* vol. 30 (1997).

Seki, Hoken S., and Peter J. Toren. "EEA Violations Could Trigger Criminal Sanctions, Stiff Penalties are Intended to Deter Economic Espionage by Foreign Companies in the U.S." *National Law Journal,* 25 August 1997.

Seltzer, Mark D., and Angela A. Burns. "The Criminal Consequences of Trade Secret Misappropriation: Does the Economic Espionage Act Insulate Your Company's Trade Secrets from Theft and Render Civil Remedies Obsolete?" *Software Law Bulletin,* February 1999. Available in Lexis-Nexis (Legal News).

Sen, Sankar. "Cyber Crimes: Police Should Be Properly Equipped." *Statesman* (India), 10 September 2000.

Senate, S12213, 104th Cong., 2d sess., Cong. Rec. (2 October 1996), 142. Congressional Record. "Economic Espionage Act of 1996. Accessed July 2003. Available at: <http://thomas.loc.gov/cgi-bin/query/F?r104:1:./temp/~r104z29Vk0:e126131>.

Senate, S12207-08, 104th Cong., 2d sess., Cong. Rec. (2 October 1996), 142. Congressional Record. "Economic Espionage Act of 1996." Accessed July 2003. Available at: <http://thomas.loc.gov/cgi-bin/query/R?r104: FLD001:S62208-S62210>.

Senate, S12213, 104th Cong., 2d sess., Cong. Rec. (2 October 1996), 142. Congressional Record. "Economic Espionage Act of 1996." Accessed July 2003. Available at: <http://thomas.loc.gov/cgi-bin/query/F?r104:1:./temp/~r 104z29Vk0:e126131>.

Senate, S12213, 104th Cong., 2d sess., Cong. Rec. (2 October 1996), 142. "Economic Espionage Act of 1996." Congressional Record, available at http://thomas.loc.gov/cgi-bin/query/F?r104:1:./temp/~r104z29Vk0: e126131: (last visited July 2003).

Sennott, Charles M. "Business of Spying." *Star Tribune* (Minneapolis-St. Paul), 4 February 1997. Available in Dow-Jones News (Publications Library). [1997a]

"Shadowy World of Spying." *Rocky Mountain News* (Denver), 2 February 1997. [1997b]

Seper, Jerry. "4 Arrested in Denmark for Computer Hacker Scheme." *Washington Times*, 16 December 1993.

Sepura, Karen. "Economic Espionage: The Front Line of a New World Economic War." *Syracuse Journal of International Law and Commerce*, vol. 26 (Fall 1998).

Shackelford, Steve. "Note, Computer-Related Crime: An International Problem in Need of an International Solution." *Texas International Law Journal*, vol. 27 (1992).

Shapiro, Howard M. "The FBI in the 21st Century." *Cornell International Law Journal*, vol. 28 (1995).

"Shedding the Trench Coat; Despite a Cloak-and-Dagger Image, 'Competitive Intelligence' Operations are Winning Rave Reviews at Many Technology Companies." *Electronic Business*, 1 September 2001.

Sherr, James. "Cultures of Spying." *National Interest* (winter 1994/1995).

"Shift in Espionage Trends" Annual Report to Congress on Foreign Economic Collection and Industrial Espionage 2001, prepared by the Office of the National Counterintelligence Executive, available at http://www.ncix.gov/docs/fecie·fy01.pdf

Shipley, Greg. "Anatomy of a Network Intrusion." *Network Computing*, 18 October 1999. Accessed 2002. Available at: <http://www.networkcomputing. com/1021/1021ws1.html>.

Shiva, Vandana. *Protect or Plunder? Understanding Intellectual property Rights.* New York: Zed Books, 2001.

Shoichet, Catherine E. "Charges of Laboratory Theft Vex the Research World." *The Chronicle of Higher Education*, 18 October 2002.

Sieber, Ulrich. "Computer Crimes and Other Crimes Against Information Technology: Commentary and Preparatory Questions for the Colloquium of the Association Internationale de Droit Penal in Wuerzburg." *Revue Internationale De Droit Penal*, vol. 64 (1993).

The International Handbook on Computer Crime: Computer-Related Economic Crime and the Infringements of Privacy. New York: Wiley, 1986.

Silva, Jeffrey. "Legislative Relief Sought For Corporate Espionage Cases; High-Tech Companies Must Step Up Defenses." *Radio Comm. Report*, 25 September 2000.

Simensky, Melvin, et al. *Intellectual Property in the Global Marketplace. 2nd ed.* Hoboken, NJ: Wiley, 1999.

Simmonsen, Derek. "Con Artists Take Scams Online; Computer Fraud Headache For Law Enforcement." *Stuart News/Port St. Lucie News,* 16 December 2002.

Simon, Spencer. "The Economic Espionage Act of 1996." *Berkeley Technology Law Journal,* vol. 13 (1998).

Siri, Liraz. "The Internet Auditing Project." Accessed 15 September 2003. Available at: <http://www.viacorp.com/auditing.html>.

Slind-Flor, Victoria. "New Spy Act to Boost White-Collar Defense Biz." *National Law Journal,* 28 July 1997.

Sohmen, Helmut. "Critical Importance of Controlling Corruption." *International Lawyer,* vol. 33 (1999).

Solomon, Joel S. "Forming a More Secure Union: The Growing Problem of Organized Crime in Europe as a Challenge to National Sovereignty." *Dickinson Journal of International Law,* vol. 13 (1995).

Soma, John T., et al. "Computer Crime: Substantive Statutes & Technical & Legal Search Considerations." *Air Force Law Review,* vol 39 (1996).

"Transnational Extradition for Computer Crimes: Are New Treaties and Laws Needed?" *Harvard Journal on Legislation,* vol. 34 (1997).

Specter, Arlen. Statement. *See* Cooper . . . Economic Espionage: Joint . . . (1996) [Specter statement].

Specter, Arlen. Senator [PA]. "Economic Espionage Act of 1996." Congressional Record. Accessed October 2003. Available at: <http://thomas.loc.gov/cgi-bin/query/R?r104:FLD001:S62207,S62208>.

"Spies Step Up Attacks on U.S. Firms." *Irish Times,* 16 January 1998.

Staniford, Stuart, Vern Paxson and Nicholas Weaver. 'How to Own the Internet in Your Spare Time." Accessed 2002. Available at: <http://www.cs.berkeley.edu/~nweaver/cdc.web/cdc.pdf>.

Stanton, John. "Industrial Espionage Becoming 'Big Business'." *National Defense,* vol. 86 (1 July 2001).

Starkman, Dean. "Russian Hacker Enters Fraud Plea in Citicorp Case." *Wall St. J.,* 26 January 1998.

"Secrets and Lies: The Dual Career of a Corporate Spy." *Wall St. J.,* 23 October 1997.

Steele, Robert David. "Private Enterprise Intelligence." In *Intelligence Analysis and Assessment,* edited by David A. Charter, et al. London: Frank Cass & Co., Ltd., 1996.

Steiker, Carol S. "Punishment and Procedure: Punishment Theory and the Criminal-Civil Procedural Divide." *Georgetown Law Journal,* vol. 85 (1997).

Still, Torri. "A Lesson for the Valley: Thou Shalt Not Steal." *Recorder* (California), 7 October 1999.

Stoll, Cliff. *The Cuckoo's Egg: Tracking a Spy Through the Maze of Computer Espionage.* Edinburgh, Ireland: Pocket Books, 1989.

Stone, Brad. "Diving into Bill's Trash." *Newsweek,* 10 July 2000.

"The Spy Who Scrubbed Me." *Newsweek,* 24 February 1997.

Stone, Katherine V. W. "Knowledge at Work: Disputes Over the Ownership of Human Capital in the Changing Workplace." *Connecticut Law Review*, vol. 34 (2002).

"Superseding Indictment Adds Charges in Lucent Trade Secret Theft Case, Criminal Action." *E-Business Law Bulletin*, vol. 3 (June 2002).

Swartz, Jon. "Modern Thieves Prefer Computers to Guns Online Crime Is Seldom Reported, Hard to Detect." *San Francisco Chronicle*, 25 March 1997.

Tenet, George J. Director of Central Intelligence. Statement before Senate Select Committee on Intelligence. "The Worldwide Threat in 2000: Global Realities of Our National Security." 2 February 2000. See "Speeches and Testimony." Accessed 2002. Available at: <http://www.cia.gov/>.

Testimony before the *Senate Committee on Government Affairs*, 24 June 1998. Accessed 20 July 2003. Available at: <http://www.fas.org/irp/congress/1998_hr/980624-dci_testimony. htm> [Tenet testimony].

"Theft of Trade Secrets May Bring Automatic Jail Time – California, In The Courts." *Cyberspace Lawyer*, vol. 7 (July/August 2002).

Tillett, L. Scott. "DOJ, IT Industry Team to Fight Cybercrime." Accessed 4 July 2003. Available at: <http://www.cnn.com/TECH/computing/9903/23/crimefighters.idg/index.html>.

Toffler, Alvin. *Powershift: Knowledge, Wealth and Violence at the Edge of the 21st Century*. New York: Bantam Books, 1990.

Toffler, Alvin, and Heidi Toffler. *The Third Wave*. New York: Bantam Books, 1980.

War and Anti-War. East-Maitland, Australia: Warner Books, 1993.

Toren, Peter J.G. "Internet: A Safe Haven for Anonymous Information Thieves?" *St. John's Journal of Legal Commentary*, vol. 11 (1996).

Intellectual Property and Computer Crimes. New York, NY: Law Journal Press, 2003.

"The Prosecution of Trade Secret Thefts Under Federal Law." *Pepperdine Law Review*, vol. 22, no. 3 (1994).

"Trade in Secrets, The." *Bulletin*, 29 June 1994.

"Treaty Establishing the European Economic Community." *United Nations Treaty Series*, vol. 11 (25 March 1957).

Tucker, Darren S. "The Federal Government's War on Economic Espionage." *University of Pennsylvania Journal of International Economic Law*, vol. 18 (1997).

Tucker, Robert L. "Industrial Espionage as Unfair Competition." *University of Toledo. Law Review*, vol. 29 (1998).

"2 Charged with Trying to Steal Intel Trade Secrets." *Fort Worth Star-Telegram*, 4 June 1998.

Tyler, Christian. "The Enemy Within." *Financial Times* (London), 12 April 1997.

Uniform Trade Secrets Act. Uniform Laws Annotated, Title 14, sec. 433–467 (1990 & Supp. 2001).

United Nations Association of the U.S.A. *Science and Technology in an Era of Interdependence*. New York, NY: UNA-USA, 1975.

United Nations General Assembly Press Release GA/DIS/3106, 9 October 1998.

"United Nations Manual on Prevention and Control of Computer-Related Crime." *International Review of Criminal Policy*, vol. 24, nos. 43 and

44. Available at: http://www.uncjin.org/Documents/EighthCongress.html (accessed July 2003).

United States Code (USC), title 18, sec. 2710 (2000) Wrongful Disclosure of Video Tape Rental or Sales Records. U.S. Code 18 (2000) § 2710.

United States v. Morris, 928 F.2d 504 (2d Cir. 1991), cert. denied 502 U.S. 817 (1991).

United Nations Treaty Series 993. 16 December 1966.

United States Code (USC) (1994–2000).

United States Code Annotated (USCA) (1991–1999).

United States Code Service (USCS) (2000).

United States Intelligence Community. Accessed 3 July 2003. Available at: <http://www.intelligence.gov/>.

United States International Trade Commission. *Foreign Protection of Intellectual Property Rights and the Effect on U.S. Industries and Trade*, no. 2065, 1988.

United States v. Hancock, Crim. No. CR88-319A (N.D. Ga. 1988).

"University of Chicago Student Charged in Enabling Theft of TV Signals." *Chicago Sun-Times*, 4 January 2003.

University of Lethbridge (Alberta, Canada), Faculty of Management. *Management Matters*, 1 February 1997. Available in WL 7489166.

USA Patriot Act. Public Law No. 107-56. Congress. House Report 3162, 26 October 2001.

U.S. Congress. *House of Representatives*. 104th Cong., H.R. 788. Washington, DC: GPO, 1996.

    House of Representatives. 105th Cong., H.R. 2265. Washington, DC: GPO, 1997.

    Senate. 104th Cong., S.R. 359, Washington, DC: GPO, 1996.

    Senate. 105th Cong., S.R. 190, Washington, DC: GPO, 1998.

    House Permanent Select Committee on Intelligence. Staff Study. *IC21: Intelligence Community in the 21st Century*. Washington, D.C.: GPO, 1996. Accessed 2002. Available at: <http://www.access.gpo.gov/congress/house/intel/ic21/ic21_toc.html>.

United Nations General Assembly, G.A. Res. 1236, U.N. GAOR, 12th Sess., Supp. No.18 (1957), at http://ods-dds-ny.un.org/doc/ RESOLUTION/GEN/NR0/120/19/IMG/NR012019.pdf?OpenElement (last visited July 2003).

United Nations General Assembly, G.A. Res. 2131, U.N. GAOR, 20th Sess., Supp. No.14 (1965), at http://ods-dds-ny.un.org/doc/RESOLUTION/GEN/NR0/218/94/IMG/NR021894.pdf?OpenElement (last visited July 2003).

United States v. Hsu, 155 F.3d 189 (3d Cir. 1998).

United States v. Pin Yen Yang, Criminal No. 1:97MG0109 (N.D.Ohio 1997).

United States v. Yang, No. 1:97 CR 288, 1999 WL 1051714 (N.D. Ohio, Nov. 17, 1999)

United States v. Worthington, Criminal No. 97–9 (W.D. Pa. 1996).

USC, title 17, sec. 506 (1994). Criminal Offenses. U.S Code 17 (1994) § 506. USC, title 17, sec. 506 (1994). Section Name: "Criminal offenses," Title 17: Copyrights, United States Code: Containing the General and Permanent

Laws of the United States, in Force on January 4, 1995. 1994 ed., Washington: Government Printing Office, 1995–2000.

USC, title 17, sec. 906(a) (Supp. 1998). There was no changes to the 1998 Supplement. "Limitation on exclusive rights: reverse engineering; first sale" (Name of Section 906), Title 17: Copyrights, United States Code: Containing the General and Permanent Laws of the United States, in Force on January 4, 1995. 1994 ed., Washington: Government Printing Office, 1995–2000.

USC, title 18, sec. 3123 (1994). "Issuance of an order for a pen register or a trap and trace device" Title 18: "Crimes and Criminal Procedure," United States Code: Containing the General and Permanent Laws of the United States, in Force on January 4, 1995. 1994 ed., Washington: Government Printing Office, 1995–2000.

USC, title 18, sec. 1030 (2000). 18 U.S.C. § 1030 (2000) "Fraud and related activity in connection with computers." Title 18: "Crimes and Criminal Procedure" United States Code: Containing the General and Permanent Laws of the United States, in Force on January 2, 2001. Washington: Government Printing Office, 2001-. [Note: This section was modified by Public Laws 107–273 and 107–296 in 2002]

USC, title 18, sec. 1030 (2000). Fraud and Related Activity in Connection with Computers. U.S. Code 18 (2000) § 1030(a). Title 18: "Crimes and Criminal Procedure" United States Code: Containing the General and Permanent Laws of the United States, in Force on January 2, 2001. Washington: Government Printing Office, 2001-. [Note: Section 1030 was modified by Public Laws 107–273 and 107–296 in 2002.]

USC, title 18, sec. 1030 (2000). Fraud and Related Activity in Connection with Computers. U.S. Code 18 (2000) § 1030(a)(5)(A). Title 18: "Crimes and Criminal Procedure" United States Code: Containing the General and Permanent Laws of the United States, in Force on January 2, 2001. Washington: Government Printing Office, 2001-. [Note: Section 1030 was modified by Public Laws 107–273 and 107–296 in 2002.]

USC, title 18, sec. 1030(g) (2000). Fraud and Related Activity in Connection with Computers. U.S. Code 18 (2000) § 1030(g). Title 18: "Crimes and Criminal Procedure" United States Code: Containing the General and Permanent Laws of the United States, in Force on January 2, 2001. Washington: Government Printing Office, 2001-. [Note: Section 1030 was modified by Public Laws 107–273 and 107–296 in 2002.]

USCA, title 18, sec. 1832(a) (2000). [Section Name: "Theft of trade secrets" Title 18: "Crimes and Criminal Procedure," United States Code: Containing the General and Permanent Laws of the United States, in Force on January 2, 2001. 2000 ed., Washington: Government Printing Office, 2001-.

USC, title 18, sec. 1837(1) (2000). Section Name: "Applicability to conduct outside the United States" Title 18: "Crimes and Criminal Procedure," United States Code: Containing the General and Permanent Laws of the United States, in Force on January 2, 2001. 2000 ed., Washington: Government Printing Office, 2001."

USC, title 18, sec. 1839(3)(B) (Supp. V 1999). "Definition of 'trade secret'" Title 18: Crimes and Criminal Procedure, United States Code: Containing the General and Permanent Laws of the United States, in Force on January 4, 1995. 1994 ed., Washington: Government Printing Office, 1995–2000.

USC, title title 18, sec. 1905 (1994 & Supp. IV 1998). "Disclosure of confidential information generally," Title 17: "Crimes and Criminal Procedure," United States Code: Containing the General and Permanent Laws of the United States, in Force on January 4, 1995. 1994 ed., Washington: Government Printing Office, 1995"2000.

USCA, title 18, sec. 2319(b)(1) (West Supp. 1998). "Criminal infringement of a copyright" Title 18: "Crimes and Criminal Procedure" United States Code Annotated, 1994 ed., St. Paul: West Group, 1927-.

USC, title 35, secs. 100–105 (Supp. 1998), outlining the requirements for patenting an "invention." Sections 100–105 are in Chapter 10: "Patentability of Inventions," within Title 35: Patents United States Code: Containing the General and Permanent Laws of the United States, in Force on January 4, 1995. 1994 ed., Washington: Government Printing Office, 1995–2000.

USC, title 35, sec. 102 (1994), detailing the "novelty" requirement for patentability. Section 102: "Conditions for patentability; novelty and loss of right to patent" Title 35: Patents United States Code: Containing the General and Permanent Laws of the United States, in Force on January 4, 1995. 1994 ed., Washington: Government Printing Office, 1995–2000.

USC, title 35, sec. 102(b) (Supp. 1998), denying patentability if an invention is patented, described in a printed publication, publicly use, or placed on sale more than one year prior to the date of the application. Section 102: "Conditions for patentability; novelty and loss of right to patent" Title 35: Patents United States Code: Containing the General and Permanent Laws of the United States, in Force on January 4, 1995. 1994 ed., Washington: Government Printing Office, 1995–2000.

USC, title 35, sec. 103 (Supp. 1998), detailing the "non-obvious subject matter" requirement for patentability. Section 103: "Conditions for patentability; non-obvious subject matter" Title 35: Patents United States Code: Containing the General and Permanent Laws of the United States, in Force on January 4, 1995. 1994 ed., Washington: Government Printing Office, 1995–2000.

USC, title 35, sec. 115 (Supp. 1998), requiring the inventor to submit an oath stating that he believes himself to be the first inventor. Section 115: "Oath of applicant" Title 35: Patents United States Code: Containing the General and Permanent Laws of the United States, in Force on January 4, 1995. 1994 ed., Washington: Government Printing Office, 1995–2000.

USC, title 35, sec. 284 (1998), providing for damages not less than a reasonable royalty, including interest and costs. Section 284: "Damages" Title 35: Patents United States Code: Containing the General and Permanent Laws of the United States, in Force on January 4, 1995. 1994 ed., Washington: Government Printing Office, 1995–2000.

18 U.S.C. § 1837(2). "Applicability to conduct outside the United States" Title 18: "Crimes and Criminal Procedure," United States Code: Containing the General and Permanent Laws of the United States, in Force on January 2, 2001. 2000 ed., Washington: Government Printing Office, 2001.

U.S. Department of Justice. "Computer Crime and Intellectual Property Section (CCIPS)" Accessed 3 July 2003. Available at: <http://www.usdoj.gov/criminal/cybercrime>.

   "Introduction, Computer Crime and Intellectual Property Section." Accessed 4 July 2003. Available at: <http://www.cybercrime.gov/ipmanual/intro.htm>.

U.S. Department of Justice. Accessed July 2003. Available at: <http://www.usdoj.gov/>.

"U.S. Department of Justice Online." Accessed 3 July 2003. Available at: <http://www.usdoj.gov/>.U.S. Department of Justice. Press Release. U.S. Attorney, Western Dist. of N.Y., 28 August 1997.

U.S. Department of Justice. Press Release. U.S. Attorney, Western Dist. of N.Y., 28 August 1997 [1997a].

   Press Release. U.S. Attorney, Western Dist. of N.Y., 13 November 1997 [1997b].

   "The National Information Infrastructure Protection Act of 1996 Legislative Analysis," The Computer Crime & Intellectual Property Section. Accessed 4 July 2003. Available at: <http://www.usdoj.gov/criminal/cybercrime/1030_anal.html>.

U.S. Department of State Overseas Security Advisory Council. *Guidelines for Protecting U.S. Business Information Overseas.* Washington, D.C.: GPO, 1992.

U.S. Department of Justice. Computer Crime and Intellectual Property Section (CCIPS). "What Does CCIPS Do?" Accessed July 2003. Available at: <http://www.usdoj.gov/criminal/cybercrime/ccips.html>.

Use of Electronic Media for Delivery Purposes. U.S. Securities and Exchange Commission, Docket 1091, File No. S7-31-95, no. 22 (6 October 1995).

U.S. General Accounting Office. "Economic Espionage: Information on Threat from U.S. Allies." *GAO/T-NSIAD-96-1141*, 28 February 1996.

"U.S. Losing High-Tech Secrets to 'Student' Spies: FBI." *Straits Times* (Singapore), 8 April 1997.

USSID (United States Signals Intelligence Directive)18. "Procedures for NSA collection of data on US persons." Accessed 2002. Available at: <http://www.gwu.edu/~nsarchiv/NSAEBB/NSAEBB23/07-01.htm>.

U.S. Statutes at Large, vol. 35 (1909). *Act of 4 March 1909.*

   vol. 98 (1984). *Counterfeit Access Device and Computer Fraud and Abuse Act of 1984.*

   vol. 105 (1991). *Intelligence Authorization Act of Fiscal Year 1991.*

   vol. 110 (1996). *Economic Espionage Act of 1996.*

   vol. 96 (1982). Public Law No. 97-180.

   vol. 105 (1992). Public Law No. 102-561.

   vol. 108 (1994). Public Law No. 103-325.

   vol. 110 (1996). Public Law No. 104-253.

Vaknin, Sam. "Analysis: The Industrious Spies – II." *United Press International, Financial News,* 14 May 2002 [2002a].

"Analysis: The Industrious Spies – III." *United Press International, Financial News,* 15 May 2002 [2002b].

Veltrop, James. "Trade Secret Misappropriation a Federal Crime." *Intellectual Property Today,* June 1997.

Vickery v. Welch, 36 Mass. (1 Pick.) 523, 526 (1837).

Venzke, Ben N. "Economic/Industrial Espionage." Accessed 3 July 2003. Available at: <http://www.computercrimeconsultants.com/news1.htm>.

"Veridian Targeted by Spy?" *Intelligence Online,* no. 441, 5 December 2002.

Vise, David A., and Daniel Eggen. "FBI Warns of Cyber-Attack Threat: U.S. 'Very Concerned' About Vulnerability of Infrastructure." *Washington Post,* 21 March 2001.

Vistica, Gregory. "Inside the Secret Cyberwar: Facing Unseen Enemies, the Feds Try to Stay a Step Ahead." *Newsweek,* 21 February 2000.

Vrana, Deborah. "University of Chicago Student Arrested for Document Piracy." *Chicago Tribune,* 3 January 2003.

Waguespack, Michael J. Director of the NACIC. Letter. Accessed 13 January 1997. Available at: <http://www.nacic.gov/dirlett.htm> [Waguespack letter].

Walker, Nigel. *Punishment, Danger and Stigma: The Morality of Criminal Justice.* Oxford: Basil Blackwell, 1980.

Wall, David. *Crime and the Internet: Cybercrimes and Cyberfears.* London; New York: Routledge, 2001.

Cyberlaw. Harlow: Longman, 2000.

Cyberspace crime. Aldershot, Hants, England; Burlington, VT: Ashgate, 2003.

Waller, Douglas. "Spying: 'Halt! Friend or Foe?'" *Time,* 6 March 1995.

Waller, Spencer W., and Noel J. Byrne. "Changing View of Intellectual Property and Competition Law in the European Community and the United States of America." *Brooklyn Journal of International Law,* vol. 20 (1993).

Warner, William T. "Economic Espionage: A Bad Idea." *National Law Journal,* 12 April 1993.

Waterschoot, Paul. "Overview of Recent Developments in Intellectual Property in the European Union." In *International Intellectual Property Law and Policy, vol. 4,* edited by Hugh C. Hansen. Yonkers, NY: Juris Publishing, 2000.

Watson, Bruce W. *United States Intelligence: An Encyclopedia.* New York: Garland, 1990.

Weisner, Don, and Anita Cava. "Stealing Trade Secrets Ethically." *Maryland Law Review,* vol. 47 (1988).

Welch, Lee Ann. *Herald-Dispatch* (West Virginia), 14 August 2002.

Welsh, Robert C., et al. *Protecting Confidential Business Information in the Digital Age.* New York: Practicing Law Institute, 2001.

"What Purchasing Managers Should Know About Trade Secrets." *Purchasing Law Report,* December 2001.

Wheeler, Scott L. "PRC Espionage Leads to 'Terf' War." *Insight on the News Magazine,* 29 October 2002.

Wilke, Clifford A. "Protecting Internet Addresses of National Banks." *Comptroller of the Currency, Alert 2000–9,* 19 July 2000.

Wine, Michael. "Cyberspace – A New Medium for Communication, Command and Control by Extremists." April 1999. Accessed 15 September 2003. Available at: <http://www.ict.org.il/articles/cyberspace.htm>.

Wingfield, Nick. "A Stolen Laptop Can Be Trouble if Owner is CEO." *Wall St. J.*, 19 September 2000.

Winkler, Ira. *Corporate Espionage.* New York: Prima Publishing, 1997.

Winter, Christine. "Security, Inside Out; Firm's Product Protects Networks From Disgruntled Employees." *Sun-Sentinel* (Florida), 27 August 2002.

Winton, Ben. "Intel Theft a Frame-Up?" *Arizona Republic,* 25 September 1995.

WIPO. "Member States." Accessed 3 July 2003. Available at: <http://www.wipo.org/members/index.html>.

Wiretap Reports. Accessed 2002. Available at: <http://www.uscourts.gov/wiretap.html>.

"Woman Pleads Guilty." *Houston Chronicle,* 31 July 1998. Available in Dow-Jones News (Publications Library).

Woodward, John D. Jr. *Superbowl Surveillance: Living Up to Biometrics.* Santa Monica, CA: RAND, 2001.

Woolsey, James R. "Former CIA Director Woolsey Delivers Remarks at Foreign Press Center." 7 March 2000. Accessed 3 July 2003. Available at: <http://cryptome.org/echelon-cia.htm>.

"World Forum Designed to Combat International Crime, Corruption." *The Metropolitan Corporate Counsel* (Mountainside, NJ), May 2000.

World Information Technology and Services Alliance (WITSA). "Digital Planet 2000: The Global Information Economy. Accessed 3 July 2003. Available at: <http://www.WITSA.org/DP2000sum.pdf>.

World Intellectual Property Organization. "About Intellectual Property." Accessed 28 February 2003. Available at: <http://www.wipo.org/about-ip/en/>.

Worldwide Threat Assessment Brief to the Senate Select Committee on Intelligence. Accessed 1 July 2003. Available at: <http://www.fas.org/irp/congress/1996_hr/s960222p.htm>.

"Worming Out the Truth." *Economist,* 4 November 2000.

Wray, Stefan. "On Electronic Civil Disobedience." *Peace Review,* vol. 11 (1999).

Wright, Steve. "An Appraisal of Technologies of Political Control." Working document. European Parliament, Scientific and Technological Options Assessment (STOA). Accessed 9 September 2003. Available at: <http://cryptome.org/stoa-atpc.htm>.

Yates, Ronald E. "Cold War: Part II, Foreign Intelligence Agencies Have New Targets – U.S. Companies." *Chicago Tribune,* 29 August 1993 [Yates 1993a].

    "Corporate Cloak-and-Dagger Spying – Either by Rival Businesses or Foreign Governments – Can Cut Right to the Heart of a Vulnerable Corporation, But Congress Is Considering Ways to Strike Back." *Chicago Tribune,* 1 September 1996.

    "U.S. Intelligence Retools to Fight New Brand of Espionage." *Chicago Tribune,* 30 August 1993 [Yates 1993b].

Yellen, Dwight, and Frank S. Kalamajka. "Reviewing Current Issues on Trade Secrets." *New York Law Journal*, 1 April 2002.

Young, Jeffrey. "Spies Like Us." *Forbes*, 3 June 1996.

Yushkiavitshus, Henrikas. "Law, Civil Society, and National Security: International Dimensions." In *The Information Revolution and National Security: Dimensions and Directions*, edited by S. Schwartzstein. Washington, DC: Center for Strategic and International Studies, 1996.

Zuckerman, M.J. "Cracking Down on the Outlaws of Cyberspace." *USA Today*, 2 July 1996.

Index